Youth in Africa's Labor Market

Youth in Africa's Labor Market

Editors
Marito Garcia
Jean Fares

THE WORLD BANK
Washington, D.C.

ISBN: 978-0-8213-6884-8
eISBN: 978-0-8213-6885-5
DOI: 10.1596/978-0-8213-6884-8

Library of Congress Cataloging-in-Publication Data

Garcia, Marito, 1951-
    Youth in Africa's labor market / Marito Garcia and Jean Fares.
        p. cm.
    Includes bibliographical references and index.
        1. Youth—Employment—Africa. 2. Youth—Africa—Social conditions. 3. Labor market—Africa. I. Farès, Jean. II. Title.

HD6276.A32G37 2008
331.3'47096—dc22   2007044706

Cover painting: Paul Olaja
Cover design: Naylor Design

Contents

Figures

Tables

Foreword

About 200 million people between the ages of 12 and 24 live in Africa today, and their share of the population is rising. By 2010 youth will account for 28 percent of the population, making Sub-Saharan Africa the "youngest" region in the world. This largest-ever youth cohort means that the time has never been more urgent to invest in young people in Africa. With good policies and institutions in place, the potential to reap a dividend from a larger, younger work force with fewer dependents is great.

This book examines the challenges African youth face in their transition to work and presents a strategy for meeting these challenges. It argues that African youth start working too early and are unprepared to meet the demands of the labor market. Leaving school early—or not entering at all—limits their human capital accumulation and restricts their upward mobility, with grave implications for both individuals and national economics.

Labor is the most abundant asset of poor households in Africa. Developing this asset is therefore essential to helping households move out of poverty. Strengthening the work force can also improve the investment climate, increase economic growth, and prevent instability and violence, particularly in postconflict situations, where large numbers of unemployed youth threaten security.

This book describes how Africa's young people spend their time and presents a case for investing in youth in Africa, analyzing the two paths to working life for Africa's youth: directly (without the benefit of education) and through school. It also presents new evidence on the effects of education on employment and income in selected countries, and examines youth unemployment and its determinants. The case studies conducted in selected African countries analyze policies and programs implemented on youth employment and suggest a policy framework to help African youth successfully transition to working life.

Robert Holzmann
Director, Social Protection
Human Development Network
The World Bank

Yaw Ansu
Director, Human Development
    Department
Africa Region
The World Bank

Contributors

Lisa Dragoset is an economist at Cornell Institute for Social and Economic Research, Cornell University in Ithaca, New York, United States.

Jean Fares is a senior economist at the World Bank's Human Development Network.

Marito Garcia is a lead economist at the World Bank's Human Development Department, Africa Region.

Lorenzo Guarcello is a researcher with the Understanding Children's Work project—a joint World Bank, ILO, and UNICEF project.

Florence Kondylis is an economist in the Department of Economics, QMUL and CEP–London School of Economics, United Kingdom.

Scott Lyon is a researcher with the Understanding Children's Work project—a joint World Bank, ILO, and UNICEF project.

Marco Manacorda is a professor at the Department of Economics, RHUL and CEP–London School of Economics, United Kingdom.

Daniel Parent is a professor of Economics at McGill University, Montreal, Canada.

Furio Rosati is the Director of Understanding Children's Work project—a joint World Bank, ILO, and UNICEF project.

Cristina Valdivia is a researcher with Understanding Children's Work project—a joint World Bank, ILO, and UNICEF project.

Lars Vilhuber is a research fellow at the Cornell Institute for Social and Economic Research, Cornell University in Ithaca, New York, United States.

Acknowledgments

This report is a collaborative effort of the Africa Human Development Technical Department, the Social Protection Team of the Human Development Network, and the Burkina Faso, Ethiopia, Tanzania, and Uganda Country Teams of the World Bank.

The report was prepared by a team led by Marito Garcia (Team Leader) and Jean Fares (Co-Task Team Leader). Contributions were made by the study team consultants: Lisa Dragoset, Martha Getachew, Martin Godfrey, Lorenzo Guarcello, Emily Kallaur, Florence Kondylis, Marco Manacorda, Anthony Okech, Barthelemy Ouedraogo, Daniel Parent, Furio Rosati, Joseph Shitundu, Ruth Uwaifo, Lars Vilhuber, and Gillian Virata. Moukim Temorov (Burkina Faso Country Team), Emily Kallaur and Caterina Ruggeri Laderchi (Ethiopia Country Team), Rest Lasway and Robert Utz (Tanzania Country Team), and Suleiman Namara and Mirey Ovadiya (Uganda Country Team) also contributed to the report.

The report was prepared under the general guidance of Laura Frigenti (Sector Manager); Yaw Ansu (Sector Director); and Robert Holzmann (Sector Director). Peer reviewers were Emmanuel Jimenez, Linda McGinnis, and Wendy Cunningham.

The participants of the one-day workshop on youth in Africa's labor market held in Washington, D.C., provided valuable guidance to the study team and commented on initial drafts of the country case studies. The team is particularly grateful to Emmanuel Jimenez, Robert Holzmann, M. Louise Fox, Setareh Razmara, Stefano Scarpetta, Pia Peeters, Harold Alderman, Viviana Mangiaterra, Linda McGinnis, Maurizia Tovo, Wendy Cunningham, Daniel Kwabena Boakye, members of the Africa Labor Market Analysis Thematic Group, the Children and Youth Thematic Group, and Laura Brewer (International Labour Organization Geneva).

The country case studies were funded partly by the Trust Fund of the ESSD-Social Protection Window. This support is gratefully acknowledged.

Abbreviations

AGETIP	Agence d'Exécution des Travaux d'Intérêt Public
BEUPA	Basic Education in Urban Poverty Areas
BOLSA	Bureau for Labour and Social Affairs (Ethiopia)
COBET	Complementary Basic Education in Tanzania
ESDPIII	Education Sector Development Plan III
GDP	gross domestic product
GTZ	German Agency for Technical Cooperation
HIV/AIDS	human immunodeficiency virus/acquired immune deficiency syndrome
ILFS	Integrated Labor Force Survey
ILO	International Labour Organization
LICUS	low-income countries under stress
MDGs	Millennium Development Goals
MOLSA	Ministry of Labour and Social Affairs (Ethiopia)
NGOs	nongovernmental organizations
PEAP	Poverty Eradication Action Plan
PEVDT	Promotion of Employment-Oriented Vocational and Technical Training
ReMSEDA	Regional Micro and Small Enterprises Development Agencies
SFSI	Standard Files Standard Indicators Database
SHLS	Survey of Household Living Conditions

TVET	technical and vocational education and training
UCW	Understanding Children's Work
UNICEF	United Nations Children's Fund
VETA	Vocational Education and Training Authority, Tanzania

Executive Summary

Youth and Africa have received increased attention in recent policy discussions and World Bank work, as articulated in the Africa Action Plan and the *World Development Report 2007: Development and the Next Generation*. The Africa Action Plan offers a framework to support critical policy and public action led by African countries to achieve well-defined goals, such as the Millennium Development Goals (MDGs). The *World Development Report's* main message is that the time has never been better to invest in young people living in developing countries. It offers a three-pillar policy framework for investing in and preserving the human capital of the next generation. Both frameworks respond to the desire to find solutions to Africa's development challenges and to prepare for and benefit from the next generation of workers, parents, and leaders.

This report examines the challenges Africa's youth face in their transition to working life and proposes policies for meeting these challenges. It presents evidence from case studies of 4 countries—Burkina Faso, Ethiopia, Tanzania, and Uganda—and from household data on 13 countries. The four case studies include a stocktaking of existing policies and programs to address youth employment and labor markets.

The overarching message of the report is the call to further invest in the human capital of youth in Sub-Saharan Africa to take advantage of the large youth cohorts there. Youth in Africa leave school too early and enter the labor market unprepared, limiting their contribution to economic growth and increasing their vulnerability to poverty and economic hardship.

Why Focus on the Transition to Work for Youth in Africa?

Youth undergo several transitions between the ages of 12 and 24. During this period, some young people move from primary to secondary education. Others leave school and start to work. Decisions made during this period affect young people's acquisition of human capital. These decisions have enormous consequences for their future prospects, as well as those of their communities.

The difficulties youth encounter in entering the work force and developing the skills needed to ensure gainful and productive employment can have profound effects on countries' investment climates and prospects for growth. An educated and healthy work force provides incentives for investment; unskilled and disillusioned youth make returns to investment low and uncertain. For this reason, national governments and regional bodies have placed this issue squarely on their policy agenda for this decade.

Africa's Window of Opportunity

The demographic transition in Sub-Saharan Africa makes youth the most abundant asset the region has or will have in the near future. About 200 million young people between the ages of 12 and 24 live in Africa today; unlike in the rest of the developing world, the share of youth in the population will continue to rise in Africa. Since the 1950s the youth population in Sub-Saharan Africa has more than quadrupled (UN 2005). This rapid rate of growth has pushed the absolute size of the youth population in Sub-Saharan Africa beyond that of many other regions. By 2010 youth will represent about 28 percent of Sub-Saharan Africa's population, making it the "youngest" region in the world. By 2030 Africa is projected to have as many youth as East Asia and by 2050 could also exceed the youth population in South Asia.

This largest-ever youth cohort is more educated and healthier than previous cohorts. Other regions that have seen such an important demographic transition (such as East Asia and Latin America) have had mixed records dealing with it. East Asia, which put the right policies and institutions in place, was able to reap the demographic dividend from a large work force with fewer dependents. In fact, some observers have suggested that up to a third of the Asian miracle growth is attributable to this demographic dividend. In Latin America similar demographic dynamics did not yield better development outcomes.

This opportunity no doubt involves risks. Africa's youth cohort today faces new challenges, such as HIV/AIDS and global competition. Changes in economic conditions and global forces have increased competition and demand for higher skills, increasing the returns to education, particularly higher levels of education, in countries that are growing.

Youth Face Several Challenges in Their Transition to Work

Africa's youth follow two paths in their transitions to working life. Some go to work directly, with little benefit of formal schooling. Others join the work force after a time in the formal school system. Many young people enter the labor market unprepared, making them more vulnerable to demographic and demand changes affecting the labor market. Few youth earn wages and many work in the informal sector. In rural areas most young people are in unpaid family work, are underemployed, or both. In urban areas many young people are unemployed, some of them for long time periods. Those who work are more likely than adults to be stuck in low-productivity jobs. The low-skilled are most vulnerable to weakening demand. Young women have difficulty participating in the labor force. They become discouraged workers and engage in nonmarket activities.

African Youth Enter the Labor Market too Early and too Unprepared

Early entry into the labor market limits Africans from accumulating the human capital they need to get good jobs. The difficulties they face finding work or participating in the labor force mean that the benefits of earlier investments are not fully realized. Safeguarding and building on these investments will greatly increase the likelihood that Africa benefits from its youth bulge. It will reduce the threat to its security and future development. And because labor is the most abundant asset of the poor, making labor more productive will help move Africans out of poverty.

A substantial proportion of young people in most Sub-Saharan African countries never enter school, moving directly into the labor force. In fact, the incidence of child labor in Sub-Saharan Africa is the highest in the world. In 29 African countries for which data are available, an average of 35 percent of children under the age of 15 work. Exposure to the job market in childhood or early adolescence can have a strong negative impact on future labor market experience and earning potential. Today's child laborers will represent the weakest part of tomorrow's adult labor force.

African youth enter the labor market lacking skills. Illiteracy among 15- to 24-year-olds is alarmingly high; in Burkina Faso, Ethiopia, and Mozambique more than 75 percent of out-of-school youth have no education at all. Despite enormous improvements in education over the past decade, the primary completion rate in the region—59 percent— remains the lowest in the world. This education gap remains a major hindrance for Africa's youth as they transition into working life.

Africans who do transition from school to work experience very long periods of inactivity, implying significant labor market entry problems. In 8 of the 13 countries reviewed (Cameroon, Ethiopia, The Gambia, Kenya, Malawi, Mozambique, São Tomé and Principe, and Zambia), young people face about five years of inactivity before finding work; youth in Uganda are inactive for more than three years on average. The transition duration is just one year in Côte d'Ivoire and almost seven years in Mozambique, suggesting that vulnerability to unsuccessful transition varies greatly across countries. Male youth stay in school longer and attain higher education levels than females. They start the transition to work later than females in both urban areas (except in Kenya) and rural areas (except in Kenya and Uganda). Urban youth start working later and have higher education attainment than rural youth.

Youth Are Most Vulnerable to Demographic and Macroeconomic Conditions

By the age of 24, most Africans have left school and started to work. The proportion of youth at work versus those still in school ranges widely across countries: in Kenya and Malawi, more than 40 percent of youth remain in school, and more youth are in school than at work, while in Burkina Faso and Burundi, more than 70 percent of youth work. Transition to work is often difficult because of the lack of strong employment creation in several countries in Sub-Saharan Africa and because of several youth-specific factors. These factors include the growing numbers of new entrants into the labor force, market and policy failures that disproportionately affect youth, and the lack of skills required to match the changing nature of labor demand as a result of globalization and technological changes.

Increases in the relative size of the youth cohort and the number of new entrants into the work force hurt the employment prospects of youth. Cross-country analysis shows that a 1 percent increase in the share of youth in the population increases youth unemployment by 0.5 percentage points. Evidence from Burkina Faso, Ethiopia, and Tanzania confirms this link.

A close investigation of the labor market for youth also reveals important market segmentation by urban and rural residence or gender, a result of market and policy failures reducing youth flows between different segments of the labor market. Evidence from Ethiopia documents how employment among low-skilled youth is more vulnerable to economic shocks and demographic changes. In Burkina Faso those who start to work with little or no education are unlikely to move to better occupations years after entry.

The Policy Response: Broaden Employment Opportunities, Enhance Youth Capabilities, and Offer Youth Second Chances

Applying the *World Development Report 2007* framework to Africa requires increasing employment opportunities for youth in order to safeguard and further develop their skills, providing youth with the capability to choose among opportunities by equipping them with the right skills and improving their access to information and credit, and giving them second chances, so that no one is left behind.

Broadening Opportunities for Employment

Economic growth is key to broadening opportunities. It increases employment for everyone—and has a disproportionately large effect on youth. The recent economic expansion in several countries in Sub-Saharan Africa will have positive effects on youth. In Ethiopia the evidence shows that youth employment responds positively to increased demand for labor, partly offsetting the pressure of a large cohort of new entrants. A good investment climate—which lets the private sector expand and helps trade flourish—will support economic expansion. These general policies are necessary to promote youth employment opportunities, but they are not sufficient. Youth would also benefit from policies that mitigate the market and policy failures responsible for labor market rigidity and segmentation, particularly along the skills and urban-rural dimensions.

Increasing Youth's Capabilities

Youth need to be prepared to take advantage of potential opportunities and to create opportunities on their own though self-employment and entrepreneurial activities. Preparation for employment starts with basic good-quality education, which provides the foundation for future human capital accumulation and the later acquisition of vocational skills in schools, training institutes, and the workplace (World Bank 2006).

In general, higher levels of education are associated with an easier transition to work. But for youth in Africa, education does not always reduce unemployment; in some countries the unemployment rate among educated youth is very high. Over time, however, as youth gain work experience, higher levels of education increase the employment incidence and enhance occupational mobility. In Tanzania, after controlling for experience, the incidence of employment among urban men with the highest level of education is about 26 percentage points higher than that of men with no education. In Burkina Faso the initial occupations of youth vary little with education levels, but young people with higher levels of education are more likely to move to better occupations over time.

In Burkina Faso and Tanzania, school enrollment is negatively affected by adverse income shocks to households, the low education of the household head, and difficulty in access to education, measured by distance to school. Because poor households are more likely to be income-constrained, when faced with negative income shocks, they are more likely to take their children out of school and send them to work. Other households may not realize the incentives for investing in education, partly because parents with low educational attainment tend to understate the benefits of children's schooling.

Providing a Second Chance

Poverty, adverse economic conditions, ill health, employment shocks, and inadequate schools force many young people to leave school, bringing early investment to a halt and frustrating their efforts to prepare for work and develop their livelihoods. In Africa, an estimated 95 million young men and women with no education are either unemployed, in low-paying jobs, or totally withdrawn from the labor force. These youth need a second chance.

Policy makers are concerned about the difficulties African youth are facing in their transition to work and their need for a second chance. They recognize the consequences for the future development of youth as well as for the development of the economies in which they live. Despite this recognition, the response to the problem has been fragmented, confined to limited interventions. The review of interventions in Burkina Faso, Ethiopia, Tanzania, and Uganda shows that most second-chance interventions are small in scale, unevaluated, and face severe challenges for sustainability and scalability.

The Way Forward

Youth are one of Africa's most abundant assets. Only by safeguarding early investments and further developing this resource will the region be able to reap the benefit of its unprecedented demographic transition. This window of opportunity is wide open for policies that ensure that countries can move forward to achieve more rapid growth and poverty reduction. Failing to do so will be costly for this generation and for future generations.

This report offers some guidance to policy makers searching for solutions to address youth employment issues. The approach is based on a policy framework that encompasses the complexity of youth issues and incorporates lessons from international experience. The analyses and the surveys of interventions in Burkina Faso, Ethiopia, Tanzania, and Uganda ground the proposed framework in these countries' realities and provide the background for further empirical examination. The report lays the foundation for mainstreaming youth employment within the World Bank's operations and supporting the policy dialogue with countries.

PART 1

Youth in Africa's Labor Market: A Synthesis

Marito Garcia and Jean Fares

CHAPTER 1

Why Is It Important for Africa to Invest in Its Youth?

Marito Garcia and Jean Fares

Youth are the most abundant asset Sub-Saharan Africa has—or will have in the near future—because of the demographic transition in the region. About 200 million young people between the ages of 12 and 24 live in Africa today, and their number is growing. Investing in youth will greatly increase the likelihood that Africa will benefit from its youth bulge, and it will reduce the threat to its security and future development. Because labor is the most abundant asset of the poor, improving labor's productivity is the best way to reduce poverty.

Investment in children's education and health has increased primary enrollment and reduced health risks in several countries in the region. But African youth still enter the labor market early and unprepared, limiting their human capital accumulation and upward mobility. The difficulties of finding work can limit the benefits of investments in their education.

Economic growth and overall employment creation are necessary to improve employment outcomes for youth as well, but these conditions are not sufficient. Policy makers need to ensure that youth can take full advantage of the opportunities that growth presents and to minimize policy and market failures that affect youth disproportionately. Policies are needed to help young people develop skills and to increase their access to information and credit so that they are able to make better choices among available opportunities. The most vulnerable young people should be granted second-chance opportunities to ensure that no one is left behind.

Why Focus on the Transition to Work?

Youth undergo several transitions between the ages of 12 and 24. During this period some young people move from primary to secondary education. Others leave school and start to work. Decisions made during this period affect young people's human capital and future prospects, as well as the development of the communities and regions where they live.

One of the most important decisions youth make is when to leave school. Those who leave too early enter the labor market unprepared. They are more vulnerable to shocks, less likely to find work, and more likely to get stuck in low-quality jobs, with few opportunities to develop their human capital and move to better employment. Because labor is the most abundant asset of poor households in Africa, ensuring its proper development when youth are most able to learn and develop is essential to helping families move out of poverty.

The difficulties youth encounter entering the work force and developing the skills needed to ensure gainful and productive employment can have profound effects on countries' investment climates and growth prospects. For this reason, national governments and regional bodies have placed this issue prominently on their policy agenda for this decade.

Africa's Demographic Transition Creates a Window of Opportunity

The developing world today has the largest youth cohort ever—1.2 billion people between the ages of 12 and 24. According to most global population projections, the world will not see a cohort this large again in the foreseeable future (World Bank 2006).

Unlike in the rest of the developing world, the share of youth in the population will continue to rise in Sub-Saharan Africa. Since the 1950s the youth population in Sub-Saharan Africa has more than quadrupled (figure 1.1; UN 2005). The share of youth in the population in Sub-Saharan Africa is projected to increase to about 28 percent in 2010, higher than in any other region in the world. By 2035 Sub-Saharan Africa is projected to have as many youth as East Asia, and by 2050 could also exceed South Asia.[1]

Demographic factors—such as changes in fertility and mortality rates—are key to understanding the processes underlying the increase in

Figure 1.1. Africa's Youth Population Is Projected to Grow Faster Than That of Any Other Region in the World

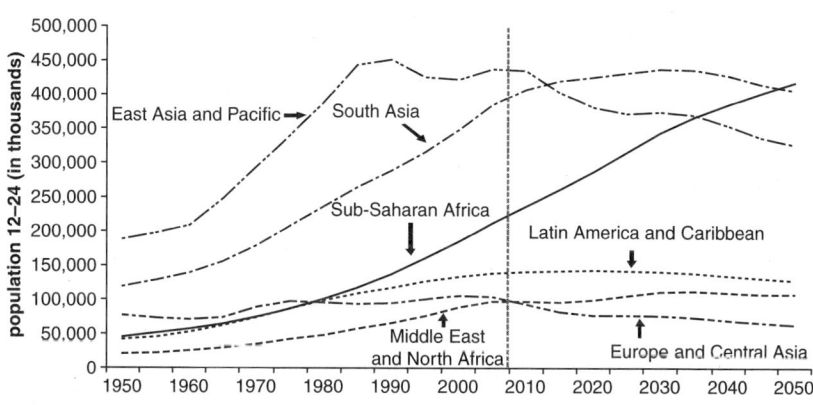

Source: UN (2005).

the size of the youth cohort. In some countries, such as the Democratic Republic of Congo and Kenya, where fertility rates are high and late to decline, the youth population is projected to continue to increase rapidly over the next several decades. Other countries, such as Senegal, are projected to experience slower growth, with the youth population leveling off shortly after 2030 (Lam 2006). These projections are subject to constant revisions and are affected by several shocks, including the prevalence of HIV/AIDS (box 1.1).

Everything else equal, a large cohort reduces labor market opportunities for youth. In Europe and the United States, which experienced large demographic shifts after World War II, wages and employment for youth fell as the relative size of the youth cohort grew (Freeman 1979; Korenman and Neumark 2000). Evidence from a large set of developing countries suggests that the estimated elasticity of youth unemployment to the relative youth cohort size is about 0.5 (O'Higgins 2003). This means that a 1 percent increase in the cohort size increases youth unemployment by 0.5 percentage points. Microanalysis from household surveys in Ethiopia and Tanzania indicates that the increase in the youth share in the local labor market leads to a significant decline in the youth employment rate (see chapter 5).

A large youth cohort also presents an opportunity for the region, however. The rapid rise in the ratio of the working to the nonworking populations in East Asia between 1965 and 1990 may have played an important role in driving the East Asian "economic miracle" (Bloom and Williamson 1998). Since Sub-Saharan Africa will be faced with similar

Box 1.1

HIV/AIDS Is Projected to Reduce the Size of the Youth Cohort in Southern Africa

The population projections of the UN Population Division include projections about AIDS mortality and the potential impact of antiretroviral treatment. They incorporate the Joint United Nations Programme on HIV/AIDS (UNAIDS) model used to project the course of the epidemic in the 60 countries with the highest HIV prevalence (UNAIDS 2002). A second set of hypothetical projections is made based on the assumption that there is no AIDS mortality.

Comparison of the two sets of projections indicates that AIDS mortality has a substantial impact on the size of the youth population in Botswana, South Africa, and Zambia. There is little difference in the two projections in 2000, but by 2010 the projections begin to diverge. In Botswana, for example, the youth population is projected to peak around 2005 under the medium-variant projection; under the "no AIDS" projection, it would have continued increasing for several more decades. In Zambia AIDS is projected to reduce the size of the youth population by about 15 percent by 2015.

AIDS Is Expected to Reduce the Size of the Youth Cohort in Botswana, South Africa, and Zambia

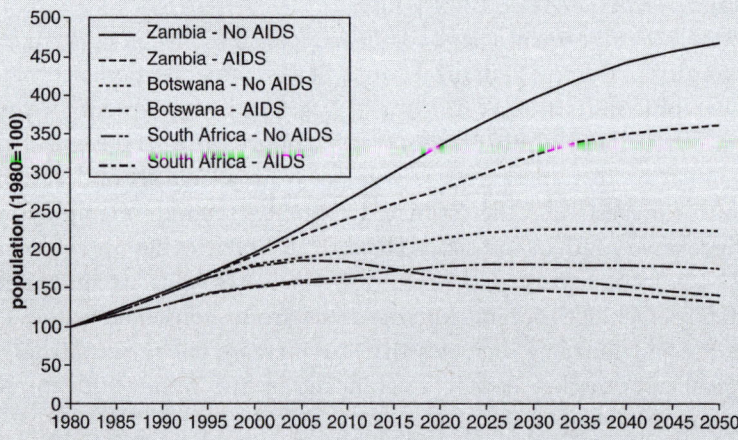

Source: Lam 2006.

demographic dynamics, setting macroeconomic and labor market policies that will help it reap this demographic dividend is essential.

The Level of Educational Attainment Has Risen—and Returns to Education Are Rising in Some Countries

The average years of educational attainment in Sub-Saharan Africa doubled between 1960 and 2000 (Barro and Lee 2000). Although Sub-Saharan Africa has the lowest primary completion rate of any region, at only 59 percent in 2003, enormous progress is being made. According to the *2005 Global Monitoring Report*, since 1990, 8 of the developing world's 10 top performers in annual increases in primary completion rates have been in Africa (Benin, Eritrea, Ethiopia, Guinea, Mali, São Tomé and Principe, Togo, and Malawi). Primary completion rates in these countries have grown by more than 5 percent a year, well above the low-income country average of 0.8 percent a year. All of these countries, which started from a very low base, have enjoyed dramatic growth in enrollment: Ethiopia's primary gross enrollment rate, for example, doubled in just 10 years, from 37 percent in 1995 to about 74 percent in 2005. These improvement rates far exceed anything achieved by today's developed countries at a similar stage of development (World Bank 2005).

The larger cohorts of primary school finishers are increasing the pressure on secondary school enrollment. Between 1990 and 2003, the increase in the cohort size and the primary completion rate was reflected by an increase of more than 160 percent in the number of primary school graduates in Sub-Saharan Africa, adding significant pressure at higher levels of education (World Bank 2006).

In Uganda the share of youth that completed primary school increased while the share of those without primary education shrank between 1992 and 2002; the share of youth with some secondary education almost doubled. With this increase, the economic returns to secondary education rose, reflecting the significant demand for higher skills in the workplace (figure 1.2). In 1999 males in Uganda with primary education earned 30 percent more and males with secondary education earned 140 percent more than those who did not complete primary school. For females the returns were even greater: females with primary education earned 49 percent more and females with secondary education earned 150 percent more than those who did not complete primary school (Vilhuber 2006). These figures indicate large increases over the already high returns to education estimated with data from 1992.

Figure 1.2. Economic Returns to Secondary Education Are High and Rising Faster Than Educational Attainment in Uganda

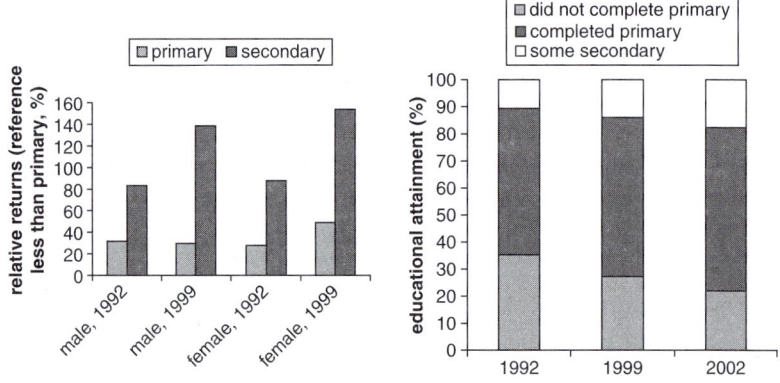

Source: 1999 Uganda National Household Survey data; see chapter 11.

Despite Progress, Significant Challenges Remain

Despite considerable progress in the region, youth continue to face challenges in successfully transitioning to work, including high involvement in child labor, low educational attainment, predominantly informal employment opportunities, low human capital investment outside of school, high illiteracy rates, and other barriers.

- *Child labor.* The incidence of child labor in Sub-Saharan Africa is the highest in the world. In 29 African countries for which data are available, an average of 35 percent of children under the age of 15 work outside the home (figure 1.3). These estimates are likely to understate child labor because of the difficulties of capturing various activities children undertake outside the market and because of the short spells of work that may be missed by surveys. The variation across countries in the region is significant, with extremely high levels of child labor in Sierra Leone and Togo.

- *Low educational attainment.* As a result of early entry into the work force, the out-of-school population has very low educational attainment in most countries in Sub-Saharan Africa (figure 1.4). In Burkina Faso, Ethiopia, and Mozambique, more than 75 percent of out-of-school youth have no education at all. In almost all countries in the region, a majority of out-of-school youth did not finish primary school.

Figure 1.3. Too Many Children Are Working in Many Sub-Saharan African Countries

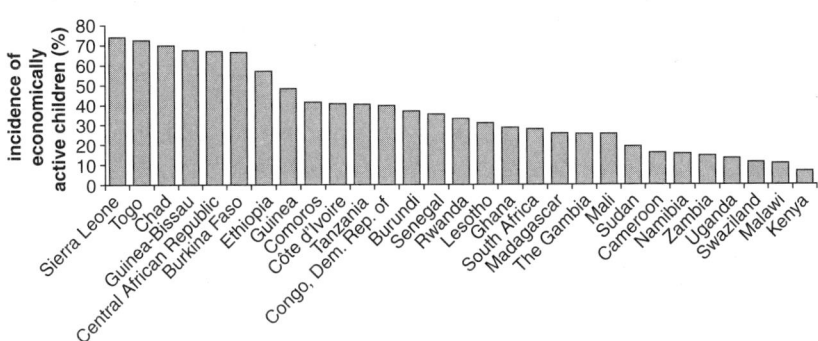

Source: Fares and Raju 2006.

Figure 1.4. The Level of Education among Out-of-School Youth in Africa Is Low

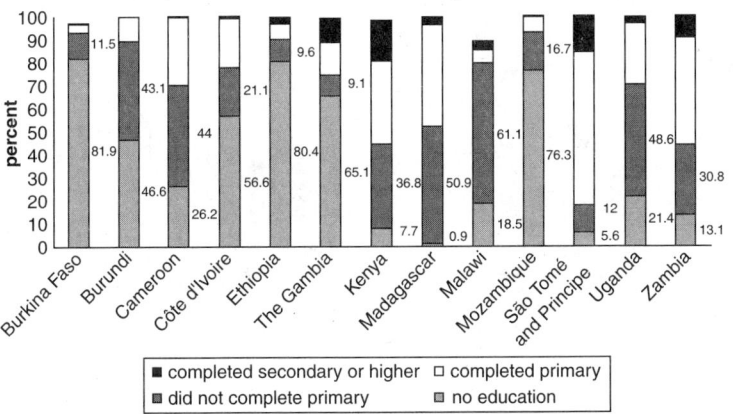

Source: Understanding Children's Work calculations based on World Bank Standard Files and Standard Indicators datasets; see chapter 7 in UN (2005).

Educational attainment figures tell only part of the story, because they fail to capture the low quality of education. In several countries less than half of women 15–24 with some primary schooling can read a simple sentence. In Namibia more than 80 percent of children finish primary school, but less than 20 percent master the material covered. (See figure 1.5.)

- *Predominantly informal employment creation.* The incidence of self-employment among youth is high (figure 1.6). In some countries, including Burundi, The Gambia, and Zambia, almost all rural youth

Figure 1.5. The Level of Literacy Varies Widely in Sub-Saharan Africa, with Higher-Income Countries Tending to Have Higher Literary Rates

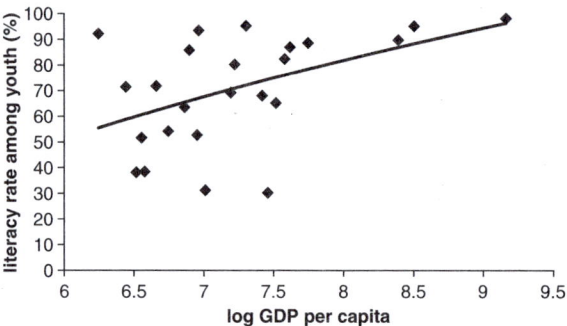

Source: Fares and Raju 2006.

Figure 1.6. Most African Youth Work in the Informal Sector or Are Self-Employed

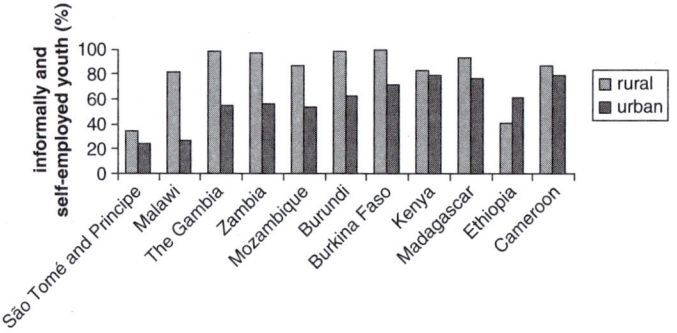

Source: Understanding Children's Work calculations based on World Bank Standard Files and Standard Indicators datasets, see chapter 7.

employment is in the informal and self-employment sectors. In urban areas some young people work in paid employment, but even there almost 80 percent of youth in Cameroon and Kenya work in the informal sector or are self-employed.

- *Low investment in human capital.* Investment in human capital outside of school has lagged. In the formal sector, skill development schemes continue to be supply-driven and disconnected from the demands of the labor market (Adams 2006). In the informal sector, traditional apprenticeship is still the main mechanism for skill development for new entrants. The strength of the traditional apprenticeship is its practical orientation, self-regulation, and self-financing. It reaches those who lack the educational requirement needed for formal training and is generally cost-effective. Apprenticeship tends to be biased against young women, however, and perpetuates the use of traditional and outdated technologies (World Bank 2006).

- *High illiteracy among 15–24-year-olds.* Literacy rates vary widely in Sub-Saharan Africa. Several countries, including Cape Verde, Côte d'Ivoire, Kenya, South Africa, and Tanzania, have raised literacy rates above 90 percent; in others the literacy rate among youth is estimated to be as low as 30 percent. Literacy among youth increases with income (figure 1.5). Large variations even among countries with similar income levels point to the significant challenges countries face in developing young people's skills and integrating youth into the work force.

- *Barriers to youth entry into the labor market.* In 2003 more than 18 million youth in Sub-Saharan Africa—21 percent of the work force—were unemployed. This figure rose 32.5 percent between 1993 and 2003. In rapidly growing urban areas, the level of youth unemployment is three to four times that of adults. In other areas, a large proportion of the population, particularly females, remains outside the labor market. Among females who are not in school, more than 50 percent in Mozambique and 60 percent in Ethiopia are outside the labor force (see chapter 5). These high estimates may be attributable to measurement problems, particularly for young girls and women working within their own households. In Tanzania the majority of young females report that the main reason they are not looking for work is their household responsibilities.

The Policy Response

A successful policy response to the challenge of youth employment rests on three pillars: broadening opportunities for young people to accumulate and preserve human capital, increasing the capability of youth to take advantage of work opportunities, and providing a second chance, so that no one is left behind.

Broadening opportunities to acquire human capital is essential to continue the progress already made on primary education. More needs to be done to increase access to postprimary education and enhance the quality of education. The challenge in the labor market is to create jobs that allow youth to protect and continue to develop their human capital. Beyond schools, youth need access to skill development through apprenticeship schemes, both formal and informal, and vocational education driven by the needs in the labor market. The large stock of low-skilled youth (child laborers, school drop-outs, and former soldiers) facing difficulties accessing the labor market calls for a system of second chances to reintegrate youth into the work force. The costs of failure are tremendous.

Broadening Opportunities in the Labor Market

Broadening opportunities in the labor market for youth not only allows young people to put the skills acquired in school to use, it also helps ensure that they continue to acquire and develop the skills needed to earn a good livelihood. Because youth tend to learn most in their early years of work experience, the difficulties they face entering employment can lead to deterioration in their human capital and the loss of early investment in skill development—with long-lasting effects on their future work.

Economic growth and general job creation will expand the opportunities for youth to find work. In Ethiopia the estimated youth employment elasticity of demand is positive, exceeding one in several instances (figure 1.7). But general policies will not be sufficient to smooth the transition to work, because market and policy failures limit young people's ability to take advantage of opportunities (see chapter 6). The demographic pressure

Figure 1.7. Less-Skilled Youth Are Most Vulnerable to Changes in the Supply of and Demand for Labor in Ethiopia

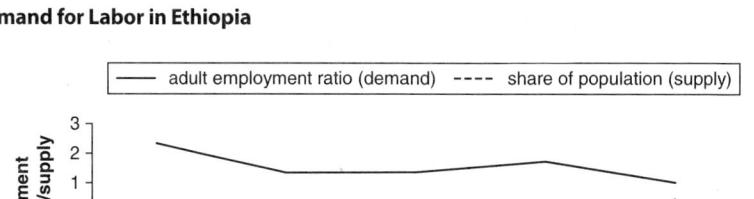

Source: World Bank calculations, based on chapter 9 in this report.

from the large youth cohort entering the labor market will adversely affect youth employment in Africa. Policies need to ensure that demand will offset these pressures and allow the market to absorb these new cohorts into productive employment.

Increasing the Capability of Youth to Take Advantage of Work Opportunities

Increasing youth capability starts with providing young men and women with the relevant skills and information they need to enter work. Because many youth start work too early, they do not have the chance to accumulate the minimum level of human capital needed to be well prepared in their transition to the labor market. In Ethiopia less-skilled youth are much more vulnerable than other youth to fluctuations in economic conditions and to supply pressures from changes in the size of the youth cohort (figure 1.7). Improving their skills, in school and beyond, is necessary to protect them from supply and demand shocks.

Youth need to be empowered so they can work for themselves and create jobs for others. Empowering them to do so requires improving the business climate and increasing youth access to credit and information.

Giving Youth a Second Chance

Many youth in Sub-Saharan Africa need a second chance. Weather, economic, and political fluctuations are common, and youth are most vulnerable to these shocks. Many young people are infected with HIV; others are AIDS orphans. Because youth experiment early on in their careers, they are more mobile and more likely to change jobs or residence than other workers. But doing so involves risks. Giving youth a second chance will permit them to better manage these risks, allowing them to recover from shocks and move to more productive opportunities.

Second-chance opportunities are particularly important for the estimated 95 million unskilled youth in Africa who are out of school and either unemployed or underemployed.[2] Governments everywhere in Africa are considering providing them with a second chance, through well-targeted training programs or direct employment creation. Some countries are implementing short-term interventions needed as a bridge response. Long-term policies that increase the opportunities and the capability of youth are also taking shape in some countries. With almost half of Africa's youth in need of second-chance opportunities, these policies need to be a priority.

Notes

1. The UN *World Population Prospects* projects that Sub-Saharan Africa will have more youth than any other region by 2050. Projections over long horizons are very uncertain and unreliable, however.

2. This estimate is based on the assumption that the average share of unskilled youth in Sub-Saharan Africa is equal to the estimated average share of unskilled youth in the 13 countries with available data on educational attainment.

CHAPTER 2

Transitions to Working Life for Africa's Youth

Marito Garcia and Jean Fares

Africa's youth follow two paths in their transitions to working life. Some go to work directly, without benefit of formal schooling. Others join the work force after spending time in the formal school system.

A substantial proportion of young people in most Sub-Saharan African countries never enter school, moving directly into the labor force. The incidence of child labor in Sub-Saharan Africa is the highest in the world. In 29 African countries for which data are available, an average of 35 percent of children under the age of 15 work (Fares and Raju 2006). Early exposure to the job market in childhood or early adolescence can have a strong negative impact on future labor market experience and earning potential. Today's child laborers will represent the weakest part of tomorrow's adult labor force.

Africans who transition from school to work experience very long periods of inactivity, implying significant labor market entry problems. In 8 of the 13 countries reviewed (Cameroon, Ethiopia, The Gambia, Kenya, Malawi, Mozambique, São Tomé and Principe, and Zambia), young people face about five years of inactivity before finding work; youth in Uganda are inactive for more than three years on average. The transition duration is just one year in Côte d'Ivoire and almost seven years in Mozambique. These large differences indicate that the vulnerability of young people to unsuccessful transition varies greatly across countries.

School nonentrants are a great policy concern because of their vulnerability to undesirable transition outcomes. School nonentrants are among the groups most vulnerable to child labor, therefore, finding satisfactory employment as adults cannot be separated from the issue of child labor.

The size of the group of school nonentrants varies widely across countries. In one broad group of countries, at least 90 percent of children attend school for at least some period of time. In a second group of countries, the percentage of children and youth not transiting through the school system is much higher, ranging from 17 percent in Cameroon to 70 percent in Burkina Faso. In 5 of the 13 countries examined in this report, more than 40 percent of 13-year-olds are working (table 2.1). In Burkina Faso and Uganda, more than 63 percent of 10-year-olds are out of school and working.

The average age at first job for children never attending school varies greatly across countries. In Kenya children begin work at about 15; in Ethiopia, Mozambique, and São Tomé and Principe children begin work at 16–17. In contrast, children begin work at about 8 years old in Burkina Faso and at 10 in Burundi. In Zambia about 23 percent of children are already working by age 10, and like Burundi, 42 percent are working by the time they reach 13.

Of the world's 250 million child workers, one-third live in Africa. Africa has the highest incidence of child labor in the world, and it has more child workers than any other region of the world. Twenty-five percent of child workers ages 5–14 live in Africa—more than in Asia

Table 2.1. Age of First Job and Percentage of Children Working in Selected Countries

Country	Age at first job	Percentage of 10-year-olds working	Percentage of 12-year-olds working	Percentage of 13-year-olds working
Burkina Faso	8.4	63.6	66.0	68.3
Burundi	10.2	22.5	35.5	42.2
Cameroon	11.2	32.7	30.6	32.1
Côte d'Ivoire	11.5	13.7	10.1	8.9
Ethiopia	16.5	15.4	13.7	17.0
Kenya	14.8	8.2	16.4	17.5
Mozambique	17.1	3.9	6.7	13.2
São Tomé and Principe	16.3	9.1	10.8	13.5
Uganda	13.8	63.6	66.0	68.3
Zambia	14.5	22.5	35.5	42.2

Source: Understanding Children's Work calculations based on World Bank Standard Files and Standard Indicators datasets; see chapter 7.

(18.7 percent) or Latin America (17.0 percent). Child labor has been declining everywhere in the world but Africa (ILO 2006). This trend is linked to a combination of factors, including economic decline, war, famine, and HIV/AIDS.

In West Africa the need for children to find work has led to child migration to Benin. Eight percent of children 6–16 in West Africa are reported to have left their households to work in Benin. Children who are orphans or in foster care are more likely than other children to work (Kielland and Tovo 2006). Wars, famine, and the spread of HIV/AIDS in Sub-Saharan Africa have increased the number of orphans, potentially increasing the number of child workers.

The incidence of child labor poses an enormous challenge in Sub-Saharan Africa. Working can have deleterious effects on children's health, education, and moral well-being, with effects that persist over the lifecycle (Bhalotra 2003).

In Tanzania a nonnegligible proportion of the population starts to work at an early age, either dropping out of or never attending school. In Ethiopia, where the rate of child labor force participation may be the highest in the world, more than 40 percent of 5- to 9-year-old urban males are involved in economic activities (figure 2.1; Cockburn 2002). More than a third of all 5- to 14-year-olds in Ethiopia—more than 5 million children—were at work in economic activity in 2001. Child labor is also widespread in Burkina Faso. The problem is particularly serious in rural areas, but even in urban areas about 10 percent of children work.

Most African children who work are unpaid family members, particularly in rural areas. As children grow older, they engage in more wage employment and are more likely to work as paid domestic helpers, although wage employment is still limited. In Ethiopia most child laborers

Figure 2.1. Child Participation in the Labor Force Is High, Particularly among Rural Males in Ethiopia

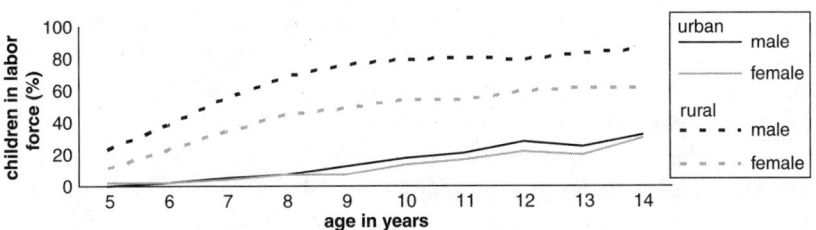

Source: Understanding Children's Work calculations based on Ethiopia Labor Force Survey 2001; see chapter 9.

work in the agriculture sector (table 2.2). Urban children also work, many of them in the service sector. As they age, children move away from agriculture into other sectors, such as services and manufacturing, although movement is more limited in rural than in urban areas.

Average hours worked differ by gender and location. Females and urban dwellers work fewer hours than males and rural workers. Younger children work longer hours than older children, probably because they are more likely to work as unpaid family workers. As children grow older and move into paid sectors, employers reduce the number of hours worked to levels profitable for them, taking into account the fact that children's productivity diminishes after a certain threshold. The hours of paid employment are usually less than the desired numbers of hours, especially among service workers and paid agricultural workers (see chapter 9).

Poverty and Large Income Shocks Push Children into the Work Force

A wide body of literature examines child labor. Some studies find a nonlinear relationship between child labor and household poverty in Africa (Andvig 2000). This relation is explained by the fact that a household needs to reach a certain level of assets to create employment opportunities for children; the poorest households may lack sufficient assets to create job opportunities. The incidence of child labor may therefore first increase with rising income and then decrease (Bhalotra and Tzannatos 2002).

Other factors that may cause children to work are related to market and institutional problems. Parents may make children work to replace lost income in bad times (Jacoby and Skoufias 1997). Children from land-rich households are more likely to work than are children of small landowners or landless agricultural workers, because the marginal product of family labor increases with the level of assets or capital (Bhalotra and Heady 2000).

What causes children to go to work? How do changing economic conditions affect children's labor participation? Examination of behavior in Burkina Faso holds some answers. Among children 12–14 in urban areas, labor force participation declines with per capita household income (table 2.3). Gender also affects participation, with males 4.5 percentage points less likely than females to participate in the labor force (chapter 9). Labor force participation is less sensitive to changes in income in households in which the head is more educated and more sensitive in households in

Table 2.2. Type and Sector of Employment of Child Workers by Age Group, Gender, and Urban-Rural Location in Ethiopia

Age group	Work modality (%)[a]					Sector (%)[b]				Average weekly working hours
	Domestic employee	Wage employee	Self-employed	Unpaid family worker	Other employment	Agriculture	Manufacturing	Services[c]	Other[d]	
5–9										
Male	0.1	1.6	0.7	97.4	0.2	99.0	0.2	0.7	0.2	38.4
Female	0.2	0.3	0.8	98.2	0.4	96.0	0.7	2.3	1.0	32.1
Urban	5.0	1.7	7.8	76.9	8.6	56.1	5.5	26.2	12.2	26.0
Rural	0.1	1.1	0.6	98.0	0.2	98.4	0.3	1.0	0.3	36.2
10–14										
Male	0.5	4.6	2.0	92.5	0.5	94.9	0.6	3.7	0.8	34.1
Female	1.6	1.3	3.6	92.9	0.7	84.6	4.0	8.4	3.0	27.1
Urban	10.5	6.0	5.8	61.4	6.2	25.3	11.4	45.4	17.9	26.3
Rural	0.4	3.1	1.9	94.3	0.3	94.4	1.5	3.4	0.8	31.6

Source: Understanding Children's Work calculations based on Ethiopia Labor Force Survey 2001.

a. Percentage distribution of employed population in each age group.

b. Percentage distribution of employed population in each age group. Sector breakdown based on ISIC Revision 3 if information is available.

c. Services include wholesale and retail trade, hotels anc restaurants, transport, financial intermediation, real estate, public administration, education, health and social work, other community services, and private household services.

d. Other sectors include mining and quarrying; electricity, gas, and water; construction; and extraterritorial organizations.

Table 2.3. Effect of Poverty and Household Income Shocks on Labor Force Participation of Urban Dwellers Ages 12–14 in Burkina Faso

Dependent variable: Whether the individual works or is unemployed and looking for work, individuals age 12 to 14 living in urban areas

	Males				Females			
	[1]	[2]	[3]	[4]	[5]	[6]	[7]	[8]
Household income decreased between survey year and year before	0.045	0.049	0.037	0.121	0.053	0.062	0.026	0.060
	(0.028)	(0.029)	(0.029)	(0.046)	(0.027)	(0.032)	(0.028)	(0.044)
Decrease in income × head's education	—	-0.005	—	—	—	-0.016	—	—
		(0.003)				(0.022)		
Decrease in income × income in bottom quintile	—	—	0.077	—	—	—	0.275	—
			(0.086)				(0.116)	
Decrease in income × household size	—	—	—	-0.007	—	—	—	-0.001
				(0.003)				(0.003)
30–59 minutes away from elementary school	0.031	0.031	0.031	0.033	-0.024	-0.024	-0.020	-0.024
	(0.042)	(0.042)	(0.042)	(0.042)	(0.040)	(0.040)	(0.040)	(0.040)
60+ minutes away from elementary school	0.008	0.007	0.006	0.000	0.446	0.446	0.458	0.446
	(0.143)	(0.144)	(0.139)	(0.141)	(0.172)	(0.172)	(0.168)	(0.172)
30–59 minutes away from secondary school	0.031	0.031	0.032	0.030	0.015	0.015	0.015	0.015
	(0.031)	(0.031)	(0.031)	(0.031)	(0.030)	(0.030)	(0.030)	(0.030)
60+ minutes away from secondary school	0.061	0.061	0.054	0.065	0.049	0.049	0.037	0.050
	(0.061)	(0.061)	(0.061)	(0.061)	(0.063)	(0.063)	(0.061)	(0.063)
N	1575	1575	1575	1575	1692	1692	1692	1692

Source: Calculations based on Survey of Household Living Standards, 2003; see chapter 8.

Note: Columns 1 (male) and 5 (females) represent the base model. Variants of the model are given in columns 2, 3, and 4 for males and 6, 7, and 8 for females simulating increase or decrease in incomes.

— Not available.

the bottom quintile of the income distribution. The effect is large for females, whose labor force participation increases 27.5 percentage points when household income drops (table 2.3). Similar results emerge if self-reported changes in income are used as the measure of household welfare.

The School-to-Work Transition of Africa's Youth Is Long and Difficult

The transition from school to work is by no means a linear process, with individuals leaving school once and for all before beginning their working lives. For individuals who never re-enter school, the starting point of the transition is well defined. The end point of the transition is more difficult to define. Individuals may experience periods of employment and periods of unemployment; they may change jobs or possibly stay out of work permanently. Young people may take temporary jobs, work on the household farm or in the family enterprise, or perform household chores for lack of better work opportunities or for the potential return these initial work experiences provide in terms of future employment and income prospects.

These problems are particularly relevant in developing countries, where women's labor force participation (at least in the market) is low and underemployment, self-employment, home production, and casual employment are widespread. In addition, school-leaving time is endogenous and probably influenced by expectations about the transition to work and the kind of job that will be obtained at the end of the transition.

Integrating the analysis of optimal school-leaving age with that of employment search and labor force participation provides a better understanding of this transition period. To measure the school-to-work transition, this report develops a new indicator, based on the difference between the average school-leaving age and the average age of first entry into work (annex 6A describes the features and limitations of this indicator). In the absence of the longitudinal data generally available in developed countries, this study uses cross-sectional data to measure the length of the transition. Under appropriate assumptions, the available data allow the parameters of interest to be identified.

The length of the school-to-work transition varies across countries (table 2.4). The average school-leaving age ranges from 15.9 years in São Tomé and Principe to 19.0 years in Cameroon; the average age at first job ranges from 18.4 years in Côte d'Ivoire to 24.4 years in Malawi.

Table 2.4. Duration of the School-to-Work Transition in Selected Countries

Country	Beginning point of transition (average age of dropping out of school)	End point of transition (average age of entry into work)	Length of transition (years)
Burkina Faso	17.1	18.6	1.5
Burundi	18.8	20.7	1.9
Cameroon	19.0	23.8	4.8
Côte d'Ivoire	17.4	18.4	1.0
Ethiopia	18.0	23.4	5.4
Gambia, The	17.4	23.2	5.8
Kenya	17.7	22.6	5.3
Madagascar	17.2	19.0	1.8
Malawi	18.8	24.4	5.6
Mozambique	16.7	23.4	6.7
São Tomé and Principe	15.9	21.3	5.4
Uganda	18.0	21.3	3.3
Zambia	17.5	22.4	5.0

Source: Understanding Children's Work calculations based on World Bank Standard Files and Standard Indicators datasets for various years between 1994 and 2001; see chapter 7.
Note: Estimated probabilities calculated on the basis of the age at which work participation rate is at its maximum. Reference age group is 5–24 for all countries except Madagascar, for which the reference group is 10- to 24-year-olds.

The total transition duration is just one year in Côte d'Ivoire and almost seven years in Mozambique. These data suggest that the vulnerability of young people to unsuccessful transition varies greatly by country. The new indicator can help identify the age range that policy should focus on in each country.

For all 13 countries, the starting point of the transition is relatively late. This is due largely to the high average age of school entry and grade repetition in these countries, where the average grade 1 pupil is more than 8 years old. The relatively high school-leaving age is particularly noteworthy given low school enrollment rates in Sub-Saharan Africa. In Burkina Faso, for example, at age 17.1 years, the average age of dropout, just 15 percent of the cohort is in school (figure 2.2). The late average school-leaving age suggests the importance of the selection process associated with initial enrollment. Because the leaving age probably reflects delayed entry, intermittent attendance, and grade repetition, it is not indicative of a high level of human capital accumulation.

The average age of labor market entry varies more across countries than does the average age of leaving school, suggesting that the transition

Figure 2.2. The Late Age of School Leaving Is Not an Indication of High Educational Attainment in Burkina Faso

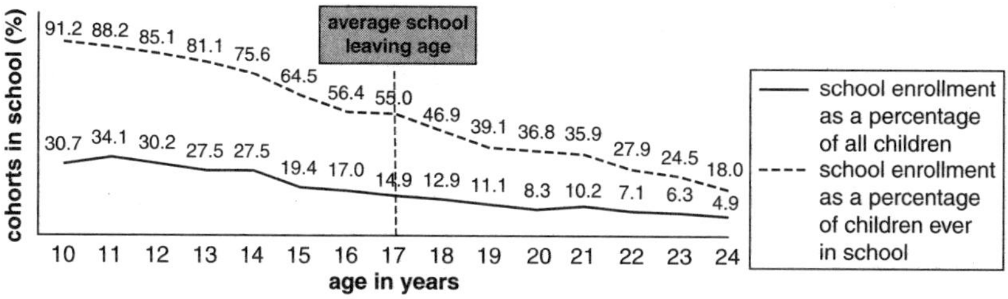

Source: Understanding Children's Work calculations based on World Bank Standard Files and Standard Indicators datasets.

from school to work is affected more by the process of finding a job than by the age at which one leaves school. The transition to work appears to depend on both residence and gender as well as the interaction between the two (table 2.5). Female youth tend to leave school earlier and transit to work more slowly than males. Rural youth tend to start the transition earlier and find employment more quickly than urban youth.

Four patterns emerge from the data:

- Male youth stay in school longer (and perhaps reach higher educational attainment) than female youth. They thus start the transition to work later than females in both urban areas (except in Kenya) and rural areas (except in Kenya and Uganda).
- Urban youth have higher educational attainment than rural youth. The transition starts later in urban areas for both males (all countries) and females (all countries except São Tomé and Principe).
- Location appears to affect the length of the transition for female but not male youth. Labor market entry takes longer for female youth in urban areas than in rural areas (except in Côte d'Ivoire and São Tomé and Principe); there is no consistent pattern in length of transition by location for male youth. The transition for female rural youth is particularly short in Burkina Faso and Madagascar, at only one year.
- Gender appears to be related to the duration of the transition in urban but not rural areas. Urban males make the transition to work more quickly than urban females (except in Côte d'Ivoire). There is no consistent pattern by gender in rural areas.

Table 2.5. Length and Timing of Transition from School to Work by Gender, Residence, and Country

Country	Rural males			Rural females			Urban males			Urban females		
	Average age leaving school	Mean age at first job	Length of transition	Average age leaving school	Mean age at first job	Length of transition	Average age leaving school	Mean age at first job	Length of transition	Average age leaving school	Mean age at first job	Length of transition
Burkina Faso	17.2	20.7	2.2	15.2	15.0	1.1	17.3	20.7	2.0	15.9	17.0	3.3
Burundi	19.0	24.4	1.0	17.0	17.0	3.0	20.0	24.5	3.2	17.4	19.3	4.8
Cameroon	19.8	26.5	3.6	19.2	20.4	3.7	20.0	25.0	4.3	19.4	21.8	6.9
Côte d'Ivoire	16.9	18.3	2.3	16.0	18.2	3.7	19.0	20.7	1.6	17.2	19.0	1.3
Ethiopia	19.0	21.8	4.4	17.5	19.5	2.8	20.0	23.8	3.4	18.8	23.8	4.5
Gambia, The	17.9	23.4	3.4	15.8	17.4	2.6	19.2	24.8	6.2	18.9	21.6	6.6
Kenya	18.2	21.6	4.8	18.9	21.5	4.2	19.0	21.6	4.0	19.7	23.2	5.6
Madagascar	17.7	20.0	1.5	16.0	16.0	1.0	18.5	20.5	2.2	16.7	17.2	2.3
Malawi	19.4	24.9	4.1	17.9	22.9	5.9	20.0	24.9	4.2	19.9	24.3	6.0
Mozambique	16.9	23.9	6.1	15.1	20.5	5.5	17.4	24.0	5.6	16.2	23.1	6.9
São Tomé and Principe	17.3	23.2	4.6	15.8	22.0	7.2	17.5	21.0	4.4	15.8	19.9	6.7
Uganda	17.6	—	2.9	17.4	—	3.1	18.1	—	2.5	18.7	—	4.6
Zambia	18.1	24.3	3.0	15.9	19.8	4.0	18.7	24.4	5.7	17.0	21.1	7.4

Source: Author calculations based on World Bank Standard Files and Standard Indicators datasets; see chapter 7.
Note: Data are from various years between 1994 and 2001.
— Not available.

The duration of the transition from school to work varies widely across countries, and accounting for the differences is not easy. An initial examination of some factors—gross domestic product (GDP) growth (a proxy for the ability of the economy to absorb school leavers), income distribution, openness to trade (as proxied by the ratio of exports plus imports to GDP), and the share of industrial value added in total value added (a proxy for differences in the structure of national economies)—showed no significant results. Only GDP growth showed some correlations; all other factors were uncorrelated with the length of the transition, suggesting that factors specific to the youth labor market may be more important in determining transitions than macro differences. A more in-depth analysis combining individual, household, and institutional characteristics will be necessary to explain cross-country differences.

CHAPTER 3

How Do Africa's Young People Spend Their Time?

Marito Garcia and Jean Fares

To craft policies that address youth-related issues, policy makers need to understand how Africans between the ages of 15 and 24 spend their time. Some youth are still in school, but by age 24 the majority have left school and begun to work. In Malawi 64 percent of 15- to 19-year-olds are in school; by age 20 this proportion drops to 18 percent. By age 24 most rural (but not urban) youth are already working and beginning to raise families. In Madagascar, for example, 72 percent of rural and 37 percent of urban 24-year-olds are working (see chapter 7).

Not Many Youth Are in the Labor Market and Employed

Youth unemployment, the most common measure of youth labor market status, varies significantly across countries, ranging from about 1 percent in Uganda to 15 percent in Mozambique.[1] In Sub-Saharan Africa whether a young person has a job often determines whether his or her household falls above the poverty threshold. This measure is included as an indicator for monitoring the United Nations (UN) Millennium Development Goal to "develop and implement strategies for decent and productive work for youth."

Unemployment can be captured by an unemployment ratio or an unemployment rate. Each measure has a slightly different implication.

The youth unemployment *rate* (unemployment as proportion of the youth in the labor force) does not provide a full description of the difficulties youth face in the labor market. In fact, in countries with widespread poverty, looking at the unemployment rate may be misleading, because most youth cannot afford to remain unemployed. Their difficulties in the labor market may be better reflected by measures of the quality of employment or measures of underemployment.

The unemployment *ratio* (unemployment as a proportion of the total youth population) varies across countries. Youth unemployment is almost nonexistent in Burundi, The Gambia, and Malawi, where less than 1.5 percent of all 15- to 24-year-olds are unemployed. In contrast, the unemployment ratio exceeds 9 percent in Cameroon, Côte d'Ivoire, Kenya, Mozambique, São Tomé and Principe, and Zambia. These levels of unemployment are still relatively low, perhaps suggesting that unemployment is a poor measure of welfare in developing countries.

Unemployment as a proportion of the population is generally higher for young adults (ages 20–24) than for teenagers (15–19)—not surprisingly, given that teenagers are more likely to be in school. Once in the workforce, teenagers have a harder time than young adults finding employment. Therefore, while the employment ratio is higher for young adults than for teenagers (except in São Tomé and Principe), the unemployment rate of young adults is lower than that of teenagers (except in Burkina Faso, Burundi, and Malawi).

Unemployment measures understate the total extent of the youth unemployment problem, for several reasons. First, they fail to capture discouraged workers. Second, and of particular relevance in Sub-Saharan Africa, these measures fail to capture people who are too poor to be unemployed and who therefore must take up work regardless of its quality or level of remuneration. Third, unemployment indicators do not capture underemployment. According to the very broad definition of employment used in generating estimates of employment, anyone who is undertaking economic activity for an hour or more during the reference week is considered employed, even if he or she is actively looking for additional work. Many young people in Sub-Saharan Africa who are categorized as employed are working fewer hours than they would like.

The level of joblessness (defined as the sum of unemployed and inactive workers) is arguably a better measure of the youth employment disadvantage, as long as inactivity does not include home production.[2] In contrast to unemployment, which is relatively low in some countries, joblessness is high, reflecting the significant proportion of inactive young people. Joblessness exceeds 20 percent in Cameroon, Ethiopia, The Gambia, Kenya, Malawi, Mozambique, and São Tomé and Principe; it is less than 10 percent in only one country in this study (Burundi). The driving indicator for joblessness is youth inactivity.

A Large Proportion of Youth Are "Inactive"

In a few countries, the proportion of young people working is high. Youth employment is 78 percent in Burkina Faso, 70 percent in Burundi, and 62 percent in Madagascar. But in most countries a large proportion of youth is inactive—they are neither in the labor force (employed or unemployed) nor in school.[3] Youth inactivity is particularly high in Ethiopia, at 59 percent, and Mozambique, at 45 percent. In 8 of the 13 countries reviewed, at least 20 percent of youth are inactive.[4]

Inactivity appears to have an important gender dimension: in all 13 countries, female youth are more likely to be inactive than their male counterparts. Income does not appear to be correlated with inactivity: both Ethiopia and Madagascar are very poor countries, but the rate of inactivity among youth in Ethiopia exceeds 50 percent while the rate in Madagascar is just 3 percent.

The data do not allow discouraged workers (people who have given up looking for work or who never entered the labor market because of meager job prospects) to be distinguished from people involved in nonwork activities or noneconomic work (fetching water and wood, cooking, taking care of children, keeping house). Most inactive young people indicate spending time on noneconomic work, but so do young people in the labor force; inactivity does not therefore necessarily reflect a choice of domestic work over labor market involvement.

Many Young People Are in School

The percentage of youth (15–24) in school only (not also working) ranges from 11 percent in Burkina Faso to 42 percent in Kenya. Most of these youth belong to higher income groups and are pursuing secondary, post-secondary, or tertiary education.[5]

The proportion of young people in school varies widely across countries, although it does not exceed 50 percent in any of the 13 countries reviewed. Kenya and Malawi have the highest percentage of youth in school, while Burkina Faso and Ethiopia have the lowest (13.7 percent and 22.3 percent respectively). The low proportion of students in school does not necessarily imply low school enrollment because many youth have completed their education. There is, however, a correlation between the proportion of in-school youth and school attainment in the countries studied.

Education and employment do not appear to be complementary because a relatively small number of young people combine school and work. This figure ranges from 2 percent in Cameroon to 10 percent in Uganda. This fact is surprising and may reflect the nature of the data available.

Young Women Have Lower Rates of School Attainment, School Enrollment, and Employment Than Young Men

Gender differences in time use are stark (table 3.1). The percentage of males in school is more than twice that of females in Mozambique, and it is markedly higher in Côte d'Ivoire, Ethiopia, and The Gambia. In only two countries, Madagascar and São Tomé and Principe, does female education participation approach that of males.

Females are overrepresented among inactive young people in most countries in Sub-Saharan Africa. This may reflect the fact that engagement in household activities, which are usually assigned to females, are classified as inactivity.[6]

Male employment exceeds female employment in 9 of the 13 countries reviewed (all but Burundi, The Gambia, Uganda, and Zambia), although the differences are not always large. There is no clear pattern by gender in terms of unemployment. For example, only 14 percent of women are employed in Ethiopia, while nearly 70 percent are employed in Burkina Faso. Three percent of Burundi women are inactive versus 67 percent of Ethiopian women, despite similar levels of development (see table 3.1). Employment, unemployment, and inactivity rates for males also differ across countries. These large differences in levels of inactivity suggest the need to look more closely at the definition of inactivity and to focus on country-specific solutions.

Gender differences in unemployment are noteworthy in five countries (Côte d'Ivoire, Madagascar, Mozambique, São Tomé and Principe, and Zambia), but there is no systematic pattern in terms of labor market advantage. Females are more likely than males to be unemployed in Côte d'Ivoire, Madagascar, and Mozambique, while males are more likely than females to be unemployed in São Tomé and Principe and Zambia.

Table 3.1. Time Use among Male and Female Youth in Selected Countries
(percent)

Country	Only in school		Only working		Unemployed		Inactive		Jobless (unemployed + inactive)	
	Male	Female	Male	Female	Male	Female	Male	Female	Male	Female
Burkina Faso	13.7	8.7	80.0	75.9	3.8	4.6	1.1	10.3	4.9	14.9
Burundi	28.4	23.1	67.4	72.8	0.9	0.7	3.3	3.5	4.2	4.2
Cameroon	36.3	28.4	45.0	41.0	13.3	12.0	2.5	16.9	15.8	28.9
Côte d'Ivoire	33.8	17.8	49.7	45.2	8.6	10.5	7.9	26.5	16.5	37.0
Ethiopia	22.3	13.7	25.5	14.3	3.5	4.4	48.7	67.6	52.1	72.1
Gambia, The	37.8	19.6	31.7	42.6	1.8	1.2	27.5	35.8	29.3	37.0
Kenya	48.4	36.0	23.5	18.3	10.1	10.8	18.0	34.9	28.1	45.7
Madagascar	25.1	21.5	64.2	60.7	5.9	11.8	1.7	4.4	7.6	16.2
Malawi	54.8	31.5	23.3	19.8	2.1	0.8	19.1	47.8	21.3	48.6
Mozambique	26.1	11.2	27.7	16.0	12.5	16.8	32.6	55.8	45.1	72.6
São Tomé and Príncipe	24.3	22.4	45.6	16.9	13.1	9.5	15.3	50.0	28.4	59.4
Uganda	38.6	29.7	41.8	54.3	1.0	0.5	3.8	10.7	4.8	11.2
Zambia	37.2	22.7	37.8	39.3	13.4	9.6	10.7	28.0	24.1	37.6

Source: Understanding Children's Work calculations based on World Bank Standard Files and Standard Indicators datasets; see chapter 7.

The proportion of females in school is similar across the 13 countries: the difference between the country with the highest enrollment and the country with the lowest enrollment is 27 percentage points. In contrast, the proportion of males in school varies widely, with a 41 percentage-point difference between the countries with the highest and lowest enrollments.

Rural Youth Are Less Likely Than Urban Youth to Be in School

Young people in rural areas use their time very differently from their counterparts in urban areas in all 13 countries (table 3.2). Urban youth enjoy greater educational opportunities, staying in school longer and joining the labor force later than rural youth. Educational involvement is much higher for urban youth (except in Kenya) and employment much lower (except in Ethiopia and Kenya).

Unemployment is more common among urban youth (except in São Tomé and Principe), presumably because of the wage differentials between the urban and rural sector. The difference in youth unemployment is very large in most countries: the unemployment ratio for urban young people is more than three times the ratio for rural young people in Burkina Faso, Burundi, Ethiopia, Mozambique, Uganda, and Zambia and twice the ratio for rural young people in Cameroon, Kenya, and Madagascar. Rural youth unemployment is 2 percent or less in Burkina Faso, Burundi, Ethiopia, The Gambia, Malawi, and Uganda. These figures underscore the fact that youth unemployment is overwhelmingly an urban phenomenon in Sub-Saharan Africa.

There is no clear pattern by urban-rural location in terms of inactivity: rates of inactivity are higher among urban young people in eight countries and lower in five.[7] Differences across urban areas in terms of the proportion of youth in school are much smaller than in rural areas, and differences in employment are greater across rural areas than urban areas. However, unemployment and inactivity vary across countries, with no location-specific bias.

Time Use Varies by Income Group

How does household income affect the ways that youth in Sub-Saharan Africa spend their time? In most countries in the region, youth in households with higher incomes are more likely to remain in school (figure 3.1). An exception is Kenya, where school enrollment is lower among youth from the highest income quintile than it is among youth from lower quintiles.

Table 3.2. Time Use among Rural and Urban Youth in Selected Countries

(percent)

Country	Only in school		Only working		Unemployed		Inactive		Jobless (unemployed + inactive)	
	Rural	Urban	Rural	Urban	Rural	Urban	Rural	Urban	Rural	Urban
Burkina Faso	4.3	34.8	89.6	36.6	1.3	14.5	3.9	13.2	5.2	27.8
Burundi	23.3	58.6	73.9	14.8	0.1	11.6	2.7	15.0	2.7	26.6
Cameroon	23.7	48.3	55.2	20.1	9.5	18.5	9.2	11.2	18.7	29.7
Côte d'Ivoire	14.9	34.8	69.1	28.3	4.1	14.4	11.9	22.6	16.0	37.0
Ethiopia	12.1	46.1	18.4	26.4	2.0	13.5	67.5	14.1	69.6	27.6
Gambia, The	20.5	37.0	56.0	16.9	0.8	2.3	21.1	43.3	21.9	45.5
Kenya	45.4	27.3	17.2	36.2	8.3	19.6	29.1	16.9	37.4	36.5
Madagascar	16.9	39.6	72.3	37.1	6.2	16.1	2.2	5.4	8.3	21.4
Malawi	40.5	55.1	22.3	14.8	1.2	2.8	35.7	26.4	36.9	29.1
Mozambique	14.9	29.8	22.0	20.2	8.4	36.1	54.3	12.8	62.7	48.9
São Tomé and Príncipe	14.7	29.3	35.4	28.4	15.3	8.6	33.7	31.8	49.1	40.3
Uganda	32.7	40.6	51.7	31.7	0.4	2.3	4.3	21.9	4.7	24.2
Zambia	25.4	35.8	53.1	16.6	5.8	19.8	14.8	27.4	20.7	47.3

Source: Understanding Children's Work calculations based on World Bank Standard Files and Standard Indicators datasets; see Chapter 7.

33

Figure 3.1. Time Use by Income Quintile Varies across Countries

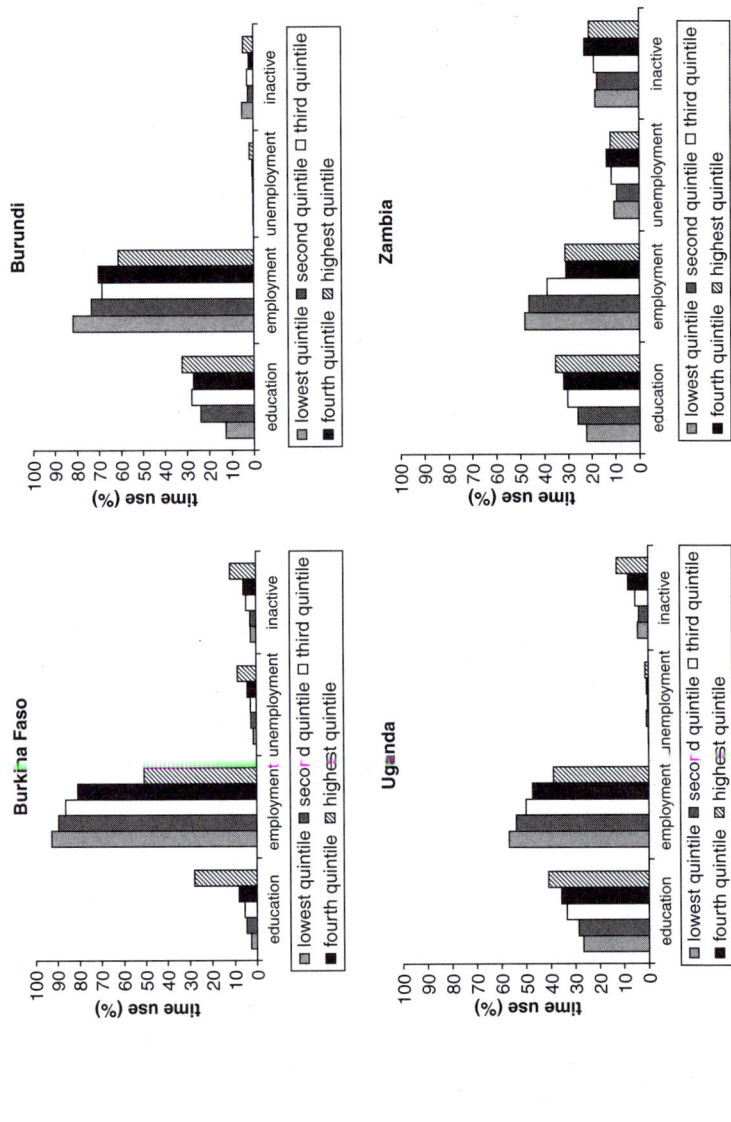

Source: Understanding Children's Work calculations based or World Bank Standard Files and Standard Indicators datasets; see chapter 7.

Table 3.3. Time Use among Teenagers and Young Adults in Selected Countries
(percent)

Country	Only in school		Only working		Unemployed		Inactive		Jobless (unemployed + inactive)	
	15–19	20–24	15–19	20–24	15–19	20–24	15–19	20–24	15–19	20–24
Burkina Faso	14.2	6.9	76.1	80.2	3.8	4.7	4.7	7.6	8.6	12.3
Burundi	31.5	16.1	64.3	79.7	0.6	1.1	3.6	3.1	4.2	4.2
Cameroon	43.4	19.3	33.7	53.8	11.9	13.5	7.8	12.2	19.7	25.7
Côte d'Ivoire	34.1	14.4	39.9	56.8	9.2	10.0	16.7	18.7	26.0	28.7
Ethiopia	25.5	6.3	13.1	29.7	3.0	5.5	58.5	58.5	61.4	64.0
Gambia, The	40.3	13.4	29.7	46.8	1.4	1.6	27.6	36.9	29.1	38.5
Kenya	64.9	11.2	10.0	35.3	8.5	13.2	16.7	40.3	25.1	53.5
Madagascar	36.0	8.5	49.9	77.0	7.7	10.4	2.7	3.5	10.4	13.9
Malawi	64.4	17.6	8.6	35.7	0.5	2.5	26.2	43.8	26.7	46.3
Mozambique	28.5	5.6	11.4	34.2	14.6	15.0	44.9	44.7	59.5	59.6
São Tomé and Principe	37.9	5.7	18.2	47.0	13.2	9.0	29.5	36.3	42.7	45.3
Uganda	47.3	14.5	33.0	70.6	0.4	1.2	6.5	8.6	6.9	9.8
Zambia	46.0	10.0	26.9	52.5	9.0	14.2	17.2	23.0	26.2	37.2

Source: Understanding Children's Work calculations based on World Bank Standard Files and Standard Indicators datasets; see chapter 7.

Figure 3.2. Time Use by Patterns of Young People Vary across Age Groups and Countries

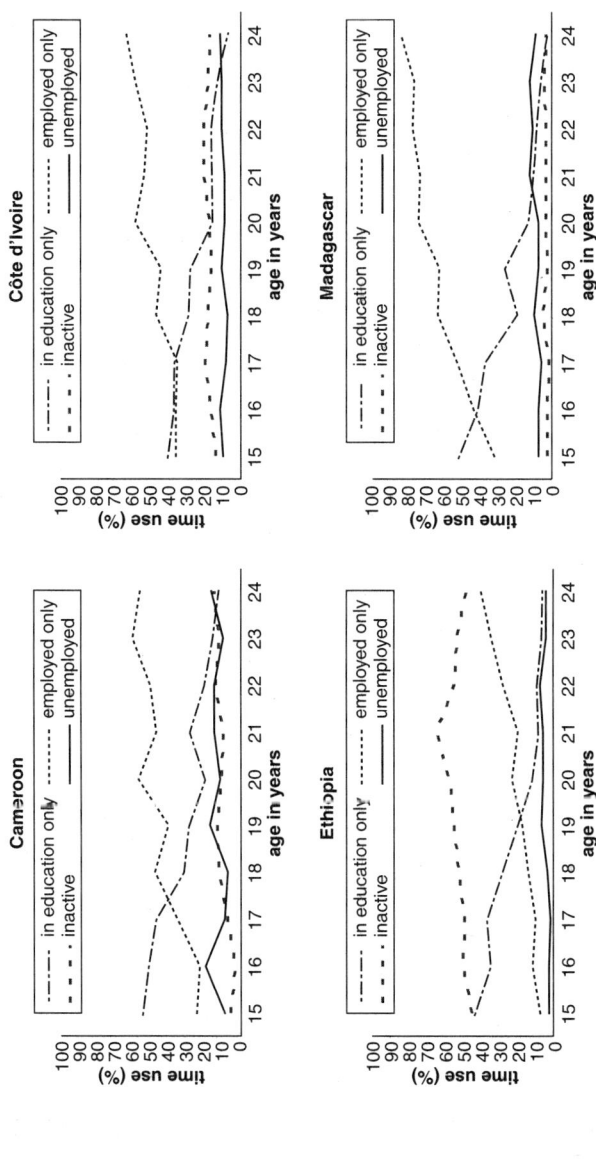

Source: Understanding Children's Work calculations based on World Bank Standard Files and Standard Indicators datasets; see chapter 7.

The proportion of the population that is working is lower among youth from households in higher income quintiles. Kenya is the exception, with higher employment for youth from higher income quintiles.

Income and unemployment seem to be positively correlated. This result is consistent with the notion that the poor cannot afford not to work and that as income rises, people can afford to spend time searching for a job. Alternatively, this correlation may simply reflect the level of education.

Inactivity does not appear to be systematically correlated with income. In Kenya and Mozambique, inactivity falls in higher income quintiles, while in Burkina Faso, Burundi, and Uganda it rises.

Teenagers and Young Adults Use Their Time Differently

Not surprisingly, teenagers (15–19) and young adults (20–24) spend their time differently, with larger percentages of young adults in the labor force (employed or unemployed) (table 3.3).[8] Age group differences are largest in Kenya and Malawi, where initial education enrollment is relatively high; they are smallest in Burkina Faso, Burundi, and Ethiopia, where initial school enrollment is very low and the transition to work begins at an early age. In most countries the proportion of 15- to 19-year-olds in school is low, with more than half of all children either never having entered school or else dropping out before the age of 15.

Across countries, as age increases the percentage of people employed rises and the percentage of people in school falls (figure 3.2). Unemployment appears to remain relatively constant across age groups. In 11 of the 13 countries (except Cameroon and Madagascar), inactivity levels exceed unemployment levels for all age groups. The patterns of inactivity differ across countries, however. In Ethiopia, for example, inactivity rises until the age of 21 before falling, while in Côte d'Ivoire the level of inactivity remains virtually constant across age groups.

Notes

1. See chapter 7 for details.
2. Unlike unemployment, joblessness reflects both unemployed and discouraged workers.
3. An employed person is one who is engaged in paid employment. This category includes employees and the self-employed. This category should include unpaid family members who hold jobs in a market-oriented establishment, irrespective of the number of hours worked during a reference period.

However, some countries set a minimum time criterion for including unpaid family labor among the employed. Usually, if a person works for more than seven hours a day, he or she is considered employed. An unemployed person is a person who does not have work, is currently available for work, and is seeking work. An inactive person is a person who is neither in the labor force (employed or unemployed) nor in school.

4. Data in this section are drawn from chapter 7.

5. Data in this section are drawn from chapter 7.

6. Some forms of economic work, such as fetching water, are also included in this category.

7. The issue of inactivity among youth requires an in-depth analysis that is beyond the scope of this report. In rural areas, where service coverage is typically less extensive, a large proportion of "inactive" young people may actually be performing chores such as fetching water and wood. In urban areas, where the burden of household chores is typically lower, discouraged workers may constitute a larger proportion of the inactive population.

8. The unemployment rate is actually higher for teenagers, because they are more likely to be in school and therefore outside the labor force.

CHAPTER 4

The Effect of Education on Income and Employment

Marito Garcia and Jean Fares

Policy makers almost everywhere recognize the benefit of education, and improving education is at the forefront of their concerns, particularly in developing countries. Despite the positive returns to education, however, educational attainment remains low in most countries in the region.

While in general, higher education is associated with an easier transition to work, for youth in Africa (and other regions), it does not always reduce unemployment. In some countries the unemployment rate among educated youth is very high. Over time, however, as youth gain experience, education increases the employment incidence and enhances occupational mobility.

How Does Education Affect Income?

The literature is large on returns to education in developed and developing countries. Most estimates indicate a positive and significant effect of years of education on individual and household earnings. The estimated effects in Africa are in line with those observed in other regions. New evidence suggests that returns increase with the level of education and that returns to higher education have been rising.

According to conventional wisdom, given the low number of educated people in Africa, demand should exceed supply, creating high returns to education. Simple ordinary least squares estimates of the returns to an extra year of schooling range from 7 to 20 percent in Kenya, Nigeria, and South Africa (see Knight, Sabot, and Hovey 1992 for Kenya; Aromolaran 2002 for Nigeria; Mwabu and Schultz 1996 for South Africa). The average return to an additional year of schooling in Sub-Saharan Africa is estimated at about 12 percent (Psacharopoulos and Patrinos 2004).

How accurate are these estimates? Most studies of the returns to education in Africa use estimation methods that do not adequately deal with the endogenous nature of the schooling decision. Of concern is the bias in the estimates due to unmeasured determinants that are correlated with both schooling and earnings.[1] Some analyses for Burkina Faso and Rwanda improve on simple ordinary least squares estimates by using semi-parametric forms, accounting for the endogenous choice of sector of employment and correcting for selectivity (see Kalzianga 2002 for Burkina Faso; Lassibille and Tan 2005 for Rwanda). Even with such corrections, however, the estimated returns in these countries are still high.

Only a few studies have tried to deal with the endogenous nature of schooling using the instrumental variables approach. Once these corrections are made, the evidence continues to show high returns to schooling in Kenya, South Africa, and Tanzania (see Kahyarara and others 2004 on Kenya and Tanzania; Dabalen 1998 on Kenya and South Africa). Some methodological problems remain, however, because the validity of some of the instruments used (such as distance to school and parents' education) has been questioned (Staiger and Stock 1997). Estimates made based on the case studies of Burkina Faso and Uganda show positive returns to education, particularly for tertiary education, as well an increase in these returns over time (see chapters 8 and 11 in part II for full regression results for each country).

Returns to Education Are High and Increase with Years of Education

Simple ordinary least squares estimates of the relationship between education and earnings in Burkina Faso show that literacy has a very large effect on household income and that the correlation between average household income and average household educational attainment is strong.[2] The estimated annual return to education is 11.5 percent, with the effect of one additional year of education rising as the household's education level increases (figure 4.1).

Two patterns are evident. First, urban households at all levels of education report higher earnings than rural households, with the urban-rural gap narrowing at higher levels of education. Second, although the relationship between education and income is very well approximated by a linear term

Figure 4.1. Household Earnings Increase with Educational Attainment in Burkina Faso

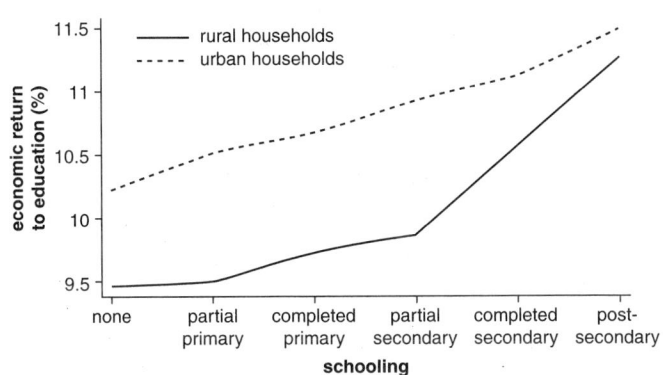

Source: Authors' calculations; see chapter 8.

in urban areas, in rural areas the return to schooling increases markedly for individuals with some partial secondary education. (It may be, of course, that individuals with more education are systematically different from those with less education.)

Simple cross-sectional estimates overstate the true effect of household education on household income. The use of instrumental variables could mitigate the sources of bias in the estimates. But even after using instrumental variables, including the distance from primary and secondary school and a regional fixed effect, to mitigate the sources of bias, the relationship between average household educational attainment and income remains strong.

Returns Have Risen over Time, Particularly for Secondary Education
Table 4.1 presents a simple estimation for the differences in income for males and females with primary education and those with more than primary education in Uganda. The estimation is done separately for different age groups in 1992 and 1999. The results reveal three important patterns:

- The returns to primary education are positive and significant for all age groups except people 40 and older.
- The returns to secondary education are large and exceed those to primary education.
- The returns to primary education seem to have declined between 1992 and 1999 while the returns to secondary education rose dramatically. Even after controlling for sources of endogeneity, returns to secondary education remain large and significant.

Table 4.1. Effect of Primary and Secondary Education on Wages, by Age Group, 1992 and 1999, in Uganda

Age group	Year	Primary education	Secondary education
20–30	1992	0.554***	0.789***
		(0.120)	(0.119)
	1999	0.071	0.876***
		(0.146)	(0.147)
30–40	1992	0.394***	0.997***
		(0.146)	(0.145)
	1999	0.396**	1.528***
		(0.158)	(0.152)
40–50	1992	0.174	0.920***
		(0.159)	(0.158)
	1999	0.073	1.196***
		(0.182)	(0.183)

Source: 1999 Uganda National Household Survey data; see chapter 11.
Note: Standard errors are in parenthesis.
**significant at 0.01 level; ***significant at 0.05 level.

Not all of the countries in Sub-Saharan Africa have enjoyed Uganda's high and increasing returns to education. In Ghana and Nigeria, the returns to an additional year of education have been estimated to be as low as 5 percent (Uwaifo 2005; Glewwe 1996). This may reflect the fact that Uganda experienced significant economic growth in this period while Nigeria suffered from economic stagnation.

How Does Education Affect Employment?

Much international evidence supports the notion that higher educational attainment leads to better employment outcomes, such as higher wages and lower unemployment. For youth, however, this relationship is not always evident. In some countries in Sub-Saharan Africa, secondary and tertiary education are not associated with lower unemployment rates among youth (figure 4.2). Youth with secondary or tertiary education in Burundi, Cameroon, Côte d'Ivoire, Kenya, Madagascar, and Nigeria have higher rates of unemployment than youth with lower educational attainments. Indeed, in 13 of the 14 countries studied, the rate of unemployment is higher among youth with at least some schooling than among those with no schooling, even though a smaller proportion of school entrants are in the labor force.

In Ethiopia the marginal effect of education on the probability of working was estimated using a probit model of employment on a set of control

Figure 4.2. More Education Does Not Always Reduce the Rate of Unemployment among Youth

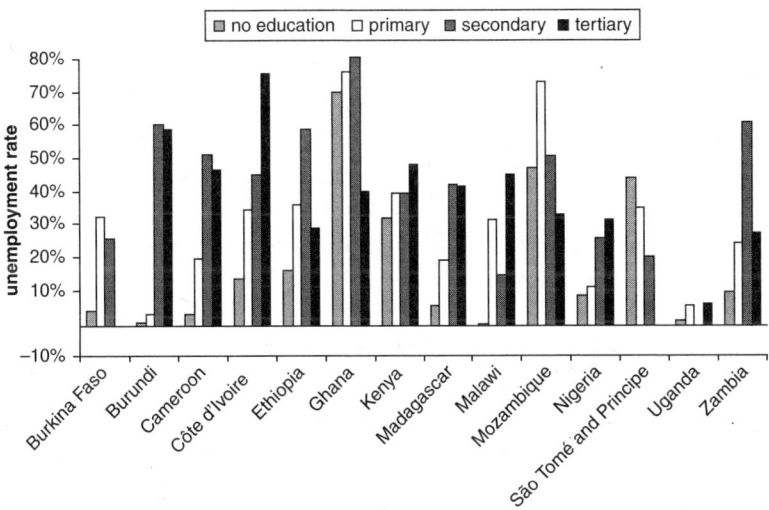

Source: World Bank calculations using basic data from various household surveys from each country; see chapter 7.

variables for urban and rural areas (the full regression results are presented in chapter 9). The results reveal a negative relationship between education and the employability of youth. One possible explanation for this unexpected outcome is that the more educated youth are, the higher their reservation wage and returns to job search. Better-educated youth may be searching for work and not yet employed.

But there is also evidence of skill mismatches. In Ethiopia 21 percent of wage job vacancies posted with employment services remained unfilled between 1997/98 and 2001/02. According to the Ministry of Labor and Social Affairs, this can be attributed to a lack of qualified workers, to employers' desire for workers with substantial experience, and to the negative attitude of job seekers toward certain jobs (in particular, unwillingness to relocate from urban to rural areas).

With Time, More Education Improves Employment Outcomes

Controlling for experience, urban men in Tanzania with the highest level of education are 26 percentage points more likely to be employed than urban men with no education. Similar results emerge for other outcome variables. Unemployment shows some positive association with education when controls for experience are included, but the differences are not statistically significant. Individuals with tertiary education are about 41 percentage points more likely to be active than those with no education, after controlling for their potential experience in the labor market.

Except for the very few youth who complete secondary education, most workers in Sub-Saharan Africa enter the labor force in similar occupations; education appears to have little effect. Youth who lack skills get permanently stuck in dead-end jobs. In contrast, those with more education make a more rapid transition to better occupations (evidence on upward occupational mobility in Burkina Faso is presented in chapter 8). Education thus has a positive effect, even though the port of entry is similar for the vast majority of workers.

Technical and Vocational Training Could Ease the Transition to Work

Increasing attention has been given to technical and vocational training in Ethiopia as a way to increase the employment and employability of youth. In 2003 about 8,000 youth—about 2 percent of all youth—indicated that they had undertaken training. What impact did this training have?

The effects of job training were estimated using a model that conditions on observable variables, including educational level, control variables, and a dummy for training. The results show that training increased the probability of being employed by about 25 percent in urban areas and 20 percent in rural areas.[3]

What Effect Does Education Have on Development?

Education also has an impact on development, including health outcomes. HIV prevalence in Zambia, for example, is much lower among 15- to 19-year-olds with secondary and tertiary education than it is among youth with less education (Coombe and Kelly 2001). Several studies based on theoretical developments in endogenous growth provide evidence of the role education plays in improving household welfare and society at large. Education and the accumulation of human capital create externalities— that is, they benefit not only the direct beneficiaries but other people as well (Ray 1998). Investing in education is associated with higher growth rates (Mankiw, Romer, and Weil 1992).

What Keeps Educational Attainment Low?

Despite the important returns to education, educational attainment remains low in most countries in Sub-Saharan Africa (see chapter 3). For the region as a whole, 18 percent of young men and 27 percent of young women are illiterate, making Sub-Saharan Africa the second-most illiterate region in the world, after Asia.[4] In some countries in the region, a large proportion of children never went to school (see chapter 2). Evidence from the case studies shows that low parental education, low household income, and lack of access to school are severe constraints to school enrollment in Burkina Faso and Tanzania.

Among 10- to 14-year-olds in Burkina Faso, 70 percent of girls and 60 percent of boys have no formal education. In Ethiopia, which has the lowest educational attainment in the world, 6.6 million people never attended school. Three-quarters of youth 15–24 possess only a primary education or less; just 28 percent of 6- to 9-year-olds and a little more than half of 10- to 14-year-olds are enrolled in school. Only about 40 percent of Ethiopian children complete primary education and just 13 percent are enrolled in secondary education. The average adult man in Ethiopia completed only 1.8 grades and the average woman just 0.88 grades, and just 5 percent of the population has secondary or higher education. Similar results are found in the other country studies. In Tanzania, for example, more than 15 percent of rural youth lack any education.

Microanalyses of Burkina Faso and Tanzania identify three main determinants of school enrollment: household income, the education of the household head, and access to education, as measured by distance to school. In Tanzania the education of the household head increases the probability of school enrollment for both males and females in both urban and rural areas (table 4.2). One year of additional education of the household head increases the likelihood of a son enrolling in school by 5 percentage points in urban areas.

In Burkina Faso enrollment in primary education is correlated with having a household head with at least primary education, but there is no strong relationship between enrollment at 15–18 (usually secondary education) and the level of education of the household head. This pattern strongly suggests that educational attainment is highly correlated across generations within households. Low intergenerational mobility creates a poverty trap because education is a strong predictor of income and vice versa.

Other studies on Africa point to similar results. Parental education appears to have a positive effect on children's school attendance and a negative effect on the probability and extent of child labor (Bhalotra and Tzannatos 2002). Children of less-educated parents are more likely to go to work than to school, and these children grow up to be less-educated

Table 4.2. Determinants of Schooling for Urban and Rural Youth by Gender in Tanzania

Variable	Urban		Rural	
	Male	Female	Male	Female
Adult employment rate	−0.337	−0.045	−0.217	0.019
	(0.258)	(0.104)	(0.181)	(0.165)
Percentage of youth in the population	0.003	0.076	0.128	−0.123
	(0.136)	(0.085)	(0.134)	(0.112)
Time to school	0.111	0.142**	−0.010	−0.041***
	(0.068)	(0.063)	(0.008)	(0.006)
Training	−0.171***	−0.083***	−0.058	−0.063*
	(0.035)	(0.029)	(0.037)	(0.038)
Migrant	−0.060***	−0.076***	0.032	−0.001
	(0.022)	(0.017)	(0.021)	(0.017)
Education of household head	0.058***	0.025***	0.023***	0.017***
	(0.005)	(0.004)	(0.003)	(0.003)
Number of observations	1,743	2,360	3,939	3,947

Source: Integrated Labor Force Survey 2000/01; see chapter 10.
Note: Standard errors are in parenthesis.
*significant at 0.10 level; **significant at 0.05 level; ***significant at 0.01 level.

parents who send their own children to work (Ilahi, Orazem, and Sedlacek 2000; Emerson and de Souza 2000). There is also evidence that school attendance rates are higher when the expected benefits of attending school increase (Bedi and Marshall 2001).

The employment status of the household head and household income are also important determinants of schooling for children. Household income quintile is negatively correlated with schooling, though the effects are sometimes modest and occur only at higher levels of education in Burkina Faso. Econometric analysis shows that household income quintiles affect enrollment of youth who are in secondary or tertiary school.[5]

Income shocks are also important determinants of schooling. Children in Burkina Faso from households that experience a negative income shock are less likely than other children to enroll in school. The effect is strongest for households in the lowest income quintile. In Tanzania the adult employment rate is negatively correlated with schooling, suggesting that as adults face more problems in the labor market, school enrollment of their children also declines.

An important factor behind school enrollment and attainment in Burkina Faso is the time it takes to get to school (primary or secondary).[6] School enrollment for both males and females 15–18 decreases as the time it takes to get to school increases. The estimated effects were negative and significant in 1993, 1999, and 2003 (chapter 8). The effect of distance to school on enrollment in Tanzania is mixed. It is not significant for young boys. For girls it increases the likelihood of enrollment in urban areas and reduces it in rural areas.

HIV/AIDS is also forcing children to leave school. Many youth are infected with HIV, especially in eastern and southern Africa, where neglect of millions of children whose family members have HIV/AIDS is fueling school dropout. These children, especially those who are orphaned, enter the labor force very early and are more likely to be exploited or abused. Dropping out of school exposes these children to a lifelong cycle of poverty and abuse.

Recent surveys from Tanzania show that orphans are more likely than other children to withdraw from school (Subbarao and Koury 2004) and that children suffer de facto discrimination in access to education from the moment HIV/AIDS affects their family. These children often leave school to perform household chores or grieve and are unable to return for lack of money to pay for uniforms, books, or other school-related items.

Notes

1. Griliches (1977) was one of the first to examine the bias in ordinary least squares estimates.

2. Most analyses of returns to education use wages and salaries of individuals. The microanalysis of Burkina Faso used household income because of the small proportion of Burkinabes reporting earnings from formal paid employment. Using individual measures of earnings would have decreased the sample size dramatically, limiting the representativeness of the sample.

3. Because this method does not control for the selection process into training, the estimates should be interpreted as the average treatment effect on those who went through the training rather than the average effect on the population as a whole.

4. Several countries, including Kenya, Tanzania, and Uganda, plan to reduce the illiteracy rate in the labor force to less than 10 percent by 2015. Côte d'Ivoire and Ethiopia expect to reduce the illiteracy rate among working women to 30 percent by 2015.

5. This finding of effects at only higher levels of education for the lowest income quintiles in Burkina Faso may not apply to other Sub-Saharan African countries. The effects of household income on schooling are typically significant and positive at all levels.

6. For evidence on the effect of distance to school in developed countries, see Card (1995a). For evidence from developing countries, see Muraközy and Halpern (2005).

CHAPTER 5

Working in Bad Jobs or Not Working at All

Marito Garcia and Jean Fares

By the age of 24, most youth in Africa have left school and started to work. The proportion of youth at work versus those still in school ranges widely across countries (see chapter 3). In Kenya and Malawi, more than 40 percent of youth (15–24) remain in school, and more youth are in school than at work. In Burkina Faso and Burundi, more than 70 percent of youth work.

What Makes the Transition to Work Difficult for Youth?

The lack of strong employment creation in several countries in Sub-Saharan Africa has limited opportunities for youth in their transition to work, particularly in the wage sector. Strong labor demand is necessary to broaden youth opportunities, but it is not sufficient, because of several special challenges youth face:

- The decline in demand for labor in Africa is disproportionately affecting young people.
- A large youth cohort is adding pressure to the labor market of new entrants.
- Internal migration is leading to higher urban unemployment among youth.

- Market failures have a disproportionate impact on youth, particularly females.
- Lack of education is making the low skilled most vulnerable.

Demand for Labor Has Not Kept Up with Supply

Structural adjustment, the global recession, and changes in technology have reduced the demand for labor. Most of the African countries adopting structural adjustment measures have retrenched large numbers of public sector workers, increasing unemployment. Changes in the economic environment and in the demand for labor have also had a negative impact on youth employment opportunities. Technology has increased the demand for higher-order skills and reduced the need for unskilled labor. All of these changes have had a disproportionately large effect on young people.

Rapid Population Growth Has Increased the Number of Youth Entering the Job Market

International evidence suggests that increases in the relative cohort size have an adverse effect on youth employment outcomes (see chapter 1). In Tanzania the increase in the size of the youth cohort has increased the incidence of unemployment among urban youth, particularly among urban females (tables 5.1 and 5.2). In Ethiopia, the size of the youth cohort has significantly reduced the probability of their employment (table 5.3).

The number of people looking for work in Sub-Saharan Africa is expected to increase by 28 percent in the next 15 years, adding about 30 million people to the pool of job seekers. The increase in job seekers may make it

Table 5.1. Determinants of Urban and Rural Youth Unemployment in Tanzania

	Urban		Rural	
Variable	Male	Female	Male	Female
Adult employment rate	−0.019	0.039	−0.334	−0.199
	(0.233)	(0.115)	(0.088)	(0.087)
Percentage of youth in total population	0.039	0.240	0.020	−0.030
	(0.123)	(0.094)	(0.065)	(0.059)
Migrant	0.011	−0.010	0.026	−0.011
	(0.020)	(0.019)	(0.010)	(0.009)
Education of household head	−0.021	−0.016	−0.001	−0.002
	(0.004)	(0.004)	(0.002)	(0.001)
Number of observations	1,964	2,360	3,939	3,947

Source: Integrated Labor Force Survey 2000/01; see chapter 10.
Note: Figures are probit estimates based on 10- to 24-year-olds, using the regionwide definition of local labor market. Standard errors are in parentheses.

Table 5.2. Determinants of Urban and Rural Youth Inactivity in Tanzania

Variable	Urban		Rural	
	Male	Female	Male	Female
Adult employment rate	−0.052	−0.325	−0.085	−0.137
	(0.172)	(0.100)	(0.095)	(0.099)
Percentage of youth in total population	0.118	0.062	−0.185	0.027
	(0.091)	(0.082)	(0.070)	(0.067)
Migrant	0.047	−0.002	−0.000	0.016
	(0.015)	(0.016)	(0.011)	(0.010)
Education of household head	−0.020	−0.009	−0.000	0.001
	(0.003)	(0.004)	(0.002)	(0.002)
Number of observations	1,964	2,360	3,939	3,947

Source: Integrated Labor Force Survey 2000/01; see chapter 10.
Note: Figures are probit estimates based on 10- to 24-year-olds, using the regionwide definition of local labor market. Standard errors are in parentheses.

Table 5.3. Employment Response to Demographic and Economic Shocks for Females by Location and Education in Ethiopia

Item	Never attended school	Has primary education or less	Has some lower secondary education	Completed lower secondary school	Has some higher education
Urban					
Female	−0.149	−0.203	−0.222	−0.181	−0.141
	(−3.62)	(−4.08)	(−5.8)	(−4.21)	(−10.73)
Adult employment ratio	2.341	1.349	1.369	1.734	1.023
	(2.71)	(5.40)	(7.26)	(4.69)	(2.83)
Percentage of youth in total population	−5.208	−3.069	−1.652	−1.992	0.463
	(−2.53)	(−5.24)	(−2.28)	(−2.43)	(0.48)
Rural					
Female	−0.251	−0.204	−0.178	−0.128	−0.164
	(−15.3)	(−7.54)	(−5.30)	(−2.63)	(−2.56)
Adult employment ratio	0.640	0.337	0.453	1.443	0.224
	(2.14)	(2.33)	(2.53)	(4.88)	(0.52)
Percentage of youth in total population	0.846	0.459	−0.261	−1.734	0.818
	(1.25)	(1.12)	(−0.79)	(−2.16)	(0.61)

Source: Ethiopia Central Statistical Agency 2001; see chapter 9.
Note: Figures are probit estimates based on 10- to 24-year-olds, using the regionwide definition of local labor market. Other regression variables are not displayed. Standard errors are in parentheses.

even more difficult for youth to find work in urban areas. Pressure is expected to be milder in rural areas, where most new entrants can be absorbed by the agriculture sector.

Many Africans are moving from rural areas to urban centers in search of greater opportunities. Many of these migrants find little or no opportunity and end up unemployed. In Tanzania the rising proportion of youth in the labor market together with increasing urbanization have reduced the labor market prospects of recent cohorts of urban workers. Young male migrants in Tanzania are more likely to be unemployed than nonmigrants (see table 5.2). Similar results are found in the other country studies.

Young Women Are at a Particular Disadvantage, in Terms of Both Schooling and Employment

Female youth in Sub-Saharan Africa have lower levels of school attainment, school enrollment, and employment than males. In most of the Sub-Saharan African countries examined, male enrollment is twice that of females. Only in Madagascar and São Tomé and Principe does female enrollment approach that of males (see chapter 3). Females are significantly overrepresented among the inactive population in most countries, and male employment exceeds female employment in all countries except Burundi, The Gambia, and Zambia (though the differences are not always large). Female youth tend to leave school at an earlier age and transit to work more slowly than male youth.

This gender bias has discouraged many women from looking for work. In Tanzania the proportion of discouraged workers is higher among women than men. Since 2001 unemployment rates have fallen for young men but risen for young women in many countries in Sub-Saharan Africa, including Burkina Faso and Ethiopia.

In Ethiopia international migration is higher for women than men. In 2001, 98 percent of the 5,015 Ethiopian workers given permits to work in two destination countries were women; more than half were young women engaged in domestic work (see chapter 9). Most women were relatively well skilled, with 74 percent having completed grade 12. The fact that secondary school graduates seek jobs as domestic workers abroad suggests that women are at a disadvantage in the local labor market. Female youth of all ages in Ethiopia are more likely to be unemployed and much more likely to be jobless than male youth.

In Tanzania labor force participation is highest among women with at least some primary education (59 percent) and lowest for those with secondary education (32 percent). In contrast to men, uneducated women are less likely to participate in the labor force than those with some primary, with only 55 percent of uneducated women participating. Female inactivity shows a *U*-shaped relation, first falling with education and then rising. The pattern may be explained by the fact that uneducated women have few opportunities and better-educated women have high reservation wages or face discrimination. Many women are not allowed to work at a level that matches their level of education, become discouraged, and drop out of the labor force.[1]

In Tanzania labor supply has no effect on unemployment among urban males but does affect unemployment among urban females. Labor demand has no effect on activity by urban males but has a strong negative effect on activity by urban females. These results imply that if labor demand drops or labor supply increases, women are more likely than men to become inactive.

In Ethiopia there is a negative and significant gender bias in employment probability among youth, in both urban and rural areas (see table 5.3). The gender bias in employment is smallest for the least- and most-educated urban youth. In rural areas the gap between males and females decreases with education.

Youth Are Vulnerable in the Labor Market

As a result of the challenges they face as they transition to work, youth are often left vulnerable. Few earn wages and most are in the informal sector. In rural areas most young people are in unpaid family work and underemployed. In urban areas unemployment—including long-term unemployment—looms large. Low-skilled youth are vulnerable to weakening demand and young females have difficulties participating in the labor force.

Lack of Education Increases Youth Exposure to Shocks

Employment is less sensitive to changes in overall demand conditions (measured by the adult employment ratio) and to changes in the size of the youth cohort among youth who are more educated in Ethiopia (see table 5.4). Put differently, youth with lower skill levels are more vulnerable to economic and demographic change. If these results are typical of other countries in the region, low-skilled youth—a large proportion of the youth population in Sub-Saharan Africa—stand to suffer disproportionately from the increased size of the youth cohort and to shocks to demand.

Table 5.4. Response of Youth Employment to Demographic and Economic Shocks for Females by Level of Education and Urban-Rural Location in Ethiopia

	Never attended school	Has primary or less	Has some lower secondary education	Completed lower secondary school	Has some higher education
Urban					
Female	−0.149	−0.203	−0.222	−0.181	−0.141
	(−3.62)	(−4.08)	(−5.8)	(−4.21)	(−10.73)
Adult employment ratio	2.341	1.349	1.369	1.734	1.023
	(2.71)	(5.40)	(7.26)	(4.69)	(2.83)
Percentage of youth in total population	−5.208	−3.069	−1.652	−1.992	0.463
	(−2.53)	(−5.24)	(−2.28)	(−2.43)	(0.48)
Rural					
Female	−0.251	−0.204	−0.178	−0.128	−0.164
	(−15.3)	(−7.54)	(−5.30)	(−2.63)	(−2.56)
Adult employment ratio	0.640	0.337	0.453	1.443	0.224
	(2.14)	(2.33)	(2.53)	(4.88)	(0.52)
Percentage of youth in total population	0.846	0.459	−0.261	−1.734	0.818
	(1.25)	(1.12)	(−0.79)	(−2.16)	(0.61)

Source: Calculations based on Ethiopia Labor Force Survey 2000; see chapter 9.
Note: Figures are probit estimates based on 10- to 24-year-olds, using the regionwide definition of local labor market. Standard errors are in parentheses.

Poor Health Limits Employment Opportunities

Several studies have documented the importance of heath for productivity, school performance, and several other basic biometric and economic indicators. All over the world youth are at the greatest risk for many diseases, especially sexually transmitted infections. People between 15 and 24 have the highest reported rates of HIV, chlamydia, gonorrhea, and other sexually transmitted infections. People 15–24 now make up more than one-quarter of all the people living with HIV/AIDS (UNAIDS/WHO 2005). Worse still, more than half of the world's 5 million people who became infected with HIV in 2003 were 15–24.

In Africa an estimated 1.7 million people 10–24 become infected with HIV every year. A large percentage of young people in Tanzania (11–46 percent; Tanzania National Bureau of Statistics 2003) cite health issues as one of the main reasons for their inactivity. These figures are consistent with the very high prevalence of HIV among youth in Tanzania (2–5 percent for men, 6–9 percent for women). Prevalence is similar in Uganda (6.7–9.0 percent for women, 2.6–5.1 percent for men). HIV is less prevalent among youth in Burkina Faso and Ethiopia but is still widespread.

Few African Youth Earn Wages

Measures of employment provide little information about the conditions young people face in the labor market. New data from selected countries allow some indicators of work conditions to be created.

Young workers fall into four main groups: wage employees, informal sector employees, the self-employed, and other employment.[2] The distribution of youth workers across these groups varies across countries (table 5.5). Informal work accounts for the majority of young workers in Burkina Faso, Burundi, Madagascar, and Uganda, self-employment is the leading work modality for youth in Cameroon, Malawi, and Mozambique, and wage employment is most important in Ethiopia and São Tomé and Principe. Both self-employment and informal employment are significant in The Gambia and Kenya.

The work modalities of young people differ dramatically from those of adults. Young people are much less likely to be involved in wage employment (except in Ethiopia and São Tomé and Principe) and much more likely to work in the informal sector (except in Malawi and São Tomé and Principe). Adult workers thus enjoy more job security and social protection and are less exposed to the instability and risks associated with the informal sector. The fact that few younger workers are self-employed

Table 5.5. Modality of Employment by Youth and Adults in Selected Countries
(percentage of all workers)

Country	Wage employment		Informal employment		Self-employment		Other employment	
	Youth	Adults	Youth	Adults	Youth	Adults	Youth	Adults
Burkina Faso	3.2	7.6	90.9	59.3	5.8	32.5	0.1	0.7
Burundi	1.7	5.8	85.3	39.5	12.8	54.2	0.2	0.5
Cameroon	8.2	16.4	26.1	14.5	65.7	69.1	—	—
Ethiopia	46.7	75.7	27.8	17.0	17.8	3.8	7.7	3.6
Gambia, The	10.1	19.2	46.1	13.8	42.7	65.8	1.1	1.1
Kenya	17.9	30.8	44.4	19.7	37.6	48.6	0.1	0.8
Madagascar	7.8	15.9	68.1	31.1	22.8	50.6	1.4	2.3
Malawi	18.8	26.7	7.1	5.1	70.3	64.9	3.8	3.3
Mozambique	15.1	16.6	—	—	53.5	69.6	1.2	0.5
São Tomé and Principe	63.2	57.8	28.8	41.5	—	—	8.0	0.7
Uganda	3.2	7.6	90.9	59.3	5.8	32.5	0.1	0.7
Zambia	9.5	23.9	51.8	16.9	37.8	58.3	0.9	1.0

Source: Understanding Children's Work calculations based on World Bank Standard Files and Standard Indicators datasets.
Note: Youth are 15–24. Adults are 25–50. Data for Côte d'Ivoire are unavailable.
— Not available.

(except for Cameroon, Malawi, and Mozambique) suggests that they find it difficult to start a business, perhaps because of lack of capital.

In all 13 countries people from the highest income quintile are most likely to earn wages (see chapter 7). Nevertheless, even for this quintile wage employment is not the dominant sector in all the countries. In Kenya and Madagascar, for example, even among people from the highest income quintile, the most important sector is the informal sector. The high level of self-employment (in Cameroon, Malawi, and Mozambique, for example) may be a sign that workers have difficulty entering the labor market.

In nearly all Sub-Saharan countries, few workers are engaged in wage employment, even in urban areas (table 5.6).[3] The high level of informal employment in most countries (except Malawi) represents a cause for concern. Informal work in rural settings is associated mainly with agriculture and is typically low paid and seasonal. In urban settings informal work often involves insecure, nonfamily work, in settings in which labor and safety regulations do not apply, leaving workers susceptible to exploitation.

In Tanzania most young adults (20–24) end up in nonwage employment, usually in the informal sector, where working conditions are poor (table 5.7). Most rural youth work in agriculture. Many are unpaid laborers on their own farms or family farms. Youth in most urban areas also work in the agricultural sector, although many, particularly in Dar es Salaam, earn wages.

Some urban young adults are self-employed, and there is evidence that many more would like to work for themselves but cannot because of lack of capital (chapter 10). This barrier is particularly true in rural areas and cities other than Dar es Salaam, but even in the capital, having social networks or coming from a higher-income family does not increase the chance of accessing capital, because most families lack collateral for loans (see chapter 10).

As they get older, young males are more likely to be found in wage employment, particularly in Dar es Salaam but also in most other urban areas, where the proportion of male employees rises from 15 percent for teenagers to about 22 percent for young adults. This incidence is still lower than that of adult males. Among employed female young adults, 36 percent in Dar es Salaam and 19 percent in other urban areas work as employees (see table 5.7).

In Ethiopia more than 80 percent of rural teenagers and 60 percent of young adults are unpaid workers (figure 5.1). Policies that provide income transfers to these families would be likely to reduce early entry into work and allow children to attend school. In urban areas in Ethiopia, the largest

Table 5.6. Modality of Employment of Rural and Urban Youth, in Selected Countries
(percentage of all workers)

Country	Rural				Urban			
	Wage employment	Informal employment	Self-employment	Other employment	Wage employment	Informal employment	Self-employment	Other employment
Burkina Faso	0.4	94.8	4.8	0.0	27.9	57.0	14.4	0.7
Burundi	1.8	83.3	14.8	0.1	31.3	19.6	43.3	5.8
Cameroon	6.3	18.1	68.8	6.8	15.3	56.9	22.0	5.9
Ethiopia	55.6	24.8	16.2	3.4	16.2	38.2	23.3	22.3
Gambia, The	1.2	53.1	45.0	0.8	42.3	20.7	34.7	2.4
Kenya	16.4	40.0	43.6	0.0	21.1	53.3	25.4	0.2
Madagascar	5.9	69.7	23.5	1.0	19.3	58.7	18.2	3.8
Malawi	15.0	7.1	74.5	3.3	63.8	6.8	19.8	9.5
Mozambique	11.8	—	86.7	1.5	40.2	—	53.5	6.3
São Tomé and Principe	59.5	34.3	—	6.2	66.3	24.3	—	9.5
Zambia	3.1	60.4	36.1	0.4	40.9	9.6	46.1	3.5

Source: Understanding Children's Work calculations based on World Bank Standard Files and Standard Indicators datasets.
Note: Data for Côte d'Ivoire are unavailable.
— Not available.

Table 5.7. Employment Modality by Gender, Age Group, and Urban-Rural Location in Tanzania

(percentage of all workers in age group)

Location and age group	Females					Males				
	Employee	Self-employed with employees	Self-employed, no employees	Unpaid family worker	Own farm	Employee	Self-employed with employees	Self-employed, no employees	Unpaid family worker	Own farm
Dar es Salaam										
Teenagers	52.1	0.4	26.1	15.2	6.2	40.8	0.0	27.2	22.8	9.3
Young adults	36.4	2.8	53.8	4.4	2.7	47.4	1.7	38.4	6.7	5.9
Prime-age adults	27.2	3.3	55.8	0.4	13.3	54.5	10.3	30.0	0.0	5.2
Urban										
Teenagers	16.8	1.3	11.7	20.9	49.4	15.1	0.2	16.7	5.2	62.8
Young adults	19.1	1.1	35.2	6.5	38.1	21.8	3.1	22.5	3.8	48.9
Prime-age adults	14.1	5.9	28.4	2.9	48.8	36.9	5.5	28.5	0.4	28.7
Rural										
Teenagers	1.9	0.0	1.9	5.2	91.1	3.6	0.0	2.3	3.5	90.5
Young adults	1.3	0.3	1.9	1.4	95.1	5.6	0.3	4.6	0.8	88.6
Prime-age adults	2.3	0.2	3.0	0.8	93.7	9.0	1.0	4.4	0.3	85.4

Source: Integrated Labor Force Survey 2000/01; see chapter 1.

Note: Teenagers are 15–19. Young adults are 20–24. Prime-age adults are 25–55.

Figure 5.1. Most Youth Perform Unpaid Family Work, Predominantly in Agriculture in Ethiopia

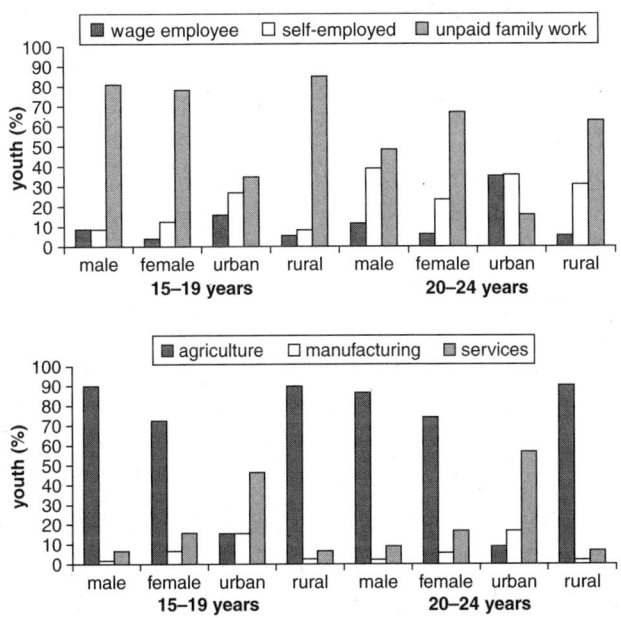

Source: Understanding Children's Work calculations based on Ethiopia Labor Force Survey 2001; see chapter 9.

proportion of teenagers work as unpaid family workers, but larger proportions of young adults are self-employed and work in the wage sector. The proportion of teenage girls and boys working in the wage sector is low.

In rural areas most Ethiopians work in the agricultural sector. In urban areas the dominant sector is services, which includes retail trade. Many of the youth employed in the service sector are involved in petty retail trade, selling products such as newspapers and beverages. These jobs yield low incomes, and some are hazardous.

Underemployment Is Prevalent in Rural Areas

Although a large portion of out-of-school youth are employed in Tanzania, 6 percent of young men and more than 10 percent of young women report being underemployed. In Ethiopia widespread underemployment is a major problem not only for youth but for the population as a whole, particularly in the rural sector. Underemployment in Ethiopia is high in rural areas, with the average worker working less than 30 hours a week.

Table 5.8. Multiple Job Holding and Underemployment by Gender, Age, and Urban-Rural Location in Burkina Faso

(percent)

Age group and job status	Male		Female	
	Urban	*Rural*	*Urban*	*Rural*
10–14				
Wants more work	11	8	6	8
Holds more than one job	8	7	3	9
15–19				
Wants more work	10	13	12	14
Holds more than one job	8	14	7	13
20–24				
Wants more work	12	16	13	20
Holds more than one job	11	18	10	21
25–34				
Wants more work	15	17	15	23
Holds more than one job	9	21	11	28
35–44				
Wants more work	15	18	15	26
Holds more than one job	9	25	13	35
45 and older				
Wants more work	18	16	16	22
Holds more than one job	17	24	16	33

Source: Survey of Household Living Standards, 2003; see chapter 8.

In Burkina Faso multiple job holding is more common in rural than in urban areas (table 5.8). Among all workers with at least two jobs, more than 92 percent live in rural areas. Not surprisingly, almost 95 percent work in the agriculture, breeding, fishing, and hunting sectors; 57 percent work as family helpers; and 41 percent are independent workers. Multiple job holding is more likely to occur as workers become older. There is little evidence of a systematic relationship between household income and the incidence of multiple job holding.

About 16 percent of all workers in Burkina Faso believe they are under-employed. The overwhelming majority of these workers hold multiple jobs. About 9 percent of people with one job and 47 percent of people with multiple jobs wish they could work more.

Youth Unemployment Is High

More than 18 million young people in Sub-Saharan Africa—21 percent of all youth (15–24)—were unemployed in 2003. This rate of youth unemployment exceeds that of all other regions except the Middle East and North Africa.

Comparing youth and adult unemployment rates provides some indication of the extent to which young workers are disadvantaged relative to adults. The unemployment rate for youth exceeds that of adults in all countries except Burundi and The Gambia (figure 5.2). Young workers are particularly disadvantaged in Cameroon and São Tomé and Principe, where the youth unemployment rate is more than five times that of adults.

Long-Term Unemployment Is a Serious Problem in Ethiopia and Tanzania

High unemployment may not represent a problem if it reflects temporary movement from one job to another or new entry into the labor market. It is a serious problem for individuals and the economy as a whole when it lasts for long periods.

In Sub-Saharan African almost all young people leave school between the ages of 15 and 24, but a large proportion do not immediately settle into

Figure 5.2. Unemployment Is Higher among Youth Than Adults in Almost All Sub-Saharan African Countries

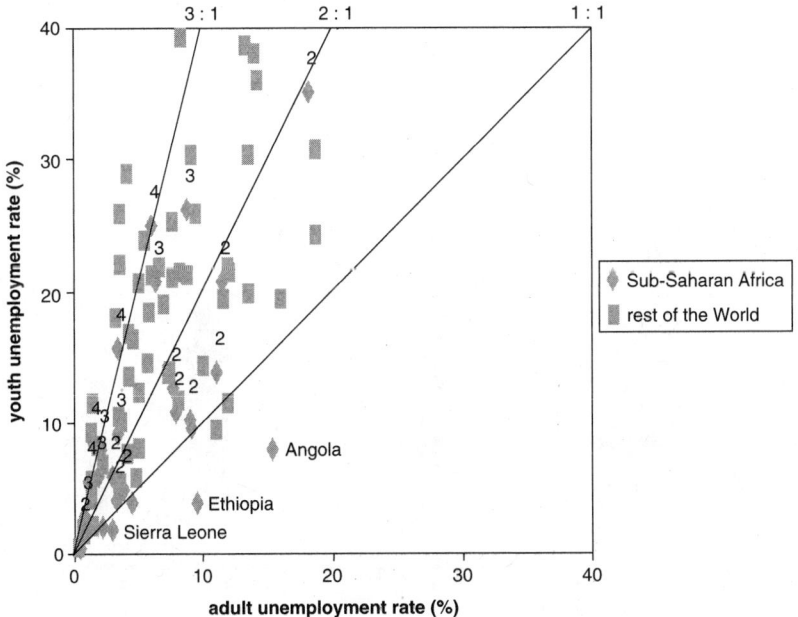

Source: World Bank 2006.

employment. The average estimated school-leaving age ranges from 15.9 to 19.0 years, and the average age at first job ranges from 18.4 to 24.4. The total estimated transition duration thus ranges from one to seven years.

Evidence from the 2003 Urban Biannual Employment Unemployment Survey of Ethiopia suggests that much urban youth unemployment is structural rather than transitory in nature. About one-third of unemployed teenagers and almost half of unemployed young adults had been without a job for at least one year at the time of the survey (figure 5.3). Even more worrisome is the fact that the share of youth with very long spells of unemployment (more than two years) increases with age.

In Tanzania more than 40 percent of unemployed young adults have been unemployed for more than two years, and more than 70 percent have been unemployed for more than a year (figure 5.4). Long-term unemployment accounts for at least half of total unemployment in Tanzania. The duration of unemployment is much longer in urban than in rural areas, and among men in urban areas, the duration of unemployment is longer among teenagers and young adults than among prime-age adults. If unemployment is mainly a long-term phenomenon, this implies that it is largely concentrated among certain population groups, raising serious distributional considerations.

Long-term unemployment increases the difficulty of entry into the work force, especially in the formal sector. Because early work experience is very important and yields high returns, lack of access to work for long

Figure 5.3. Many Urban Youth Remain Unemployed for More Than a Year in Ethiopia

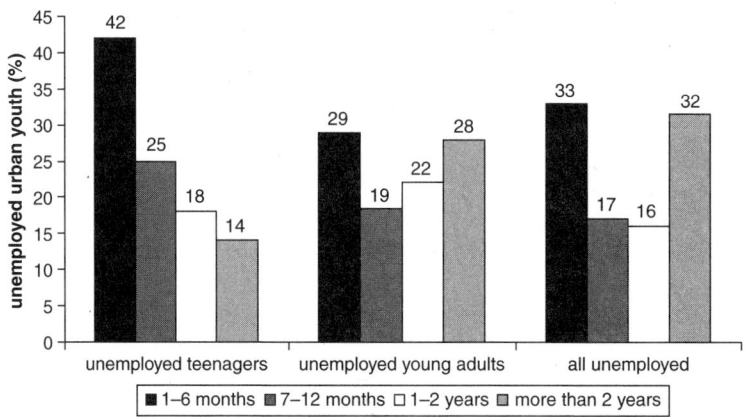

Source: 2003 Urban Biannual Employment Unemployment Survey, as cited in Denu, Tekeste, and van der Deijl 2005.

Figure 5.4. Unemployment Spells Last Much Longer in Urban Than in Rural Areas in Tanzania

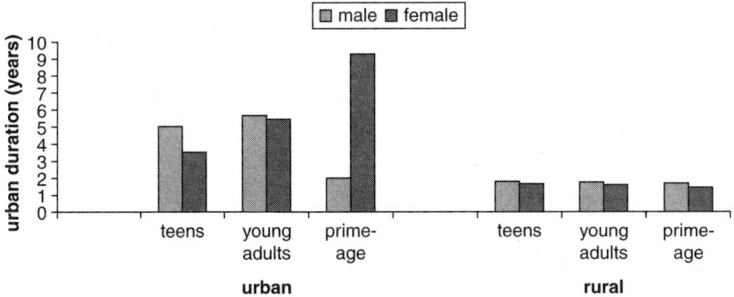

Source: Integrated Labor Force Survey; see chapter 10.
Note: Teenagers are 15–19. Young adults are 20–24. Prime-age adults are 25–55.

Figure 5.5. Young Females Are More Likely Than Young Males to Be Neither Working Nor Attending School

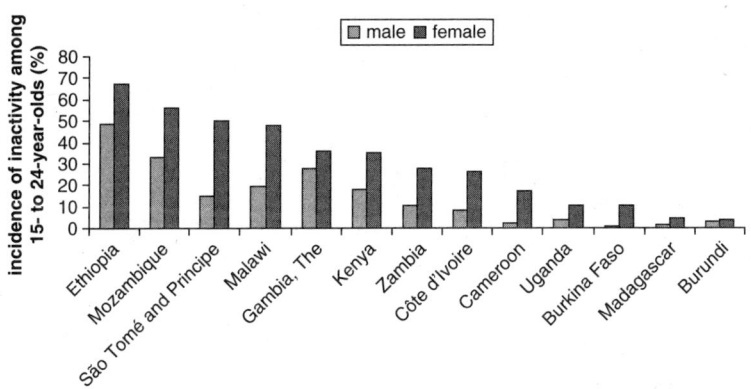

Source: Understanding Children's Work calculations based on World Bank Standard Files and Standard Indicators datasets; see chapter 7.

periods reduces human capital accumulation for young entrants, reducing their earning potential and future development.

Many Young Africans Fail to Enter the Labor Market, Particularly Women

People who are neither at work (or looking for work) nor at school are classified as inactive. The highest average rates of inactivity in Sub-Saharan Africa are in Ethiopia (59 percent) and Mozambique (45 percent) (figure 5.5). In other countries very few young people are classified as neither working nor being in school. In all countries young women are

Table 5.9. Reported Reasons for Inactivity among Male Youth in Tanzania

(percent)

Location and age group	Reason for not looking						Reason not available		
	Thought would not find	Waiting for job/ reply	Off- season	Household duties	Temporarily ill	Other	Household duties	Ill	Other
Dar es Salaam									
Teenagers	64.5	13.6	0.0	3.2	3.6	15.2	28.0	11.3	60.7
Young adults	25.6	32.5	0.0	2.7	0.0	39.3	18.7	24.7	56.6
Prime-age adults	0.0	100.0	0.0	0.0	0.0	0.0	0.0	100.0	0.0
Urban									
Teenagers	28.3	48.8	0.0	7.5	1.5	13.9	25.8	31.7	42.5
Young adults	51.8	21.8	0.0	18.0	0.0	8.3	16.9	15.7	67.4
Prime-age adults	16.2	7.0	38.3	0.0	0.0	38.5	12.6	83.4	4.0
Rural									
Teenagers	17.4	22.1	8.3	30.7	1.3	20.2	22.7	45.9	31.4
Young adults	19.9	27.9	8.7	37.6	0.0	5.9	10.5	58.6	30.9
Prime-age adults	33.8	39.4	17.7	9.1	0.0	0.0	3.2	92.1	4.7

Source: Integrated Labor Force Survey 2000/01; see chapter 10.

Note: Teenagers are 15–19. Young adults are 20–24. Prime-age adults are 25–55.

more likely than young men to be inactive. Many "inactive" young adults (20–24), especially females, may be involved in home production. Others may be discouraged because of difficulties entering the work force.

In Dar es Salaam about 25 percent of teenagers and 40 percent of young adults are neither in school nor at work; in other urban areas, about 18 percent of teenagers and of young adults are unemployed. More than 64 percent of teenage boys and 25 percent of young men in Dar es Salaam are discouraged workers (table 5.9). Among inactive females, 59 percent of teenagers and 67 percent of young women are discouraged workers. Results for other urban areas in Tanzania are lower but also high. For the country as a whole, the education of the head of household appears to be negatively correlated with inactivity, which is highest among youth with no education (27 percent).

Many inactive females report that household duties prevent them from looking for a job. Among males who claim they were not available for work, many report "other reasons." More research needs to be conducted to determine the nature of these reasons, which could include involvement in illegal activities or the need to take care of ill family members.

Notes

1. The gender bias cannot be fully captured by considering unemployment, which remains a "privilege" of more-educated girls. Inactivity also needs to be examined because less-educated females are unlikely to classify themselves as available for work, possibly due to discouragement.

2. Wage employees are people in paid employment who are remunerated by wages or salaries, commissions, piece rates, bonuses, or in-kind payments. They include regular employees and casual workers without contracts. Informal workers are people employed in semiorganized units. The International Labour Organization defines informal sector workers as own-account workers, unpaid family workers who work at least seven hours a day, and employers and employees in establishments in which less than 10 people work. Paid domestic workers are excluded. Self-employed workers are people who perform some work for profit or family gain, in cash or in kind. Remuneration depends on the profits derived from the goods and services produced (own consumption from enterprise is considered part of profits). Self-employed people make operational decisions themselves or delegate them to others while retaining responsibility for the welfare of the enterprise. Self-employment may include contributing family workers. Other employment applies to those who are not in the first three classifications.

3. In some countries—such as Ethiopia, The Gambia, and Malawi—however, the higher percentage of wage workers include casual workers without contracts.

CHAPTER 6

The Three Pillars of Policy: Lessons from International Experience

Marito Garcia and Jean Fares

Policy makers in Africa are concerned about the difficulties youth are facing in their transition to work, and they recognize the deleterious consequences of youth unemployment for both youth and the region as a whole. Despite this recognition, the response has been fragmented. Most interventions have been small-scale and face severe challenges for sustainability and scalability.

This chapter offers some guidance to policy makers searching for ways to address youth employment issues. The analyses conducted in the previous chapters and the survey of interventions in four countries in the region (presented in annexes 6B–E) ground the proposed policy framework in these countries' realities and provide the background for further empirical examination, operational work, and policy dialogue with the countries in the region. The methodology is presented in annex 6A.

The transition to work is difficult for African youth because of the large number of young people entering the labor market, their lack of skills, unfavorable economic conditions in most African countries, market failures that adversely affect youth outcomes, and a host of other factors. As suggested by the *World Development Report 2007*, a successful policy response to the challenge of youth employment rests on three pillars: broadening opportunities for young people to accumulate and preserve human capital, increasing the capability of youth to take advantage of work opportunities, and providing youth who are not initially equipped to take advantage of opportunities with a second chance, so that no one is left behind.

Pillar One: Broadening Opportunities for Employment

Spurring economic growth—Economic growth is key to broadening employment opportunities. Growth increases employment opportunities for everyone—and has a disproportionately large effect on youth. In Indonesia and Vietnam, youth benefited from new employment opportunities in the trade and manufacturing sectors (World Bank 2006). Large cohorts of young and mobile workers can, in turn, support the expansion of these sectors.

How well has Africa done in expanding economic opportunities for youth? Growth in Africa declined between the 1970s and the late 1980s (World Bank 2000), but since the mid-1990s growth in 16 countries in the region has exceeded 4.5 percent a year (World Bank 2006). Some of these countries, such as Mozambique, Tanzania, and Uganda, have diversified their economies and exports, sectors that are likely to hire more youth. Oil-producing countries have seen significant growth in GDP as a result of the sharp increase in oil prices.

Africa's performance in manufacturing has been poor (Kingdon and Knight forthcoming). Analysis of 12 countries in the region reveals that the share of industry value added in GDP was about 5 percentage points lower than the world average between 1970 and 2000. Among these countries, four saw employment in the manufacturing sector expand by more than 20 percent in the early 2000s. Others, including Kenya and Tanzania, experienced almost no growth.

Sub-Saharan Africa continues to face significant barriers to creating new jobs in the formal sector (World Bank 2004). Most youth employment is nonwage employment (see chapter 5). A key challenge is to increase nonfarm rural employment and prepare youth to move into activities off the farm. Evidence from low-income countries in other regions suggests that people with skills are more mobile than average and are likely to take advantage of opportunities off the farm.

Improving the investment climate and addressing policy failures—A good investment climate lets the private sector expand, helps trade flourish, and allows countries to attract foreign direct investment. To improve the investment climate, governments need to maintain political stability, improve the regulatory and tax climate for investment, provide needed infrastructure, and improve information on vacancies for job seekers (World Bank 2004).

These general policies are necessary to promote youth employment opportunities, but they are not sufficient. Youth would benefit from policies that mitigate the market and policy failures responsible for labor market rigidity and segmentation. In Ethiopia downward rigidity in real wages in the urban sector in times of economic reform has led to high rates of open unemployment, particularly among urban youth (Krishnan, Selassie, and Dercon 1998).

Preventing rising joblessness in order to ensure political stability—Ever-rising joblessness among youth and the desperation that accompanies it undermine the possibility of progress in countries emerging from conflict. They also risk destroying the political and social structures of countries that are currently stable, especially given demographic trends in some parts of Sub-Saharan Africa. The growing number of youth who lack the prospect of ever being able to earn a reasonable living threatens the future of the region. Until this situation changes, the likelihood of achieving genuine peace, security, and development throughout the region will remain small. At the same time, pressures to migrate, illegally and dangerously, to parts of the world where opportunities appear more promising will continue to mount, with consequences for the receiving countries (UNOWA 2005).

Pillar Two: Building Skills and Capabilities

Despite the increase in educational attainment in most Sub-Saharan African countries, youth continue to leave school unprepared to integrate into the labor market. To reduce school dropout and early transition to work, policies and programs should ease the income constraints poor families face. In Ethiopia school attendance rose after a flexible school calendar was introduced in rural areas that took into account the agriculture cycle. In Burkina Faso poor households facing adverse income shocks are likely to withdraw their children from school and send them to work (see chapter 5). Conditional cash transfers, which transfer funds to poor families as long as their children attend school or after-school programs, have been shown to increase school enrollment and reduce child labor in Brazil and Mexico (Raju 2006).

Promoting public-private partnerships and making curricula more relevant—Public-private partnerships are needed to improve the quality of primary education and increase access to lower-secondary education. Public policy could complement private initiatives by ensuring quality standards and introducing financing mechanisms to support the poor. Promotion of private schools in Kenya during the 1960s and 1970s resulted in marked expansion in secondary school enrollment. For secondary and postsecondary education, school curricula need to be made more relevant to labor market needs. Providing practical skills—by teaching subjects such as technology, economics, and foreign languages—could better equip youth for the labor market; better integrating vocational and general curricula could facilitate youth insertion into the work force.

In addition to raising enrollment, countries need to improve the quality of their education systems and the relevance of school curricula by teaching students the practical thinking and behavioral skills demanded by the labor market, using teaching methods that lead to high learning achievement and blend academic and vocational curricula (World Bank 2006). Building bridges between school and work can facilitate the transition of youth from school to the workplace.

Combining part-time schooling with work, as Germany does, has proved difficult to replicate in Sub-Saharan Africa, where the lack of institutional capacity and the small industrial sector limit the chance of success of the dual system (Johanson and Adams 2004). Youth are more likely to participate in traditional apprenticeship schemes (Adams 2006). Across most of West Africa, apprentices outnumber wage employees in informal firms (Haan and Serriere 2002). These programs could be enhanced by providing access to new technologies, improving the technical skills of master craftspeople, and certifying skills. In Kenya a voucher program in the informal sector helped improve the quality and relevance of the training offered to apprentices by giving master craftspeople access to new technologies and upgrading their skills (Riley and Steel 1999). A similar program could potentially be adopted elsewhere in the region.

Given the budget constraints facing African governments, technical and vocational education and training also need to change to allow for public-private partnerships, diversify financing for training, promote sustainability, and improve access and relevance. In Mauritius the Industrial Vocational Training Board has split the financing and provision of training and adopted a competitive model for procuring training services. Other examples from countries outside the region (such as

Argentina and Chile) illustrate how competition promotes efficient delivery and closer links to market demand, shifting the financing model for training from one that is supply driven to one that is demand driven (World Bank 2006).

Youth need to be prepared to take advantage of potential opportunities or create opportunities on their own through self-employment and entrepreneurial activities. Young entrepreneurs face several constraints to creating a venture and making it grow. Some lack entrepreneurial skills, others lack access to information and networks, almost all have difficulty accessing credit and face investment climates that make it difficult to start and run a business. Improving the climate for doing business would allow more young entrepreneurs to start their own enterprises. Programs that provide access to networks and information have been initiated in some countries in Latin America and seem promising (for example, Endeavor in Argentina, Brazil, Mexico, and Uruguay). South Africa's youth fund illustrates how public and private financial intermediaries could collaborate to provide youth with better access to credit.

Pillar Three: Offering a Second Chance So That No One Is Left Behind

Poverty, adverse economic conditions, poor health, employment shocks, and inadequate schools force many young people to leave school without acquiring the basic skills demanded in the workplace. Harsh weather and civil conflicts uproot many communities, halting early efforts youth have made to find work and develop their livelihoods. The result is a huge stock of unskilled youth who never went to school, are ill-prepared for the workplace, and are vulnerable to shocks (see chapters 2 and 3).

Estimates based on data in this study indicate that 36 percent of the 15- to 24-year-olds in the region never went to school, only 28 percent completed primary school, and only 8 percent completed secondary school. This means that about two-thirds of all youth in the labor market—some 95 million young people—lack the skills to be competitive in the labor force. These youth need a second chance.

Many countries operate second-chance programs. Some try to get out-of-school youth back in school or provide alternative mechanisms for skill development. Others attempt to directly reintegrate out-of-work youth into the work force. To limit—and justify—the fiscal burden of second-chance initiatives, all programs must be well targeted, designed to increase youth skills, and geared to the needs of the labor market.

For young people who are out of school, equivalence, literacy, and job training programs should be designed to provide the skills needed for work (World Bank 2006). Practical curricula that include both technical and life skills, flexible schedules, and less formal instruction methods are most likely to attract youth and provide them with the skills most needed in the labor market. Literacy programs have suffered from low take-up rates; they need to be more contextual and demand driven. Programs in Ghana and Senegal include postprogram follow-up to solidify literacy skills (World Bank 2006).

Job training programs are more likely to be successful if they are part of a package that includes basic education, employment services, and social services. A recent review of 19 training programs targeting youth shows that in the absence of such a package, training programs rarely improve the employment and earnings of young participants (Betcherman, Olivas, and Dar 2004). Well-targeted and comprehensive training programs, such as the Jovens program in Argentina, Chile, and Peru, have been successful in reaching the most vulnerable youth and improving their earnings and employment (World Bank 2006).

Public works programs provide good opportunities for young workers, particularly rural residents and people with low skills, to acquire initial work experience. In Senegal the Agence d'Exécution des Travaux d'Intérêt Public (AGETIP) trains and employs unemployed youth, who work on public infrastructure projects (roads, buildings, sanitation systems). The youth are hired only on a temporary basis, but the training and work experience helps them obtain more permanent employment. Public works projects also allow good targeting for other youth interventions (such as training and placement services) that may increase the likelihood that youth find better employment opportunities beyond the program.

A few evaluations have tested whether these programs improve the chances of participating in the labor market or enhance private sector employment. Evaluation of Argentina's Trabajar program suggests that such programs can have a significant impact on participants' current incomes (Ravallion and others 2005). There is also some evidence of lagged gains from past participation. Evaluation of the first seven years of the AGETIP program in Senegal finds that the number of engineering firms more than tripled, the number of construction firms increased fivefold, and 35,000 person-years of employment were generated. Poor governance can be an issue, however. Public works projects require transparency and oversight to ensure that projects target the poor, that only worthy projects are funded, that funds are used wisely, and that inexperienced youth are trained (World Bank 2006).

Responses from African Countries

A review of 68 programs in Burkina Faso, Ethiopia, Tanzania, and Uganda (presented in annexes 6B–E) reveals important differences across countries. The inventory, based on a country stocktaking exercise conducted in late 2005, is not comprehensive but is indicative of the number and range of interventions in progress at the time of the survey. The list is restricted mainly to postschooling interventions.

The inventory of programs is organized into three categories: interventions that broaden opportunities for youth, interventions that build skills and capability, and interventions that offer second chances (table 6.1).

- *Broadening opportunities* includes programs that boost overall demand for labor, such as regional and micro- and small-enterprise development programs, and interventions to remedy labor market failure, such as counseling and job search programs.
- *Building skills and capability* includes programs to improve the skills of disadvantaged youth, postschool programs that provide unemployed youth with vocational skills, entrepreneurship programs (which are bundled with credit schemes), and livelihood training.
- *Second-chance programs* include adult literacy and equivalency programs, support for marginalized young people, and public works programs.

Improving opportunities for entrepreneurs is by far the most popular type of program, in terms of both programs that target youth (except in Ethiopia) and those that target all workers. Public works programs are in place in Burkina Faso, Ethiopia and Tanzania, although they do not specifically target youth. Training programs are heavily represented among youth-specific programs in Burkina Faso, Tanzania, and Uganda, albeit with different emphases. Burkina Faso is the only country in which a rural adult literacy program appears to be in place, although Uganda has a National Adult Literacy Strategic Investment Plan and Tanzania and Uganda have second-chance/equivalency programs. Improving training systems for young people seems to be neglected, although Tanzania seems well placed to move in this direction through its skill development levy system. There may also be scope for reforming labor market regulations to encourage employers to hire more young workers.

Program Evaluation Has Been Weak

Several evaluation studies of these interventions have been conducted, but they report only outcomes, not impact. Information has been collected on

Table 6.1. Promising Interventions in Burkina Faso, Ethiopia, Tanzania, and Uganda

Category	Policy or program
Broadening opportunities	
Job creation programs	Regional Micro and Small Enterprise Development Agencies (Ethiopia)
Counseling and job search programs	Labor Exchange Center (Tanzania)
Financial incentives	FINCA Lending Programme (Tanzania)
	ZANU Finance Lending, Training, and Literacy (Burkina Faso)
Building skills and capability	
Apprenticeship systems	VETA National Apprenticeship (Tanzania)
Vocational skills training (active labor market training programs for youth)	Entoto Technical and Vocational Education and Training (Ethiopia)
	Hope Enterprises (Ethiopia)
	Community Skill Training Centers (IIZ/DW and Government) (Ethiopia)
	PEVOT-GTZ Program (Uganda)
Young entrepreneur programs	Gatsby Trust Entrepreneurship (Tanzania)
	PCY (GTZ) Small Business (Uganda)
	Tanzania PRIDE Entrepreneurship (Tanzania)
	FAARF Women's Credit (Burkina Faso)
	FAPE Employment Promotion Fund (Burkina Faso)
Programs to counteract isolation	Livelihood Skills Development Programme (Tanzania)
	BKF/98/006 Program to Retain Young People in Own Regions (Burkina Faso)
Second-chance programs	
Literacy and numeracy programs	YES Program (Uganda)
Second-chance equivalency programs	Complementary Basic Education (COBET) (Tanzania)
	BEUPA Equivalency Program (Uganda)
Public works	Dar es Salaam Solid Waste Municipal Service Delivery (Tanzania)
	Productive Safety Nets Program (Ethiopia)
	PSTP/HIMO Public Works (Burkina Faso)
	TIPE Public Works Program (Burkina Faso)
Support to disadvantaged youth	REPAGE Project for Marginalized Young People (Burkina Faso)

Source: Godfrey 2006.

the cost of various interventions, but no cost-benefit studies appear to have been conducted, and the impact of the programs was not compared with that of a control group.

Evaluation is particularly important in countries with limited resources, where resources are vitally needed for education, safe motherhood programs, contraception, and construction and repair of infrastructure. Youth employment interventions should pass two tests: their social benefits should outweigh their costs and the private return to program participants should be high.

Future Research to Fill Knowledge Gaps

This report identifies gaps in knowledge about youth in the labor market. Future analysis is needed to fill these gaps. Priority areas for future research include the following:

- Rigorous evaluations need to be conducted in order to build an evidence base from which interventions can be formed to help poor youth make successful transitions to working life. Evaluating program impact should be one of the highest priorities for donors and governments in responding to the challenge of youth unemployment.
- Surveys need to add nonstandard labor market indicators so that they fully describe what is happening in the rural labor market. Current surveys fail to capture many unpaid family workers.
- Better understanding is needed of the response of youth program interventions in rural areas and informal sectors.
- More research should be done on second-chance programs, which are particularly important in Africa given the large number of youth who never completed primary school.

Annex 6A. Methodology: Building an Indicator of the School-to-Work Transition

This annex computes a measure of the school-to-work transition in developing countries. It tries to overcome some of the problems associated with using methods applied to measure the transition in Western countries.

OECD (1998, 1999, 2000) uses the age at which 50 percent of individuals are employed to determine the end point of the transition. Measures of transition based on this definition implicitly assume that the overall portion of individuals moving into employment is at least 50 percent (otherwise no transition would ever be completed) and that the proportion of individuals who enter employment is roughly comparable across countries (otherwise this indicator is biased by differences in participation across countries). Neither of these assumptions is likely to be true, especially in developing countries.

Similar problems occur in estimating the starting point of the transition. OECD indicators implicitly assume that all children transit through the school system and that the vast majority of them stay in school at least as long as they are required to by law. This assumption is clearly not valid in most developing countries.

These assumptions represent a serious source of bias in comparing data from developing countries with very different levels of overall labor market participation in adulthood, especially among women, and of school attendance. The procedure developed for this study tries to circumvent the problems with other methods by standardizing the measures of school-to-work transition to the population at risk—that is, those who eventually transit through school and participate in the labor force.

Ideally, to model the transition process from school to work, longitudinal data should be used that provide detailed job histories that follow individuals from childhood into adulthood. Alternatively, cross-sectional data with retrospective information could be used that allow work histories to be reconstructed. In the absence of these data, which are generally lacking even in developing countries, cross-sectional data can be used to measure the length of the transition. Under appropriate assumptions, cross-sectional data allow the parameters of interest to be consistently identified.

To measure the school-to-work transition, a new indicator was developed for this report based on the difference between the average school-leaving age and the average age of first entry into work. This measure was constructed as follows. Suppose there exists an age a_{min}, such that for $a > a_{min}$, individuals never enter school and for $a \leq a_{min}$ individuals never leave school. In this case, at age a_{min} those who ever enter school are in school. Let S denote the event of being in school and SL_a the probability of leaving school at age a. Then

$$SL_a = -[P(S_{a+1}) - P(S_a)] \qquad a > a_{min} \qquad (6A.1)$$

represents the change in enrollment across two consecutive ages. Equation (6A.1) states that if, say, 90 percent of children are in school at age 10 and

80 percent are in school at age 11, then 10 percent of children must have dropped out between age 10 and 11.

Assume that for any age, $a < a_{max}$ individuals never leave work and $a \geq a_{max}$ individuals never begin work. This implies that at age a_{max}, everyone who ever will work is working. This assumption, which is less realistic than the previous one, means that exit from employment occurs before a_{max} and exit from inactivity occurs before a_{max}. Denote work by W, and denote the probability of entry into work at age a by EW_a. This equation is the increase in participation from one year to the other:

$$EW_a = P(W_{a+1}) - P(W_a) \qquad a < a_{max}. \qquad (6A.2)$$

Equation (6A.2) states that if, say, 10 percent of children are in work at age 14, and 15 percent are in work at age 15, then 5 percent of children must have started to work between the ages of 14 and 15.

One problem with these indicators is that many individuals do not enter school and many, particularly females, do not transition into work, if work is defined as participation in a market-oriented economic activity. These indexes are thus conditional on individuals ever transiting into the relevant state. Under the assumptions above, the average school-leaving age conditional on ever having been in school is

$$E(SL) = \Sigma_{a > a_{min}} a \, [SL_a/P(S_{a_{min}})] \qquad (6A.3)$$

and the distribution of age of entry into work is

$$E(EW) = \Sigma_{a < a_{max}} a \, [EW_a/P(W_{a_{max}})]. \qquad (6A.4)$$

Notice that $P(W_{a_{max}}) = S_{a < a_{max}} EW_a$, hence $\Sigma_{a < a_{max}}[EW_a/P(W_{a_{max}})] - 1$.

Similar reasoning applies to the weights in equation (6A.3).

An index of the average gap between the age of entry into work (conditional on ever entering into work) and the age of exit from school (conditional on ever being in school) is given by

$$I = E(SL) - E(EW). \qquad (6A.5)$$

A probit model was fitted (separately for males and females in each country) on the probability of being in school. The model was regressed on a polynomial in age. Fitting a probit model is useful for smoothing the age participation profiles in the presence of measurement error and small sample sizes, and it allows sample predictions to be made if necessary. The value a_{min} is identified as the turning point in the estimated age participation profile. The same procedure is carried out for the probability of working. The estimated probabilities are used to compute the indicators in equations (6A.3), (6A.4), and (6A.5).

This procedure has several drawbacks. First, although it is generally possible to ascertain whether individuals in work ever attended school, it is generally not possible to know whether those who attend school will ever get jobs. The index in equation (6A.5) is, then, the average age gap for individuals who enter work after leaving school (the true school-to-work transition age gap) only under the assumption that age of exit from school is uncorrelated with the probability of entering into work later in the life cycle, an assumption that some may not find compelling. If early school leavers are less likely to eventually find a job, the gap will be overestimated; if they are more likely to find a job, the gap will be underestimated.

A second drawback of this procedure when applied to a single cross-section is that the index is derived from a comparison of individuals of different ages at a given time and hence from different birth cohorts. The direction and magnitude of the bias are difficult to determine. If there is a secular increase in school-leaving age without relevant changes in the age of first employment across cohorts, the length of the transition period from school to work in each country may be underestimated. If the age of first employment also shows a secular increase, the bias could go in either direction. If these biases are assumed to be similar across countries, a sensible inference can be made about cross-country differences.

Annex 6B. Inventory of Selected Policies and Programs on Youth Employment and Skills Development in Burkina Faso

Government Involvement in Youth Employment Issues

In November 2004 the government established a National Agency for Employment. The new agency's functions include the following:

- Studying the problems of employment, apprenticeship, and professional training and maintaining relevant documentation.
- Organizing a system of labor market intermediation and information.
- Promoting self-employment and the emergence of viable micro-, small, and medium-size enterprises.

- Initiating and implementing programs that help young people make the transition to employment.
- Identifying the needs and possibilities for apprenticeship and training and implementing a policy of orientation and information for potential participants.
- Renovating existing systems and creating new systems for training and apprenticeship.
- Organizing and implementing recruitment of people for overseas employment.

Description of Policies and Programs

This inventory of policies and programs on youth in Burkina Faso describes 28 interventions (table 6B.1). It is a selective rather than a comprehensive inventory.

Making the Labor Market Work Better for Young People
The first category of interventions includes only public works programs in Burkina Faso. These six programs are:

- The special program of labor-intensive public works (PSTP/HIMO)
- The pilot urban infrastructure project at Kaya (BKF/90/02M/BEL)
- The public works program for employment executed by the Faso Baara agency (TIPE)
- The projects of the labor-intensive fund (HIMO)
- The street cleaning teams project in Ouagadougou
- The community participation component of the third urban project (BKF/94/06)

None of these programs specifically targets young people, and only one of them is confined to rural areas.

Improving Opportunities for Young Entrepreneurs
This is by far the largest category of interventions in Burkina Faso. The 16 projects examined in this category are:

- The promotion of female artisans
- The fund in support of the informal sector (FASI)
- The employment promotion fund (FAPE)
- The national program for the redeployment of laid-off workers (PNAR-TD)

Table 6B.1. Selected Employment-Related Programs by Category, Location, and Age Group Served in Burkina Faso

Intervention	Urban		Rural		Both		Total		
	Only young people	All ages	Only young people	All ages	Only young people	All ages	Only young people	All ages	Total
1. Making the labor market work better for young people									
1a. Counseling, job search skills									
1b. Wage subsidies									
1c. Public works programs		2		1		3		6	6
1d. Antidiscrimination legislation									
1e. Other									
2. Improving opportunities for young entrepreneurs		1	3	3	2	7	5	11	16
3. Providing skills training for young people									
3a. Apprenticeship systems									
3b. Literacy and numeracy (young adult literacy programs)				1				1	1
3c. Vocational skills (active labor market training programs for youth)			1				1		1
3d. Second-chance and equivalency programs								1	1
3e. Other									

Type of intervention									Total
4. Making training systems work better for young people									
4a. Information									
4b. Credit (to individuals or enterprises)									
4c. Financial incentives (subsidies, vouchers)									
4d. Other									
5. Programs to counteract the isolation of disadvantaged young people									
5a. Transportation									
5b. Other									
6. Improving labor market regulations to the benefit of young people						2			2
7. Programs for overseas employment of young people									
8. Comprehensive multiple-service approach								2	2
9. Other, including voluntary national service programs				1				2	2
Unclassified									
Total	0	3	5	7	3	10	8	20	28

Source: Godfrey 2006.

- The fund in support of income-earning activities for women (FAARF)
- The project in support of creating small- and medium-size enterprises (PAPME)
- Two programs to retain young people in their home regions (PDI-SYP 6ème FED and BKF/98/006)
- Centers for agropastoral development
- The fund for the insertion of young people (FIJ)
- The project in support of poverty reduction among disadvantaged and marginalized young people (REPAGE)
- The project in support of micro and small handcraft enterprises (PER-COMM)
- The project in support of rural microenterprises (PAMER)
- The national karite project (PNK)
- The fund in support of income-generating activities in agriculture (FAAGRA)
- Various interventions by the system for decentralized finance (SFD)

Only five of these interventions specifically target young people, and only six are confined to rural areas.

Making Training Systems Work Better for Young People

Few interventions in Burkina Faso focus on skills training (although entrepreneurship programs often include some training). The ZANU project is a literacy program for rural areas that aims to create permanent learning centers and libraries and to boost employment. The only other training program is a rural program that trains women in agriculture, animal husbandry, dressmaking, dyeing, and weaving.

Other Interventions

No interventions in categories 4–7 are examined in the case of Burkina Faso. Burkina Faso has two comprehensive multiple-service projects, one (PAICB/ LCP) in support of communal initiatives in the struggle against poverty, the other (PRPC) aimed at reducing poverty at the level of the community. Two voluntary service programs for young people (production brigades and the national service for development) are also in place.

How Well Have Interventions Performed?

A high proportion of interventions can be classified as having had a strong positive impact in the labor market (table 6B.2; Ouedraogo 2005). Public works programs performed well in terms of providing immediate employment, raising incomes, and improving the local economy; longer-term

Table 6B.2. Quality of Employment-Related Interventions in Burkina Faso

Intervention	0	1	2	3	Unknown	Total
1. Making the labor market work better for young people						
1c. Public works programs		2	4			6
2. Improving opportunities for young entrepreneurs		13	2		1	16
3. Providing skills training for young people						
3b. Literacy and numeracy (young adult literacy programs)			1			1
3c. Vocational skills (active labor market training programs for youth)		1				1
8. Comprehensive multiple-service approach			2			2
9. Other, including voluntary national service programs	2					2
Total		18	9		1	28

Sources: Godfrey 2006; Ouedraogo 2005.
Note: 0 = Program had negative or zero impact in the labor market (even though outcomes may have been positive).
1 = Program had positive impact in the labor market.
2 = Program had strong positive impact in the labor market.
3 = Program's positive impact exceeded its cost.
Unknown = Program not reviewed by this study.

impact in future employability is likely to depend on how the experience transfers into skills needed by the economy. Among the entrepreneurship projects, two stand out: the fund in support of income-earning activities for women (FAARF), which significantly increased women's access to credit, and the second program to retain young people in their home regions (BKF/98/006), which successfully linked them with the banking and microfinance system. The ZANU project receives a good rating for its combination of literacy, training, and finance, despite financial and organizational constraints. The two multiple-service interventions seem to have had a substantial impact on participants' incomes.

Only a third of interventions are oriented toward the disadvantaged. Five of the entrepreneurship projects target women, and one (REPAGE, the project in support of poverty reduction among disadvantaged and marginalized young people) targets the poor. The two comprehensive multiple-service projects are oriented toward the poor, while the national service program focuses on the less educated.

Only 29 percent of interventions are youth specific, and 57 percent are countrywide or urban rather than limited to rural areas. This focus may reflect the higher incidence of unemployment in urban areas.

All but one project in Burkina Faso was evaluated (table 6B.3). Evaluations, however, measured only outcomes; impact (comparing

Table 6B.3. Quality of Evaluations of Employment-Related Interventions in Burkina Faso

Intervention	0	1	2	3	Unknown	Total
1. Making the labor market work better for young people						
1c. Public works programs		6				6
2. Improving opportunities for young entrepreneurs	1	15				16
3. Providing skills training for young people						
3b. Literacy and numeracy (young adult literacy programs)		1				1
3c. Vocational skills (active labor market training programs for youth)		1				1
8. Comprehensive multiple-service approach		2				2
9. Other, including voluntary national service programs		2				2
Total	1	27				28

Sources: Godfrey 2006; Ouedraogo 2005.

Note: 0 = Program has no evaluation information on outcomes or impact.

1 = Evaluation includes basic information on gross outcomes of the intervention (number of participants, number of young people who found jobs after the intervention, improvement in earnings of participants) without considering net effects (that is, comparing with control group).

2 = Evaluation includes estimate of net impact on, for example, employment and earnings in the labor market (using control groups to measure impact) but no cost-benefit analysis.

3 = Evaluation includes net impact and cost-benefit analysis.

Unknown = Program not reviewed by this study.

outcomes of interventions with those of control groups) does not appear to have been evaluated.

Annex 6C. Inventory of Selected Policies and Programs on Youth Employment and Skills Development in Ethiopia

Government Involvement in Youth Employment Issues

Ethiopia does not have an employment policy as such. Various federal policies and laws are relevant to youth employment, however (Getachew and Kallaur 2005). These include the following:

- A National Youth Policy, officially launched in September 2004, which has a broad objective to encourage the participation of youth (defined as people 15–29) in the economic, social, and cultural life of the country and to support democratization and good governance, through (among other measures) youth participation in policy formulation and implementation, promotion of self-employment and wage

employment, creation of conditions for young people in rural areas to acquire land, reduction in disparities in educational participation by location and gender, and provision of education to out-of-school youth.
- The 2003 Labor Law, which defines the conditions for apprenticeships (for those 14 and older) and layoffs.
- An education policy, established in 1994, and an Education Sector Development Program for 2005–10 that shift the post-grade-10 system toward technical and vocational education and training, in the hope of facilitating the school-to-work transition.
- A Micro- and Small Enterprises Development Strategy, formulated in 1997, which gives priority to enterprises operated by women, school dropouts, people with disabilities, and unemployed youth.

Description of Policies and Programs

This inventory of policies and programs on youth in Ethiopia describes 13 interventions (table 6C.1). It is a selective rather than a comprehensive inventory.

Making the Labor Market Work Better for Young People

Ethiopia has several employment exchange services, run by both public and private operators. The main program is run by the regional Bureaus of the Ministry of Labor and Social Affairs (BOLSAs). The number of beneficiaries is small, with just 24,000 job seekers registered in 2001/02. The program is not youth specific, but 84 percent of those registered were 15–29, nearly two-thirds of them with at least senior-secondary education. Forty-nine regional public employment services offices offer similar services. Private employment exchange offices have also emerged in Ethiopia, governed by the Private Employment Agencies Proclamation.

A variety of public works programs are in place, including the Productive Safety Nets program. Although youth participate in public works programs, the programs do not specifically target youth, and detailed data on beneficiaries are not available.

Legal provisions in Ethiopia protect the rights of people with HIV/AIDS. These provisions cover nondiscrimination in employment.

Improving Opportunities for Young Entrepreneurs

The main government programs to encourage entrepreneurship are run by the federal Micro- and Small Enterprise Development Agency through its regional offices (ReMSEDAs). The ReMSEDAs vary in size

Table 6C.1. Selected Employment-Related Programs by Category, Location, and Age of Group Served in Ethiopia

Intervention	Urban		Rural		Both		Total		
	Only young people	All ages	Only young people	All ages	Only young people	All ages	Only young people	All ages	Total
1. Making the labor market work better for young people									
1a. Counseling, job search skills						3		3	3
1b. Wage subsidies									
1c. Public works programs				1				1	1
1d. Antidiscrimination legislation						1		1	1
1e. Other									
2. Improving opportunities for young entrepreneurs		1				1		2	2
3. Providing skills training for young people									
3a. Apprenticeship systems					1		1		1
3b. Literacy and numeracy (young adult literacy programs)						1		1	1
3c. Vocational skills (active labor market training programs for youth)	1		1				2		2
3d. Second-chance and equivalency programs									
3e. Other									

									Total
4. Making training systems work better for young people									
4a. Information									
4b. Credit (to individuals or enterprises)									
4c. Financial incentives (subsidies, vouchers)									
4d. Other									
5. Programs to counteract the isolation of disadvantaged young people									
5a. Transportation	1								
5b. Other									1
6. Improving labor market regulations to the benefit of young people								1	1
7. Programs for overseas employment of young people							1		1
8. Comprehensive multiple-service approach									
9. Other, including voluntary national service programs									
Unclassified									
Total	2	1	1	1	1	7	1	4	9	13

Sources: Godfrey 2006; Getachew and Kallaur 2005.

and type of programs offered. The Addis Ababa and Dire Dawa ReMSEDAs provide a package of services, including access to work premises, credit, information, and counseling; advice on marketing, business development, and technology; help obtaining licenses; and legal support. The ReMSEDAs include unemployed youth and women among their clients as well as existing business owners. The Addis Ababa ReMSEDA targets unemployed youth and women (though not exclusively).

Microfinance institutions, which operate in all but three regions in Ethiopia, assist young entrepreneurs by providing microcredit. Comprehensive data on borrowers are not available, and youth are not explicitly targeted for loans, making it difficult to assess the impact on youth entrepreneurship. Microfinance institutions are believed to meet only a small fraction of demand.

Providing Skills Training for Young People

A variety of schools provide skills training for young people. The Ministry of Education's formal technical and vocational education and training (TVET) system offers an alternative to the academic programs of traditional secondary schools. Including public as well as private schools operating under the formal Ministry of Education guidelines, there were 158 TVET schools in Ethiopia in 2004.

The Ministry of Agriculture runs a separate formal agricultural TVET program. In addition to the formal TVET schools, the Ministry of Education operates adult and nonformal education programs for all ages, focusing on literacy and numeracy skills. Privately run nonformal education programs, such as those by the German NGO IIZ/DVV, are also available. Some youth receive training by serving as apprentices in the private sector.

Other Interventions

Ethiopia's 25 licensed microfinance institutions provide credit to individuals. Hundreds of civil society organizations work on youth-related issues. Most of these organizations focus on HIV/AIDS and therefore fall outside the scope of this report. However, some organizations, such as the Addis Ababa Youth Association (and its counterparts in other regions), organize a variety of programs for members, including skills training programs.

The Ethiopian Labor Law stipulates that an Ethiopia national may be employed abroad if the Ministry of Labor and Social Affairs "has obtained adequate assurances that his [or her] right and dignity shall be respected in the country of employment." In accordance with this law, work permits are given to Ethiopians whose employment contracts are submitted to the ministry. About 5,000 people were given permits to work abroad in 2001/02, suggesting that only a small fraction of migrants apply for work permits. Of those who went through the formal process, most were relatively well-educated young women who were relocating to Saudi Arabia and Lebanon to work as domestics.

How Well Have Interventions Performed?

In the absence of proper evaluations, it is almost impossible to assess the quality of the interventions. However, two efforts stand out (table 6C.2). The Hope Enterprise vocational training centers appear to have had an impact exceeding their cost. The nonformal training courses run by the German NGO IIZ/DVV using government community skills training centers are based on extensive market analysis and needs assessment in the local area and are likely to have had a strong positive impact. Two

Table 6C.2. Quality of Employment-Related Interventions in Ethiopia

Intervention	0	1	2	3	Unknown	Total
1. Making the labor market work better for young people						
1a. Counseling, job search skills					1	1
1c. Public works programs						
1d. Antidiscrimination legislation						
2. Improving opportunities for young entrepreneurs		2			1	3
3. Providing skills training for young people						
3a. Apprenticeship systems						
3b. Literacy and numeracy (young adult literacy programs)						
3c. Vocational skills (active labor market training programs for youth)	1	1	1	1	1	5
5. Programs to counteract isolation of disadvantaged young people						
5b. Other	1				1	2
7. Programs for overseas employment of young people					1	1
Total	2	3	1	1	5	12

Source: Godfrey 2006.
Note: 0 = Program had negative or zero impact in the labor market (even though outcomes may have been positive).
1 = Program had positive impact in the labor market.
2 = Program had strong positive impact in the labor market.
3 = Program's positive impact exceeded its cost.
Unknown = Program not reviewed by this study.

Table 6C.3. Quality of Evaluations of Employment-Related Programs in Ethiopia

Intervention	0	1	2	3	Unknown	Total
1. Making the labor market work better for young people	1				1	
1a. Counseling, job search skills	1				2	5
1c. Public works programs						
1d. Antidiscrimination legislation						
2. Improving opportunities for young entrepreneurs	1	1				2
3. Providing skills training for young people						
3a. Apprenticeship systems						
3b. Literacy and numeracy (young adult literacy programs)						
3c. Vocational skills (active labor market training programs for youth)	1	3				4
5. Programs to counteract isolation of disadvantaged young people						
5b. Other	1					1
7. Programs for overseas employment of young people	1					1
Total	6	4			3	13

Source: Godfrey 2006.

Note: 0 = Program has no evaluation information on outcomes or impact.

1 = Evaluation includes basic information on gross outcomes of the intervention (number of participants, number of young people who found jobs after the intervention, improvement in earnings of participants) without considering net effects (that is, comparing with control group).

2 = Evaluation includes estimate of net impact on, for example, employment and earnings in the labor market (using control groups to measure impact) but no cost-benefit analysis.

3 = Evaluation includes net impact and cost-benefit analysis.

Unknown = Program not reviewed by this study.

other training interventions, the Entoto Technical and Vocational Education Training College and the Selam Technical and Vocational Center, and the Addis Ababa and Dire Dawa ReMSEDAs also seem likely to have had a positive impact.

The impact of the other seven interventions on young people's job opportunities is more difficult to assess. Public works programs are believed to be highly beneficial from a safety net perspective, but impact evaluations have not yet been conducted and the long-term effect on the employability of participants is unclear.

Some programs target women, although data on actual beneficiaries are scarce. The Addis Ababa ReMSEDA targets female entrepreneurs, and some microfinance institutions target women. Scholarships, often sponsored by nongovernmental organizations (NGOs), help some of the poorest attend training programs, as does the fee structure of the formal TVET system. Nonformal training courses (second-chance programs designed to provide basic skills) target relatively poor and vulnerable groups.

Information with which to evaluate the effectiveness of programs for Ethiopian youth is scarce and appears limited to information on outcomes and beneficiaries (table 6C.3). The full evaluation of technical and vocational education programs reportedly underway will be very welcome.

Annex 6D. Inventory of Selected Policies and Programs on Youth Employment and Skills Development in Tanzania

Government Involvement in Youth Employment Issues

A number of recent policy documents in Tanzania address youth employment (Shitundu 2005). The Vision 2025 document provides a guide to addressing overall and youth employment challenges through creative, innovative, and high-quality education and the establishment of a culture of self-development and entrepreneurship, especially among young people.

The National Strategy for Growth and Reduction of Poverty (November 2004) aims to halve the proportion of the population living below the basic needs and food poverty lines and to reduce youth unemployment by 50 percent by 2010. The strategy includes the following:

- Implementing strategies that promote employment creation and self-employment. Such strategies include investment tax incentives, especially to training institutions; microfinance; curriculum reform; and skill development.
- Promoting community-based construction and maintenance of roads.
- Increasing public investment and promoting private sector investment in key sectors of the economy.
- Strengthening institutional and individual capacity for the efficient coordination of employment policy.
- Developing apprenticeship and entrepreneurship programs targeting young people.
- Reforming and enforcing laws that increase opportunities for youth employment in both the formal and informal sectors.
- Maintaining the policy of free primary school education to encourage universal access to education for all children.
- Providing young people with life skills education, including education about HIV/AIDS.

Tanzania has also developed a National Youth Development Policy, which addresses in a participatory way the range of problems faced by young people, including employment.

Description of Policies and Programs

This inventory of policies and programs on youth in Tanzania describes 28 interventions (table 6D.1). It is a selective rather than a comprehensive inventory.

Making the Labor Market Work Better for Young People

Tanzania provides information and counseling through the Labor Exchange Center. It runs two public works programs, the Dar es Salaam Solid Waste Management Project and the Municipal Service Delivery Project, both innovative public-private partnership projects. Tanzania does not appear to have used wage subsidies or antidiscrimination legislation, which are sometimes used to help make labor markets work better for women, ethnic minorities, and people with disabilities.

Improving Opportunities for Young Entrepreneurs

The second category of interventions is the largest in Tanzania, accounting for more than half of the programs reviewed in table 6D.1. These programs include microfinance programs run by the government alone, such as the National Youth Development Fund; programs run by NGOs, such as FINCA Tanzania (the second-largest such program in Africa); programs run by the government together with donors, such as the National Income-Generating Program; and programs run by commercial banks. Some programs in this category, such as the Tanzania Gatsby Trust, are described as entrepreneurship programs; others, such as the Youth Economic Groups program, are described as microenterprise development programs.

Providing Skills Training for Young People

The third category of interventions includes the national apprenticeship program and other programs run by the Vocational Education and Training Authority (VETA), an information and communication technology-based program based in Ilonga, and a second-chance Complementary Basic Education in Tanzania (COBET) program aimed at out-of-school children as old as 18. No specific literacy/numeracy programs were identified, although COBET includes literacy and numeracy components.

Table 6D.1. Selected Employment-Related Programs by Category, Location, and Age Group Served in Tanzania

Intervention	Urban		Rural		Both		Total		
	Only young people	All ages	Only young people	All ages	Only young people	All ages	Only young people	All ages	Total
1. Making the labor market work better for young people									
1a. Counseling, job search skills						1		1	1
1b. Wage subsidies									
1c. Public works programs		2		1		1		4	4
1d. Antidiscrimination legislation									
1e. Other									
2. Improving opportunities for young entrepreneurs					3	12	3	12	15
3. Providing skills training for young people									
3a. Apprenticeship systems					1		1		1
3b. Literacy and numeracy (young adult literacy programs)									
3c. Vocational skills (active labor market training programs for youth)					1	1	1	1	2
3d. Second-chance and equivalency programs					1		1		1
3e. Other									

(continued)

Table 6D.1. Selected Employment-Related Programs by Category, Location, and Age Group Served in Tanzania (continued)

Intervention	Urban		Rural		Both		Total		
	Only young people	All ages	Only young people	All ages	Only young people	All ages	Only young people	All ages	Total
4. Making training systems work better for young people									
4a. Information									
4b. Credit (to individuals or enterprises)									
4c. Financial incentives (subsidies, vouchers)									
4d. Other						1		1	1
5. Programs to counteract the isolation of disadvantaged young people									
5a. Transportation									
5b. Other					1		1		1
6. Improving labor market regulations to the benefit of young people									
7. Programs for overseas employment of young people					1		1		1
8. Comprehensive multiple-service approach									
9. Other, including voluntary national service programs						1		1	1
Unclassified									
Total	0	2	0	1	8	17	8	20	28

Source: Godfrey 2006.

Making Training Systems Work Better for Young People

The single program in this category is the formal sector skill development levy/grant scheme. This scheme gives enterprises an incentive to train their employees by reimbursing their costs from a levy fund.

Other Interventions

The Livelihood Skills Development Program is concerned mainly with reducing risk-taking behavior, with particular emphasis on HIV/AIDS and drug abuse, and promoting healthy lifestyles. No attempts appear to have been made to make labor market regulations more hospitable to young people (by lowering minimum wages for younger workers and trainees, for example, or relaxing employment security regulations). The program for overseas employment of young people is not a migrant worker program along Asian lines but rather a set of small-scale youth exchange programs. The comprehensive multiple-service approach is part of an International Labour Organization project to promote gender equality and decent work.

How Well Have Interventions Performed?

Based on the limited information available, the quality of the programs appears to have been poor (table 6D.2). Only one intervention—the FINCA microfinance program, which targets poor families—is believed to have had an impact that exceeded its cost, and it is not clear how

Table 6D.2. Quality of Employment-Related Interventions in Tanzania

Intervention	0	1	2	3	Unknown	Total
1. Making the labor market work better for young people						
1a. Counseling, job search skills		1				1
1c. Public works programs		2			2	4
2. Improving opportunities for young entrepreneurs	1	7	2	1	4	15
3. Providing skills training for young people						
3a. Apprenticeship systems		1				1
3c. Vocational skills (active labor market training programs for youth)		1	1			2
3d. Second-chance and equivalency programs		1				1

(continued)

Table 6D.2. Quality of Employment-Related Interventions in Tanzania *(continued)*

Intervention	0	1	2	3	Unknown	Total
4. Making training systems work better for young people						
4c. Financial incentives (subsidies, vouchers)					1	1
5. Programs to counteract the isolation of disadvantaged young people						
5b. Others			1			1
7. Programs for overseas employment of young people		1				1
8. Comprehensive multiple-service approach		1				1
Total	1	13	6	1	7	28

Source: Godfrey 2006.

Note: 0 = Program had negative or zero impact in the labor market (even though outcomes may have been positive).
1 = Program had positive impact in the labor market.
2 = Program had strong positive impact in the labor market.
3 = Program positive impact exceeded its cost.
Unknown = Program not reviewed by this study.

many young people benefited from the program. Six programs—two entrepreneurship programs (PRIDE Tanzania and the Youth Economic Groups); three skills training programs (apprenticeship, information and communication technology training, and COBET); and the Livelihood Skills Development Program—are judged to have had a strong positive impact. Thirteen programs are likely to have had a positive impact that did not exceed their costs, while one credit program (the Local Government Youth and Women Development Funds) seems likely to have had no impact. The impact of the unevaluated levy/grant scheme is not known, but the scheme is unpopular with enterprises.

Less than 30 percent of the programs reviewed (mainly credit and training programs) specifically target young people, and only one program (a public works programs) targets rural areas, where the vast majority of Tanzania's young people live. A relatively small proportion of interventions are oriented toward the disadvantaged: seven programs (mainly credit and public works) target women, three target the poorest youth, and one targets the least educated youth. No programs appear to be available for young people with disabilities.

Evaluation of the programs has been weak or nonexistent (table 6D.3). No evaluation information is available on 5 interventions, the situation for 3 is unknown, and the remaining 20 report only on outcomes rather than impact.

Table 6D.3. Quality of Evaluations of Employment-Related Programs in Tanzania

Intervention	0	1	2	3	Unknown	Total
1. Making the labor market work better for young people						
1a. Counseling, job search skills		1				1
1c. Public works programs	2	2				4
2. Improving opportunities for young entrepreneurs	1	11			3	15
3. Providing skills training for young people						
3a. Apprenticeship systems		1				1
3c. Vocational skills (active labor market training programs for youth)	1	1				2
3d. Second-chance and equivalency programs		1				1
4. Making training systems work better for young people						
4c. Financial incentives (subsidies, vouchers)	1					1
5. Programs to counteract the isolation of disadvantaged young people						
5b. Other		1				1
7. Programs for overseas employment of young people		1				1
8. Comprehensive multiple-service approach		1				1
Total	5	20			3	28

Source: Godfrey 2006.

Note: 0 = Program has no evaluation information on outcomes or impact.

1 = Evaluation includes basic information on gross outcomes of the intervention (number of participants, number of young people who found jobs after the intervention, improvement in earnings of participants) without considering net effects (that is, comparing with control group).

2 = Evaluation includes estimate of net impact on, for example, employment and earnings in the labor market (using control groups to measure impact) but no cost-benefit analysis.

3 = Evaluation includes net impact and cost-benefit analysis.

Unknown = Program not reviewed by this study.

Annex 6E. Inventory of Selected Policies and Programs on Youth Employment and Skills Development in Uganda

The review for Uganda did not include a detailed inventory of interventions; analysis comparable to that in annexes 6B–D was thus not possible. Instead, this annex presents the results of a review of policies and programs affecting youth in Uganda.

Uganda has a wide range of plans, policies, and programs that affect youth employment. These include the following:

- Vision 2025, which provides a long-term perspective and aims to create a "highly trained, competent and knowledgeable labor force that is

motivated, responsible, efficient, enterprising, innovative, and industrious" and that can find "secure and well-remunerated employment."
- A Poverty Eradication Action Plan (PEAP), most recently revised in 2004, which deals with employment issues in some of its pillars—production, competitiveness, and incomes (especially improving the functioning of the labor market and the productivity of workers) and human development (especially education and skill development).
- A National Adult Literacy Strategic Investment Plan, 2002/3–2006/7, part of Uganda's Poverty Eradication Action Plan, which aims to increase literacy levels by 50 percent over the plan period.
- The promotion of youth participation in decision making, through the establishment of a National Youth Council (which has developed a strategic investment plan for 2004–07) and youth representation in local councils and parliament.
- A 1992 White Paper on Education, which remains the guiding document for the sector. This document has found practical expression in an Education Sector Strategic Plan, 2004–15, which emphasizes post-primary vocational training institutions and community polytechnics, and a 2003 Policy for Business, Technical, Vocational Education and Training (BTVET).
- An Orphans and Vulnerable Children Policy, 2005, which shifts the focus from helping individual orphans to helping the households in which they live, by providing microfinance to grow economically viable crops and other interventions.
- A Plan for Modernization of Agriculture, 2000–20, which aims to increase agricultural productivity and shift farmers from producing primarily for subsistence to producing for the market to the benefit of off-farm employment.
- A Social Development Sector Strategic Investment Plan, 2003–08, in which youth is one of the groups of special concern. The plan includes the promotion of employment and productivity.

Only four interventions have been analyzed in any detail (Okech 2005). They include the following:

- The Youth Entrepreneurs Scheme, which improves opportunities for young entrepreneurs.
- The Promotion of Children and Youth program, which also improves opportunities for young entrepreneurs.

- The Program for the Promotion of Employment-Oriented Vocational and Technical Training (PEVOT), which provides vocational skill training to young people.
- Basic Education in Urban Poverty Areas (BEUPA), which provides young people with second chances.

The Youth Entrepreneurs Scheme has imparted business skills to more than 4,000 young people, provided credit to 1,812 people between the ages of 18 and 34, and increased the capacity of intermediary institutions. The review of the program comments favorably on its achievements and impact but notes that it disbursed only 35 percent of the funds available to it. Moreover, the program focuses on elite school-leavers (those with upper-secondary school certificates or higher qualifications).

The Promotion of Children and Youth program, funded by GTZ, promotes cooperative ventures and small businesses involving young people and builds the capacity of local government in this field. The review of the program is favorable, but no evaluation evidence is cited.

The PEVOT, also supported by GTZ, is helping develop and implement reforms of vocational education and training, including a qualifications framework; improvements in financing (training levies paid by enterprises are envisaged); and short courses for the disadvantaged. This work is still in progress, with few measurable achievements to date.

The BEUPA project provides a three-year course, equivalent to primary school, and prevocational skills training for urban dropouts 9–18. It also organizes apprenticeships for participants. There is no information on its outcomes or impact.

In addition to these interventions, ongoing activities of the Ministry of Gender, Labor, and Social Development include registration and placement of job seekers, a review of obsolete labor laws, and development of a policy framework to ensure the safety and dignity of Ugandans working abroad.

The background to these interventions is a steady increase in the proportion of young people who have completed primary education (and a closing of the gender gap) since 1992. As a result of the government's universal primary education policy, Uganda now has one of the highest average levels of education in Sub-Saharan Africa.

Bibliography for Part 1

Abu-Ghaida, Dina N., and Marie Connolly. 2003. "Trends in Relative Demand for Workers with Secondary Education: A Look at Nine Countries in East Asia, Africa, and MENA." Background paper prepared for *Expanding Opportunities and Building Competencies for Young People: A New Agenda for Secondary Education*. World Bank, Washington, DC.

Acemoglu, Daron. 2003. "Patterns of Skill Premia." *Review of Economic Studies* 70 (2): 231–51.

Adams, Arvil V. 2006. "The Role of Skills Development in the Transition to Work: Lessons from Global Experience." Background paper for *World Development Report 2007*. World Bank, Washington, DC.

Andvig, J. C. 2000. "Family-Controlled Child Labor in Sub-Saharan Africa: A Survey of Research." Working Paper 612. Norwegian Institute of International Affairs (NUPI), Oslo.

Aromolaran, Adebayo B. 2002. "Private Wage Returns to Schooling in Nigeria 1996–1999." Working Paper 849. Yale University, Economic Growth Center, New Haven, CT.

Barro, Robert J., and Jong-Wha Lee. 2000. "International Data on Educational Attainment: Updates and Implications." *Oxford Economic Papers* 53 (3) 541–63.

Bedi, A. S., and J. H. Marshall. 2001. "Primary School Attendance in Honduras." *Journal of Development Economics* 69 (1): 129–53.

Betcherman, Gordon, Karina Olivas, and Amit Dar. 2004. "Impacts of Active Labor Market Programs: New Evidence from Evaluations with Particular Attention to Developing and Transition Countries." Social Protection Discussion Paper Series 0402. World Bank, Washington, DC.

Bhalotra, S. 2003. "Is Child Work Necessary?" Bristol Economics Discussion Paper 03/554. University of Bristol, Department of Economics, Bristol, U.K.

Bhalotra, S., and Chris Heady. 2000. "Child Farm Labor: Theory and Evidence." STICERD Development Economics Papers 24. London School of Economics, Suntory and Toyota International Centres for Economics and Related Disciplines, London.

Bhalotra, S., and Z. Tzannatos. 2002. "Child Labor: What Have We Learnt?" Social Protection Discussion Paper 0234. World Bank, Washington, DC.

Bloom, David E., and Jeffrey G. Williamson. 1998. "Demographic Transitions and Economic Miracles in Emerging Asia." *World Bank Economic Review* 12 (3): 419–55.

Card, David. 1995a. "Earnings, Schooling, and Ability Revisited." NBER Working Paper 4832. National Bureau of Economics, Cambridge, MA.

———. 1995b. "Using Geographic Variation in College Proximity to Estimate the Returns to Schooling." In *Aspects of Labour Market Behaviour: Essays in Honour of John Vanderkamp*, ed. L. N. Christodes, E. K. Grant, and R. Swidinsky. Toronto, Canada: University of Toronto Press.

Cockburn, John. 2001. "Child Labor versus Education: Poverty Constraints or Income Opportunities?" Working Paper. Université Laval, CREFA, Québec, Canada.

———. 2002. "Income Contributions of Child Work in Rural Ethiopia." Working Paper. Centre for the Study of African Economies Series, Oxford, U.K.

Coombe, C., and M. J. Kelly. 2001. "Education as a Vehicle for Combating HIV/AIDS." *Prospects* 31 (3): 435–45.

Dabalen, A. 1998. "Returns to Education in Kenya and South Africa: Instrumental Variable Estimates." University of California, Berkeley, CA.

Denu, Berhanu, Abraham Tekeste, and Hannah van der Deijl. 2005. "Characteristics and Determinants of Youth Employment, Underemployment, and Inadequate Employment in Ethiopia." Employment Strategy Paper. Employment Policies Unit, Employment Strategy Department. International Labour Organization, Geneva.

Emerson, Patrick, and André Portela F. de Souza. 2000. "Is There a Child Labor Trap? Inter-Generational Persistence of Child Labor in Brazil." Working Paper 471. Cornell University, Department of Economics, Ithaca, NY.

Ethiopia Central Statistical Agency. 2001. Ethiopia Labour Force Survey 1999/2000. Addis Ababa.

Fares, Jean, and Dhushyanth Raju. 2006. "Child Labor across the Developing World: Patterns, Correlations and Determinations." Background paper for *World Development Report 2007*. World Bank, Washington, DC.

Freeman, Richard B. 1979. "Why Is There A Youth Labor Market Problem?" NBER Working Paper 365. National Bureau of Economic Research, Cambridge, MA.

Getachew, Martha, and Emily Kallaur. 2005. "Youth Employment in Ethiopia: Overview and Inventory of Existing Policies and Programs." World Bank, Washington, DC.

Glewwe, Paul. 1996. "The Relevance of Standard Estimates or Rates of Return to Schooling for Education Policy: A Critical Assessment." *Journal of Development Economics* 51 (2): 267–90.

Godfrey, Martin. 2006. "Youth Employment in Sub-Saharan Africa: An Assessment of Existing Interventions." Presentation at the World Bank Youth in Africa's Labor Market Workshop, Washington, DC. February 7.

Griliches, Z. 1977. "Estimating the Returns to Schooling: Some Econometrics Problem." *Econometrica* 45 (1): 1–22.

Haan, Hans Christiaan, and Nicholas Serriere. 2002. *Training for Work in the Informal Sector: Fresh Evidence from West and Central Africa*. Turin, Italy: International Training Centre of the International Labour Organization.

Ilahi, N., P. Orazem, and G. Sedlacek. 2000. "The Implications of Child Labor for Adult Wages, Income, and Poverty: Retrospective Evidence from Brazil." World Bank, Washington, DC.

ILO (International Labour Office). 2006. "The End of Child Labour: Within Reach." International Labour Office, Geneva.

Jacoby, Hanan G., and Emmanuel Skoufias. 1997. "Risk, Financial Markets, and Human Capital in a Developing Country." *Review of Economic Studies* 64 (3): 311–35.

Johanson, Richard K., and Arvil V. Adams. 2004. *Skills Development in Sub-Saharan Africa*. Washington, DC: World Bank.

Kahyarara, G., F. Teal, A. Wambugu, and M. Söderbom. 2004. "The Dynamics of Returns to Education in Kenyan and Tanzanian Manufacturing." Development and Comp Systems 0409041, Economics Working Paper Archive. Washington University in St. Louis, MO.

Kalzianga, H. 2002. "Schooling Returns for Wage Earners in Burkina Faso: Evidence from the 1994 and 1998 Living Standard Measurement Surveys." Yale University, Economic Growth Center, New Haven, CT.

Kielland, A., and Maurizia Tovo. 2006. *Children at Work: Child Labor Practices in Africa*. Boulder. CO: Lynne Rienner Publishers.

Kingdon, G., and J. Knight. Forthcoming. "How Flexible Are Wages in Response to Local Unemployment in South Africa?" *Industrial and Labor Relations Review.*

Korenman, Sanders, and David Neumark. 2000. "Cohort Crowding and Youth Labor Markets: A Cross-National Analysis." In *Youth Employment and Joblessness in Advanced Countries,* ed. David G. Blanchflower and Richard B. Freeman. Chicago, IL, and London: University of Chicago Press for the National Bureau of Economic Research.

Knight, J. B., R. H. Sabot, and D. C. Hovey. 1992. "Is the Rate of Return on Primary Schooling Really 26 Per Cent?" *Journal of African Economies* 1 (2): 171–91.

Krishnan, Pramila, Tesfaye Gebre Selassie, and Stefan Dercon. 1998. "The Urban Labour Market During Structural Adjustment: Ethiopia 1990–1997." CSAE Working Paper WPS/98.9. University of Oxford, Center for the Study of African Economies, U.K.

Lam, David. 2006. "The Demography of Youth in Developing Countries and Its Economic Implications." Policy Research Working Paper, WPS 4022. World Bank, Washington, DC.

Lassibille, G., and J. Tan. 2005. "The Returns to Education in Rwanda." *Journal of African Economies* 14 (1): 92–116.

Llisteri, J., H. Kantis, P. Angelelli, and L. Tejerina. Forthcoming. *Youth Entrepreneurship in Latin America.* Washington, DC: Inter-American Development Bank.

Mankiw, N. Gregory, David Romer, and David N. Weil. 1992. "A Contribution to the Empirics of Economic Growth." *The Quarterly Journal of Economics* 107 (2): 407–37.

Muraközy, Balazs, and László Halpern. 2005. "Does Distance Matter in Spillover?" Discussion Papers 4857. Centre of Economic Policy Research, London.

Mwabu, G., and P. Schultz. 1996. "Education Returns across Quantiles of the Wage Function: Alternative Explanations for Returns to Education by Race in South Africa." *American Economic Association Papers and Proceedings* 86 (2): 335–39.

OECD (Organisation for Economic Co-operation and Development). 1998. "Getting Started, Settling In: The Transition from Education to the Labour Market." In *Employment Outlook 1998.* Paris.

———. 1999. *Preparing Youth for the 21st Century: The Transition from Education to the Labor Market.* Paris.

———. 2000. *From Initial Education to Working Life: Making Transitions Work.* Paris.

O'Higgins, Niall. 2003. "Trends in the Youth Labor Market in Developing and Transition Countries." Social Protection Discussion Paper Series 0321. World Bank, Washington, DC.

Okech, Anthony. 2005. "Uganda Case Study of Literacy in Education for All 2005: A Review of Policies, Strategies, and Practices." Background paper prepared for the *Education for All Global Monitoring Report 2006*. United Nations Educational, Scientific, and Cultural Organization, Paris.

Ouedraogo, Barthélemy M. 2005. "Etude sur L'Emploi au Burkina Faso." Ministry of Labor and the World Bank. Ougadougou, Burkina Faso.

Psacharopoulos, George, and Harry Anthony Patrinos. 2004. "Returns to Investment in Education: A Further Update." *Education Economics* 12 (2): 111–34.

Raju, Dhushyanth. 2006. "The Effects of Conditional Cash Transfer Programs on Child Work: A Critical Review and Analysis of the Evidence." Working Paper. World Bank, Washington, DC.

Ravallion, Martin, Emanuela Galasso, Teodoro Lazo, and Ernesto Philipp. 2005. "What Can Ex-Participants Reveal about a Program's Impact?" *Journal of Human Resources* 40 (1): 208–30.

Ray, Debraj. 1998. *Development Economics*. Princeton, NJ: Princeton University Press.

Riley, Thira, and William Steel. 1999. "Kenya Voucher Program for Training and Business Development Services." World Bank, Washington, DC.

Sanchez-Paramo, Carolina, and Norbert Schady. 2003. "Off and Running? Technology, Trade, and the Rising Demand for Skilled Workers in Latin America." Policy Research Working Paper Series 3015. World Bank, Washington, DC.

Schultz, Paul. 2003. *Evidence of Return to Schooling in Africa from Household Surveys: Monitoring and Restructuring the Market for Education*. New Haven, CT: Yale University.

Shitundu, Joseph M. 2005. "Youth Employment Inventory of Existing Policies and Programmes in Tanzania." World Bank, Social Protection Unit, Washington, DC.

Staiger, D., and J. Stock. 1997. "Instrumental Variables Regression with Weak Instruments." *Econometrica* 65 (3): 557–86.

Subbarao, K., and Diane Koury. 2004. *Reaching Out to Africa's Orphans: A Framework for Public Action*. Washington, DC: World Bank.

Tanzania National Bureau of Statistics. 2003. Tanzania Integrated Labor Force Survey. 2000/01. Dar es Salaam, Tanzania.

UN (United Nations). 2005. *World Population Prospects: The 2004 Revision. Volume II: Sex and Age Distribution of the World Population*. New York.

UNAIDS (United Nations Joint Programme of HIV/AIDS). 2002. *Report on the Global HIV/AIDS Epidemic*. Geneva.

UNAIDS/WHO (World Health Organization). 2005. *AIDS Epidemic Update*. Geneva: UNAIDS/WHO.

UNOWA (United Nations Office for West Africa). 2005. "Youth Unemployment and Regional Insecurity in West Africa." Dakar.

Uwaifo, R. 2005. "Africa's Education Enigma: The Nigerian Story." PhD dissertation, University of California, Berkeley.

Vilhuber, Lars. 2006. "The Transition from School to the Labor Market in Uganda." Preliminary outline presented at the World Bank Youth in Africa's Labor Market Workshop, Washington, DC. February 7.

World Bank. 1994–2001. Standard Files and Standard Indicators. Washington, DC.

———. 2000. *Can Africa Claim the 21st Century?* Washington, DC.

———. 2004. *World Development Report 2005: A Better Investment Climate for Everyone.* New York and Washington, DC: Oxford University Press and the World Bank.

———. 2005. *Global Monitoring Report.* Washington, DC.

———. 2006. *World Development Report 2007: Development and the Next Generation.* Washington, DC.

PART 2

Youth in Africa's Labor Market: Country Case Studies

Lisa Dragoset, Jean Fares, Lorenzo Guarcello, Florence Kondylis, Scott Lyon, Marco Manacorda, Daniel Parent, Furio Rosati, Cristina Valdivia, and Lars Vilhuber

CHAPTER 7

School-to-Work Transitions: Regional Overview

Lorenzo Guarcello, Marco Manacorda, Furio Rosati, Jean Fares, Scott Lyon, and Cristina Valdivia

As the international development community centers its attention on the Millennium Development Goals, improving outcomes for children and youth—the groups most directly related to achieving these goals—is a growing priority. Young people are especially vulnerable to exclusion from economic and societal resources, jeopardizing their future prospects and overall national progress toward realizing the goals.

Youth unemployment and underemployment are growing concerns worldwide. According to International Labour Organization (ILO) estimates (2006), youth made up 44 percent of the world's unemployed in 2005, 85 million people in absolute terms. Young workers everywhere have much higher rates of joblessness and much lower earnings than older workers. Young people are also concentrated in low-skill informal work or in hazardous forms of work that are ill-suited to their age and experience. Employment outcomes are typically the worst for former child laborers and others who leave school early, groups with the least opportunity to accumulate the human capital needed for gainful employment.

The challenge of youth employment in Africa is especially large. In Sub-Saharan Africa, young people ages 15–24 account for 37 percent of the working age population. As a result of population pressure, the number of young people in Sub-Saharan Africa in the labor force is expected to increase by about 24 million people between 2005 and 2015 (ILO 2006). Failure to address youth employment issues will have serious consequences for the economy and society. Without opportunities for young people to earn a living, intergenerational cycles of poverty will persist, further affecting societies already made vulnerable by HIV/AIDS, food insecurity, and violence.

While youth issues are the subject of growing attention, data for indicators relating specifically to youth employment remain scarce in most developing countries. The empirical basis for formulating policies and programs promoting youth employment and successful transitions from school to work is therefore limited.

This chapter is aimed at beginning to fill this gap by generating and analyzing a set of youth education and employment indicators based on World Bank Priority survey data for 13 countries in Sub-Saharan Africa.[1] Particular emphasis is placed on measuring the initial transition from school to work for different groups of young people and on identifying the factors affecting this transition.

Aggregate Trends

Countries in Sub-Saharan Africa are overwhelmingly poor. Of a total population of 650 million, 500 million are estimated to live on less than $2 a day, and 300 million live below the poverty line of $1 a day. Over the last two decades, gross national product per capita and private consumption have declined. In the past few years, signs of a turnaround have begun to show, but with large variations. Burkina Faso, Tanzania, and Uganda have experienced high per capita growth rates for more than five years. Growth in Kenya, Nigeria, and Zambia has been stagnant. And Burundi and Liberia are stuck in a poverty trap and a spiral of conflict and destruction (Betcherman and others 2005).

A small group of middle-income countries in Sub-Saharan Africa has started a demographic transition to lower fertility, but the region as a whole still has some of the highest population growth rates in the world. The population in Sub-Saharan Africa is expected to reach 854 million by 2010, an increase of 200 million from a decade earlier (Fluitman 2001). According to the ILO (2006), the labor force in the region, estimated to be 300 million in 2001, is expected to reach 400 million by 2011, adding an average of 10 million job seekers a year.

Labor Market Implications of Demographic Pressure

Traditional labor market concepts such as jobs, employment, unemployment, participation, wages, and earnings are difficult to apply to Africa, where most of the labor force works in family businesses (as owners or unpaid family workers); half work in agriculture, mostly at subsistence levels; and two-thirds live in rural areas.

The estimated labor force participation rate for youth (defined here as those ages 15–24) in Sub-Saharan Africa was above 60 percent in the last two decades, among the highest worldwide and second only to the East Asia region. These estimates would be even larger if the labor force definition included household chores undertaken by a significant proportion of women in the region. Each year 500,000 new entrants come into the labor market in Kenya, and 700,000 in Tanzania. These large cohorts will continue to add pressure to the labor market in the region.

Sub-Saharan Africa supplies the highest proportion of child labor in the world. The ILO (2003) estimates that about 38 million children between the ages of 5 and 14 are working. Put differently, about a quarter of children ages 5–14 in Sub-Saharan Africa are working, compared with 18.7 percent in Asia and 17 percent in Latin America. A high proportion of African children leave school early to work. Among children ages 10–14, 31 percent are estimated to be working. In some countries these numbers reach even higher proportions, such as 50 percent in Burundi. In West Africa the need for children to work has led to child migration. In Benin, for example, 8 percent of children ages 6–16 are reported to have left their parental households to work.

Older cohorts ages 15–24 have also seen their labor market outcomes deteriorate over the last two decades. The unemployment rate increased by almost a third between 1993 and 2003, reaching 21 percent. The ILO (2004) estimates that in 2003 more than 18 million youth in Sub-Saharan Africa were unemployed.

The estimated youth unemployment rate in Sub-Saharan Africa is among the highest in the world; only the Middle East and North Africa region has a higher youth unemployment rate (figure 7.1). The youth unemployment rate in Sub-Saharan Africa is 3.5 times higher than the adult unemployment rate, reflecting the relative disadvantage of this cohort in the job market in Africa.

The regional aggregation hides important country variation in the youth unemployment rate. A close look at a sample of selected countries in Sub-Saharan Africa shows that the unemployment rate could exceed 30 percent in countries with high urban unemployment (Mozambique

Figure 7.1. Regional Unemployment Rates, 2003

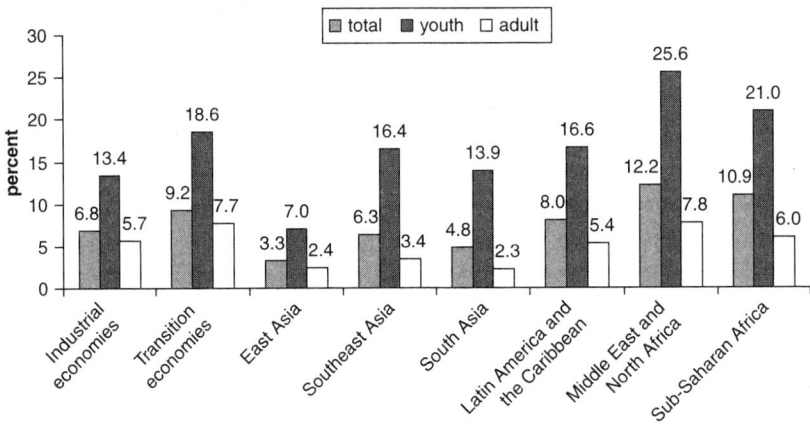

Source: ILO.

and Kenya). At the same time, countries with a large rural sector have relatively low youth unemployment (Burkina Faso and Uganda).

Links with Education
The labor force in Sub-Saharan Africa is poorly educated relative to the rest of the world. Since the 1960s, many African countries have undertaken major education expansion, but the economic stagnation in the 1970s and the decline that followed in the 1990s slowed this expansion. Education levels in Sub-Saharan Africa were comparable to those of South Asia and the Middle East and North Africa in the 1960s (figure 7.2). But by the end of the 20th century, due to slow expansion, Sub-Saharan Africa lagged behind all other regions in years of schooling.

Other indicators of the quality of human capital are alarming. Despite an improvement in the late 1990s, primary enrollment rates in Sub-Saharan Africa in 1995 fell below those in 1980. Female enrollment is very low, less than 50 percent of the total at the primary and secondary levels and just 35 percent at higher education levels. This slow progress is also reflected in a persistent high illiteracy rate at about 18 percent for young men and 27 percent for young women, second only to the South Asia region. Mixed outcomes are expected in the coming decades. By providing low-cost universal education, Kenya, Tanzania, and Uganda expect to lower the illiteracy rate in the labor force to less than 10 percent

Figure 7.2. Average Years of Schooling, by Region and Year

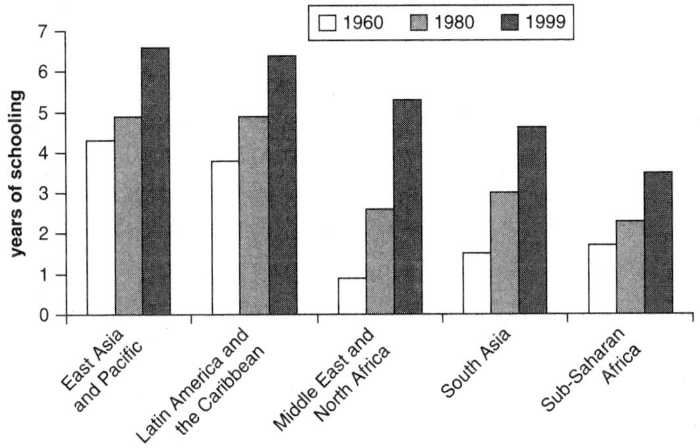

Source: World Bank 2004.

by 2015. Côte d'Ivoire and Ethiopia are still projecting about 30 percent illiteracy for their female labor forces in 2015.

Freeman and Lindauer (1999) argue that the low stock of human capital in Sub-Saharan Africa seems a natural cause for the lack of economic progress. A great deal of microeconomic and macroeconomic evidence has been accumulated linking education, productivity, and growth. A better understanding of the relationship between education and labor market outcomes for youth could shed light on the validity of this hypothesis.

There are two broad groups of young people in the labor market: those with relatively high educational attainment who are transitioning from school to work and those with little or no education who transition very early into the labor market, such as child laborers (figure 7.3). The second group predominates in all countries except Kenya, São Tomé and Principe, and Zambia, underscoring the generally low level of human capital accumulation among Sub-Saharan African youth.

Returns to Education

Returns to education, based on microevidence by Psacharaopolous (1994), have been regarded as higher than in other regions. The highest returns were estimated to be for primary school education. But Bennell (1996) and Glewwe (1991) argue that Psacharopolous' conclusion relies heavily on dated studies and unreliable data—and that more careful

Figure 7.3. Educational Attainment of Nonstudent Youth, Sub-Saharan Africa Region

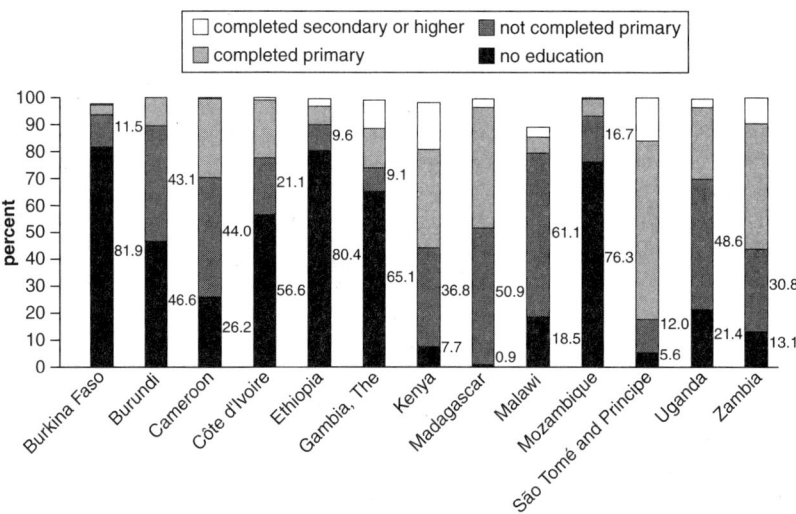

Source: Understanding Children's Work calculations based on World Bank Standard Files and Standard Indicators datasets.
Note: Some countries do not reach 100 percent because of missing data (Burkina Faso 97.5 percent, Ethiopia 99.6 percent, The Gambia 99.1 percent, Kenya 98.2 percent, Madagascar 99.5 percent, Malawi 89.2 percent, Mozambique 99.8 percent, Uganda 99.5 percent).

Mincer-type estimation of returns to education reveals modest effects. These results are more consistent with the observed stagnation or decline in school enrollment in several Sub-Saharan African countries.

According to Collier and Gunning (1999), no statistical finding supports an effect from education on farm productivity in Sub-Saharan Africa. Glewwe (1991) also estimates increasing returns to secondary and post-secondary education. While these convexities in the earning profile could reflect the scarcity of skilled labor, exacerbated by the brain drain from international migration, it could also reflect the strong selectivity bias and the lack of control for school quality.

An alternative view of the role of education is the link between education and unemployment. Considerable evidence worldwide indicates that higher educational attainment leads to better employment outcomes, such as higher wages and lower unemployment. For youth, however, this relationship is not always evident. In some countries in Sub-Saharan Africa, higher educational attainment has not led to a decrease in the unemployment rate for youth (figure 7.4). Youth with secondary and tertiary education in Burundi, Cameroon, Côte d'Ivoire, Kenya, and

Figure 7.4. Unemployment Rate for Youth by Educational Attainment in Sub-Saharan African Countries

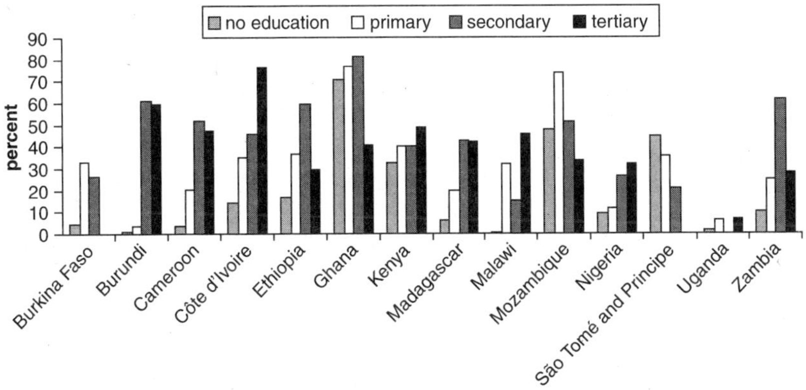

Source: Understanding Children's Work calculations based on World Bank Standard Files and Standard Indicators datasets.

Madagascar have higher rates of unemployment than youth with lower educational attainment.

Young People's Time Use

The time use profiles of young people in the Sub-Saharan Africa region appear to depend considerably on their country of residence (table 7.1).[2] Involvement in employment varies from three-fourths of young people in Burkina Faso to just one-fifth in Ethiopia, Malawi, and Mozambique. Unemployment is almost nonexistent among 15–24 year-olds in Burundi and Malawi (1 percent of this age group), but affects 10 percent or more of young people in Cameroon, Côte d'Ivoire, Kenya, Mozambique, São Tomé and Principe, and Zambia.[3] Levels of joblessness (the sum of the unemployed and inactive), arguably a better measure of youth employment disadvantage, are much higher than unemployment figures, owing to the significant proportion of young people who are inactive (absent from both the labor force and education).[4] Joblessness exceeds one-fifth in 9 of the 13 countries (Cameroon, Ethiopia, The Gambia, Kenya, Malawi, Mozambique, São Tomé and Principe, and Zambia). Only in two (Burundi and Uganda) are less than 10 percent of young people jobless.

Educational enrollment of youth varies widely but does not exceed 50 percent in any of the 13 countries. There is a negative correlation between school attendance and work across the countries considered, but this correlation is generally not strong. Education and employment

Table 7.1. Time Use Patterns for Youth Ages 15–24, by Country

	Distribution of youth by activity status (percentage)					
Country	(1) Only in education	(2) Combining[a]	(3) Only in employment	(4) Unemployed	(5) Inactive[b]	Jobless (4) + (5)
Burkina Faso	11.04	0.95	77.84	4.22	5.94	10.16
Burundi	25.48	—	70.32	0.76	3.43	4.19
Cameroon	32.24	2.27	42.99	12.62	9.87	22.49
Côte d'Ivoire	25.46	—	47.36	9.57	17.60	27.17
Ethiopia	17.84	—	19.72	3.97	58.47	62.44
Gambia, The	28.43	1.08	37.25	1.50	31.74	33.24
Kenya	41.97	—	20.79	10.47	26.77	37.24
Madagascar	23.28	2.30	62.41	8.94	3.07	12.01
Malawi	42.29	0.38	21.38	1.42	34.53	35.95
Mozambique	18.28	0.61	21.58	14.75	44.78	59.53
São Tomé and Principe	23.31	1.55	31.27	11.29	32.58	43.87
Uganda	34.04	9.66	48.23	0.73	7.35	8.08
Zambia	29.52	0.62	38.62	11.40	19.84	31.24

Source: Understanding Children's Work calculations based on World Bank Standard Files and Standard Indicators datasets.
Note: — = unavailable data, because the survey instrument structure does not permit identifying the category "combining."
a. Combining refers to youth who both work and attend school.
b. Inactive youth are youth who neither attend school nor work nor are unemployed.

do not appear complementary because only a relatively small number of individuals combine school and work. This fact is surprising and may merely reflect the data available.

These aggregates mask large variations in young people's time use by sex, residence, and age (tables 7.2–7.4). Young people in rural areas use their time very differently from their counterparts in urban areas in all 13 countries. Compared with rural youth, urban young people benefit from greater educational opportunities, staying in school longer, and joining the labor force at a later age. For the 15–24 age group, educational involvement is much higher for urban youth (except in Kenya), and employment involvement is much lower (except in Ethiopia, Kenya, Mozambique). Consistent with a Harris-Todaro model, unemployment is more common among urban youth (except in São Tomé and Principe), presumably because of the wage differentials between the urban and rural sectors. In Burkina Faso, Burundi, Ethiopia, The Gambia, Malawi, and Uganda, rural youth unemployment is 2 percent or less. There is no clear pattern in inactivity by residence; rates of inactivity are higher

Table 7.2. Time Use Patterns for Youth Ages 15–24, by Sex and Country

	(1) Only in education		(2) Combining[a]		(3) Only in employment		(4) Unemployed		(5) Inactive[b]		Jobless (4) + (5)	
Country	M	F	M	F	M	F	M	F	M	F	M	F
Burkina Faso	13.7	8.7	1.4	0.5	80.0	75.9	3.8	4.6	1.1	10.3	4.9	14.9
Burundi	28.4	23.1	—	—	67.4	72.8	0.9	0.7	3.3	3.5	4.2	4.2
Cameroon	36.3	28.4	2.9	1.7	45.0	41.0	13.3	12.0	2.5	16.9	15.8	28.9
Côte d'Ivoire	33.8	17.8	—	—	49.7	45.2	8.6	10.5	7.9	26.5	16.5	37.0
Ethiopia	22.3	13.7	—	—	25.5	14.3	3.5	4.4	48.7	67.6	52.1	72.1
Gambia, The	37.8	19.6	1.3	0.8	31.7	42.6	1.8	1.2	27.5	35.8	29.3	37.0
Kenya	48.4	36.0	—	—	23.5	18.3	10.1	10.8	18.0	34.9	28.1	45.7
Madagascar	25.1	21.5	3.1	1.6	64.2	60.7	5.9	11.8	1.7	4.4	7.6	16.2
Malawi	54.8	31.5	0.7	0.1	23.3	19.8	2.1	0.8	19.1	47.8	21.3	48.6
Mozambique	26.1	11.2	1.2	0.1	27.7	16.0	12.5	16.8	32.6	55.8	45.1	72.6
São Tomé and Principe	24.3	22.4	1.8	1.3	45.6	16.9	13.1	9.5	15.3	50.0	28.4	59.4
Uganda	38.6	29.7	14.7	4.8	41.8	54.3	1.0	0.5	3.8	10.7	4.8	11.2
Zambia	37.2	22.7	0.9	0.4	37.8	39.3	13.4	9.6	10.7	28.0	24.1	37.6

Source: Understanding Children's Work calculations based on World Bank Standard Files and Standard Indicators datasets.

Note: — = unavailable data, because the survey instrument structure does not permit identifying the category "combining."

a. Combining refers to youth who both work and attend school.

b. Inactive youth are youth who neither attend school nor work nor are unemployed.

Table 7.3. Time Use Patterns for Youth Ages 15–24, by Residence and Country

	(1) Only in education		(2) Combining[a]		(3) Only in employment		(4) Unemployed		(5) Inactive[b]		Jobless (4) + (5)	
Country	Rural	Urban	Rural	Urban	Rural	Urban	Rural	Urban	Rural	Urban	Rural	Urban
Burkina Faso	4.3	34.8	1.0	0.8	89.6	36.6	1.3	14.5	3.9	13.2	5.2	27.8
Burundi	23.3	58.6	—	—	73.9	14.8	0.1	11.6	2.7	15.0	2.7	26.6
Cameroon	23.7	48.3	2.5	1.9	55.2	20.1	9.5	18.5	9.2	11.2	18.7	29.7
Côte d'Ivoire	14.9	34.8	—	—	69.1	28.3	4.1	14.4	11.9	22.6	16.0	37.0
Ethiopia	12.1	46.1	—	—	18.4	26.4	2.0	13.5	67.5	14.1	69.6	27.6
Gambia, The	20.5	37.0	1.5	0.6	56.0	16.9	0.8	2.3	21.1	43.3	21.9	45.5
Kenya	45.4	27.3	—	—	17.2	36.2	8.3	19.6	29.1	16.9	37.4	36.5
Madagascar	16.9	39.6	2.5	1.9	72.3	37.1	6.2	16.1	2.2	5.4	8.3	21.4
Malawi	40.5	55.1	0.3	0.9	22.3	14.8	1.2	2.8	35.7	26.4	36.9	29.1
Mozambique	14.9	29.8	0.5	1.1	22.0	20.2	8.4	36.1	54.3	12.8	62.7	48.9
São Tomé and Principe	14.7	29.3	0.8	2.0	35.4	28.4	15.3	8.6	33.7	31.8	49.1	40.3
Uganda	32.7	40.6	10.9	3.5	51.7	31.7	0.4	2.3	4.3	21.9	4.7	24.2
Zambia	25.4	35.8	0.8	0.3	53.1	16.6	5.8	19.8	14.8	27.4	20.7	47.3

Source: Understanding Children's Work calculations based on World Bank Standard Files and Standard Indicators datasets.

Note: — = unavailable data, because the survey instrument structure does not permit identifying the category "combining."

a. Combining refers to youth who both work and attend school.

b. Inactive youth are youth who neither attend school nor work nor are unemployed.

Table 7.4. Time Use Patterns for Youth, by Age Group and Country

| | Distribution of youth by activity status (percentage) | | | | | | | | | | |
| | (1) Only in education | | (2) Combining^a | | (3) Only in employment | | (4) Unemployed | | (5) Inactive^b | | Jobless (4) + (5) | |
Country	15–19	20–24	15–19	20–24	15–19	20–24	15–19	20–24	15–19	20–24	15–19	20–24
Burkina Faso	14.2	6.9	1.2	0.6	76.1	80.2	3.8	4.7	4.7	7.6	8.6	12.3
Burundi	31.5	16.1	—	—	64.3	79.7	0.6	1.1	3.6	3.1	4.2	.4.2
Cameroon	43.4	19.3	3.2	1.2	33.7	53.8	11.9	13.5	7.8	12.2	19.7	25.7
Côte d'Ivoire	34.1	14.4	—	—	39.9	56.8	9.2	10.0	16.7	18.7	26.0	28.7
Ethiopia	25.5	6.3	—	—	13.1	29.7	3.0	5.5	58.5	58.5	61.4	64.0
Gambia, The	40.3	13.4	1.0	1.2	29.7	46.8	1.4	1.6	27.6	36.9	29.1	38.5
Kenya	64.9	11.2	—	—	10.0	35.3	8.5	13.2	16.7	40.3	25.1	53.5
Madagascar	36.0	8.5	3.8	0.6	49.9	77.0	7.7	10.4	2.7	3.5	10.4	13.9
Malawi	64.4	17.6	0.3	0.5	8.6	35.7	0.5	2.5	26.2	43.8	26.7	46.3
Mozambique	28.5	5.6	0.7	0.5	11.4	34.2	14.6	15.0	44.9	44.7	59.5	59.6
São Tomé and Príncipe	37.9	5.7	1.2	2.0	18.2	47.0	13.2	9.0	29.5	36.3	42.7	45.3
Uganda	47.33	14.5	12.7	5.1	33.0	70.6	0.4	1.2	6.5	8.6	6.9	9.8
Zambia	46.0	10.0	0.8	0.4	26.9	52.5	9.0	14.2	17.2	23.0	26.2	37.2

Source: Understanding Children's Work calculations based on World Bank Standard Files and Standard Indicators datasets.
Note: — = unavailable data, because the survey instrument structure does not permit identifying the category "combining."
a. Combining refers to youth who both work and attend school.
b. Inactive youth are youth who neither attend school nor work nor are unemployed.

among urban young people in eight of the countries, while in the five others the opposite holds true.[5]

Gender also appears to be an important factor in young people's time use patterns (table 7.2). In all 13 countries, males are more likely than females to continue their education longer. Differences by sex in educational involvement are often stark: male educational enrollment is double female enrollment in Mozambique and almost double female enrollment in Côte d'Ivoire, Ethiopia, and The Gambia. Only in two countries, Madagascar and São Tomé and Principe, does female educational participation approach male participation. In most of these countries females, by contrast, are significantly over-represented among inactive young people, a category that includes household chores and other forms of noneconomic work typically assigned to females.[6] Male employment exceeds female employment except in Burundi, The Gambia, and Zambia, though the differences are not always large. There is no clear pattern by sex in unemployment. In sum, large differences favoring males in education are balanced by large differences "favoring" females in inactivity, while differences by sex in labor force involvement are generally smaller. No systematic pattern across countries seems to emerge from the data.

Most obviously, time use differs with age, because the 15–24 age range is a period of transition from adolescence to adulthood and from education to working life. Comparing teenagers and young adults, there are large differences in involvement in education, with relatively few people continuing education beyond their teens into young adulthood.[7] Young adults are more represented in the labor force (both employed and unemployed), and a larger number of them are considered inactive.[8] The differences by age are most pronounced in countries where initial education enrollment is relatively high (such as Kenya and Malawi). They are least pronounced in countries (such as Burkina Faso and Ethiopia) where initial school enrollment is very low and the transition to work begins at an early age.

While almost all young people leave school in the 15–24 age range, a large proportion of them have not yet settled into employment (figure 7.5).

Status of Young People in the Labor Market

Youth Unemployment

Youth unemployment is the most important and common measure of youth labor market status. The effects of prolonged unemployment early

Figure 7.5. Changes in the Time Use Patterns of Young People by Age and Country

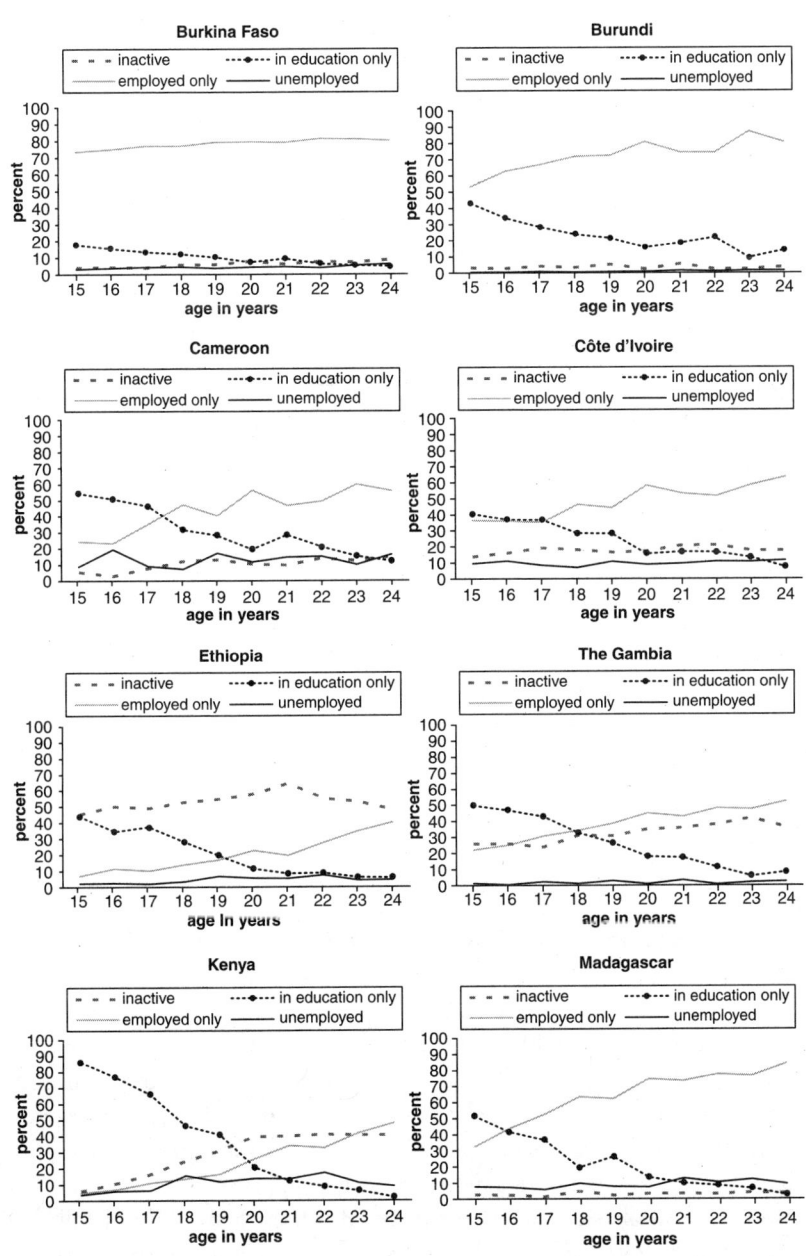

(continued)

Figure 7.5. (continued)

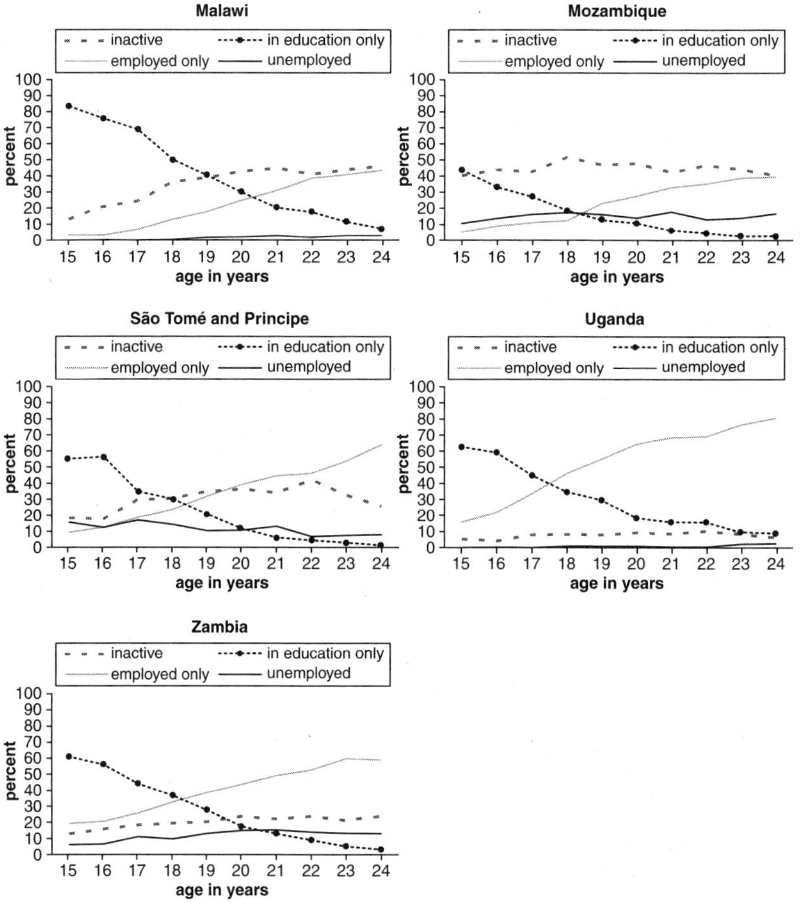

Source: Understanding Children's Work calculations based on World Bank Standard Files and Standard Indicators datasets.

in a person's working life are well-documented: it may permanently impair productive potential and therefore employment opportunities, and it can lead to serious social adjustment difficulties. Early experiences in the labor market can significantly influence lifetime patterns of employment. In Sub-Saharan Africa, whether a young person has a job can often determine which side of the poverty threshold a household falls on. Youth unemployment is included as an indicator for monitoring the Millennium Development Goal to "develop and implement strategies for decent and productive work for youth."[9]

Youth unemployment estimates need to be interpreted with caution, however, particularly in the absence of information on unemployment dynamics. Low outflows from unemployment and long durations of unemployment are likely to indicate employment problems, but high outflows and short durations may merely reflect active search on the part of youth for their preferred work. The negative effects of unemployment are therefore largely associated with prolonged spells of unemployment rather than the incidence of unemployment alone. In Sub-Saharan Africa, evidence suggests that many young people face prolonged spells of unemployment or joblessness in transitioning from school to work.

Note that the youth unemployment rate does not provide a full description of youth difficulties in the labor market. In fact, in countries with widespread poverty, the unemployment rate can be misleading, because most youth cannot afford to remain unemployed and their difficulties in the labor market might be reflected better by the quality of employment or another measure of underemployment.

There is large variation across the 13 countries in the unemployment ratio (table 7.5): more than one in ten young people are unemployed in five countries (Cameroon, Kenya, Mozambique, São Tomé and Principe, and Zambia), but in four others (Burundi, The Gambia, Malawi, and Uganda) less than 2 percent of young people ages 15–24 are unemployed. The picture changes somewhat when unemployment as a proportion of the work force (unemployment rate) is examined.

Unemployment as a proportion of population is generally higher for young adults than for teenagers, not surprising considering that teenagers are more likely to still be in school and not in the labor force. Once teenagers are in the work force, however, they often face greater difficulties in finding employment than young adults. So, the unemployment ratio of young adults is greater than for teenagers in all but São Tomé and Principe and the unemployment rate of young adults is less than that of teenagers in all but Burkina Faso, Burundi, Malawi, and Uganda.

Differences in the unemployment ratio by sex are noteworthy in Côte d'Ivoire, Madagascar, Mozambique, São Tomé and Principe, and Zambia but there is no systematic pattern in labor market advantage. Females are more likely to be affected by unemployment in Côte d'Ivoire, Madagascar, and Mozambique and males are more likely to be affected in São Tomé and Principe and Zambia (figure 7.6).

Urban youth are much more likely to be unemployed than their rural counterparts in all but Côte d'Ivoire and São Tomé and Principe, underscoring the fact that youth unemployment is overwhelmingly an urban

Table 7.5. Youth Unemployment, Inactivity, and Jobless Indicators, by Age Group and Country

Country	Unemployment ratio (as proportion of total population in the same age group)				Unemployment rate (as proportion of total work force in the same age group)				Inactivity[a] (as proportion of population in same age group)				Jobless[b] (as proportion of population in same age group)			
	15–19	20–24	15–24	25–50	15–19	20–24	15–24	25–50	15–19	20–24	15–24	25–50	15–19	20–24	15–24	25–50
Burkina Faso	3.8	4.7	4.2	1.9	4.7	5.5	5.1	2.0	4.7	7.6	5.9	6.5	8.5	12.3	10.1	8.4
Burundi	0.6	1.1	0.8	1.2	0.8	1.4	1.1	1.2	3.6	3.1	3.4	1.9	4.2	4.2	4.2	3.1
Cameroon	11.9	13.5	12.6	3.6	24.4	19.7	21.8	4.3	11.9	12.2	9.9	13.4	23.8	25.7	22.5	17.0
Côte d'Ivoire	9.2	10.0	9.6	7.7	18.7	15.0	16.8	9.0	16.7	18.7	17.6	12.9	25.9	28.7	27.2	20.6
Ethiopia	3.0	5.5	4.0	4.4	18.6	15.6	16.9	7.3	58.5	58.5	58.5	39.0	61.5	64.0	62.5	43.4
Gambia, The	1.4	1.6	1.5	8.0	4.4	3.2	3.8	9.4	27.6	36.9	31.7	14.4	29.0	38.5	33.2	22.4
Kenya	8.5	13.2	10.5	5.6	45.9	27.2	33.5	8.6	16.7	40.3	26.7	35.0	25.2	53.5	37.2	40.6
Madagascar	7.7	10.4	8.9	7.8	12.5	11.8	12.1	8.2	2.7	3.5	3.1	4.0	10.4	13.9	12.0	11.8
Malawi	0.5	2.5	1.4	1.6	5.3	6.5	6.0	2.7	26.3	43.8	34.5	39.2	26.8	46.3	35.9	40.8
Mozambique	14.6	15.0	14.8	8.8	54.7	30.2	40.0	13.3	44.9	44.7	44.8	33.1	59.5	59.7	59.6	41.9
São Tomé and Principe	13.2	9.0	11.3	3.2	40.5	15.5	25.6	4.4	29.5	36.3	32.6	26.6	42.7	45.3	43.9	29.8
Uganda	0.4	1.2	0.7	0.6	0.9	1.6	1.24	0.7	6.5	8.6	7.3	3.2	6.9	9.8	8.0	3.8
Zambia	9.0	14.2	11.4	6.6	24.5	21.2	22.5	7.9	17.2	23.0	19.8	15.8	26.2	37.2	31.2	22.4

Source: Understanding Children's Work calculations based on World Bank Standard Files and Standard Indicators datasets.

a. Inactive youth are youth who neither attend school nor work nor are unemployed.

b. Jobless is the sum of unemployed (as measured by unemployment ratio) and inactive.

Figure 7.6. Unemployment Ratios for Young People Ages 15–24, by Sex, Residence, School Attendance, and Country

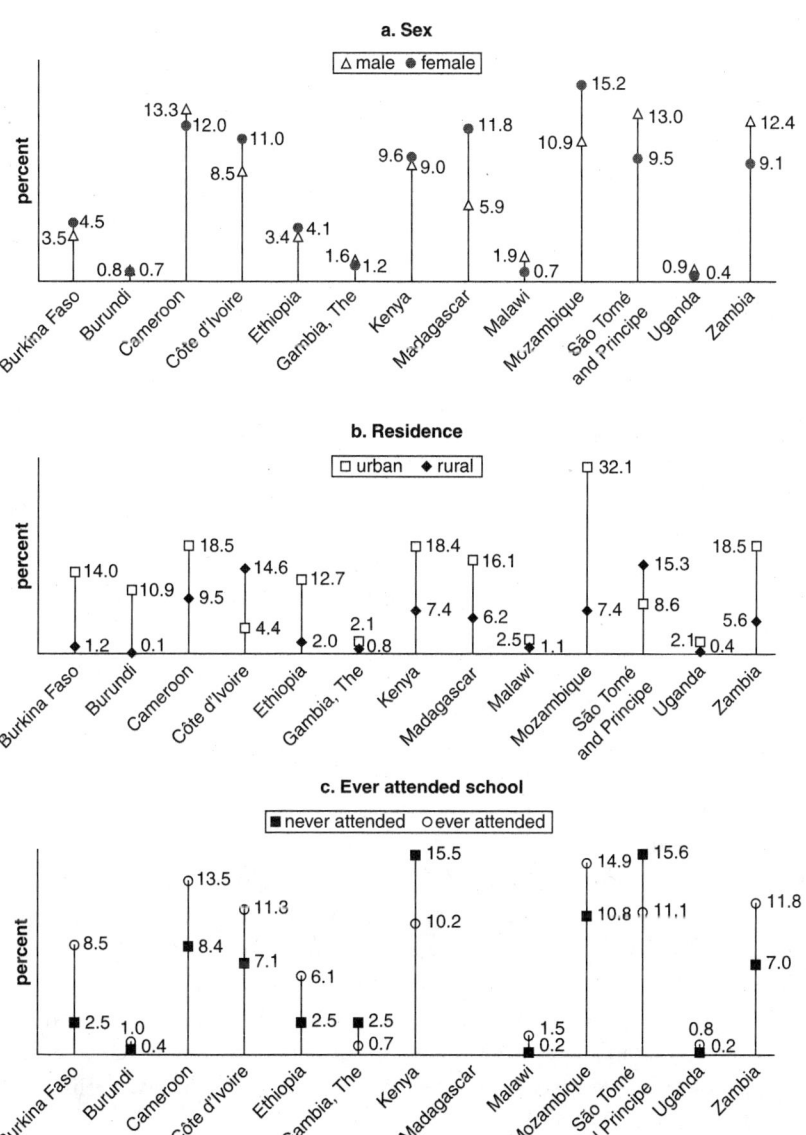

Source: Understanding Children's Work calculations based on World Bank Standard Files and Standard Indicators datasets.

phenomenon in the Sub-Saharan Africa region (figure 7.6). The difference in youth unemployment by residence is generally very large: the unemployment ratio for urban young people is at least triple that for rural young people in Burkina Faso, Burundi, Ethiopia, Mozambique, Uganda, and Zambia and at least twice that of rural young people in Kenya and Madagascar. These data highlight the different nature of the rural and urban labor markets for young people, particularly the important role that the agriculture sector plays in absorbing young rural workers. Not surprisingly, differences by residence are largest in the countries where agriculture is the most important.

Unemployment does not appear to be strongly correlated with whether a young person has had some exposure to schooling. Indeed, a larger proportion of youth with at least some schooling than youth with no schooling are unemployed in 9 of the 12 countries (data are unavailable for Madagascar; see figure 7.6), even though a smaller proportion of school entrants than nonentrants are in the labor force.

These measures of unemployment understate the extent of the youth unemployment problem, for three reasons:

- First, and most important, these measures fail to capture discouraged workers who have given up seeking work or who have never entered the labor market because of meager job prospects. Discouraged workers account for part of the young people found in the inactive category.
- Second, and particularly relevant in Sub-Saharan Africa, these measures fail to capture the group that is simply too poor to be unemployed and therefore must take up work regardless of its quality or level of remuneration.
- Third, these youth unemployment indicators do not reflect underemployment. According to the definition of employment used to generate estimates of employment, anyone undertaking economic activity for an hour or more during the reference week is considered employed, even if he or she is actively looking for additional work. It is likely, particularly in Sub-Saharan Africa, that many young people are technically categorized as employed but are putting in fewer hours than they desire.

Youth Inactivity

A very large proportion of the youth population is also inactive, neither in education nor in the labor force, in several Sub-Saharan Africa countries (table 7.1). This group is also likely to be at risk of encountering difficulties in finding and sustaining stable employment. At least one-fifth of young people are inactive in 7 of the 13 countries; inactivity is highest in Ethiopia, at 59 percent of the 15–24 age group, and in Mozambique, at 45 percent. Inactivity appears to have an important gender dimension: female youth are more likely to be inactive than their male counterparts in all 13 countries.

To what extent do inactive youth represent discouraged workers rather than people involved in noneconomic work or nonwork activities? The data do not draw a clear line between the two possibilities. Most inactive young people indicate spending time on noneconomic work (fetching water, fetching wood, cooking, child care, housekeeping), but this is also the case for young people in the labor force and therefore does not necessarily reflect a choice of domestic work over labor market involvement. Inactivity among young people has important economic and social consequences and requires in-depth analysis.

Youth Employment Characteristics

Obtaining employment does not necessarily imply successful entry into the labor market. The most vulnerable population segments simply cannot afford to be unemployed and must accept work even if difficult, hazardous, socially unacceptable, or poorly paid. Therefore, indicators reflecting the conditions of employment are also critical for assessing the labor market status of young people. Specific work quality indicators, including work intensity, job tenure, contractual and benefits coverage, workplace safety conditions, and so on are unfortunately beyond the scope of the data for the 13 countries. Data from the selected countries do, however, allow for the construction of an indicator of the general modality of work performed.

Workers fall into four main groups: wage employment, informal sector employment, self-employment,[10] and employer. The first three are of relevance for the 15–24 age group in Sub-Saharan Africa. The distribution of youth workers across these groups again depends to a large extent on their country of residence (table 7.6). Informal work accounts for the overwhelming majority of youth workers in Burkina Faso and Burundi, and it predominates in Madagascar. In rural Cameroon, Malawi, and Mozambique, self-employment is most important. In rural Ethiopia and São Tomé and Principe, wage employment is preponderate. Both informal and self-employment are important in rural areas in The Gambia and Kenya. With some exceptions, wage work is more important in urban areas, and informal (primarily agricultural) work is more important in rural areas.

Table 7.6. Employment Characteristics for the 15–24 Year-Old Age Group, by Country

Country	Rural				Urban			
	Wage	Informal	Self	Other	Wage	Informal	Self	Other
Burkina Faso	0.4	94.8	4.8	0.0	27.9	57.0	14.4	0.7
Burundi	1.8	83.3	14.8	0.1	31.3	19.6	43.3	5.8
Cameroon	6.3	18.1	68.8	6.8	15.3	56.9	22.0	5.9
Côte d'Ivoire	—	—	—	—	—	—	—	—
Ethiopia	55.6	24.8	16.2	3.4	16.2	38.2	23.3	22.3
Gambia, The	1.2	53.1	45.0	0.8	42.3	20.7	34.7	2.4
Kenya	16.4	40.0	43.6	0.0	21.1	53.3	25.4	0.2
Madagascar	5.9	69.7	23.5	1.0	19.3	58.7	18.2	3.8
Malawi	15.0	7.1	74.5	3.3	63.8	6.8	19.8	9.5
Mozambique	11.8	—	86.7	1.5	40.2	—	53.5	6.3
São Tomé and Principe	59.5	34.3	—	6.2	66.3	24.3	—	9.5
Uganda	—	—	—	—	—	—	—	—
Zambia	3.1	60.4	36.1	0.4	40.9	9.6	46.1	3.5

Source: Understanding Children's Work calculations based on World Bank Standard Files and Standard Indicators datasets.

Note: — = unavailable data, because of survey instrument structure.

What do these breakdowns say about employment quality? The generally low level of wage employment, even in urban areas, is significant, given that wage employment is typically the most sought-after form of work among young people and is most likely to offer a measure of stability and some benefits coverage. The high level of informal employment in most countries is also a quality concern. Informal work in rural settings is mainly associated with agriculture—and is typically low paid and seasonal. In urban settings, informal work frequently means insecure, nonfamily work in settings where labor and safety regulations do not apply, leaving workers susceptible to work place exploitation. In both urban and rural settings, work in the informal economy is generally a poor alternative to formal sector employment. A high rate of involvement in self-employment (for example, in Cameroon, Malawi, and Mozambique) can also be a sign of labor market entry difficulties. Evidence from South Africa, for instance, suggests that most young people are motivated to start their own businesses because of limited opportunities in the rest of the labor market.

Youth Labor Market Disadvantage

Comparing youth and adult unemployment rates provides some indication of the extent to which young workers are disadvantaged in relation to their adult counterparts in securing jobs. The youth unemployment rate exceeds the adult rate in all countries except Burundi and The Gambia (figure 7.7). Young workers appear particularly disadvantaged in Cameroon and São Tomé and Principe, where the youth unemployment rate is more than five times that of adults. Youth unemployment does not appear to be correlated with adult unemployment, suggesting that factors unique to the youth labor market are important in driving it.

Sub-Saharan Africa countries show a higher (sometimes much higher) ratio of youth to adult unemployment than do Organisation for Economic Co-operation and Development (OECD) countries (The Gambia and Burundi excepted; figure 7.8). Also striking in the comparison with OECD countries is the large variation among African countries. The reasons for this variation are not immediately apparent and merit more detailed investigation, with regard to both data and determinants.

Differences between youth and adult work characteristics also provide an indication of youth labor market disadvantages. The work performed by young people appears to differ dramatically from that performed by adults (table 7.7). Young people are much less likely to be involved in wage work (Mozambique and São Tomé and Principe excepted) and much more likely to be performing informal work (São Tomé and Principe excepted). This suggests that adult wage workers in general enjoy a greater degree of

Figure 7.7. Youth versus Adult Unemployment

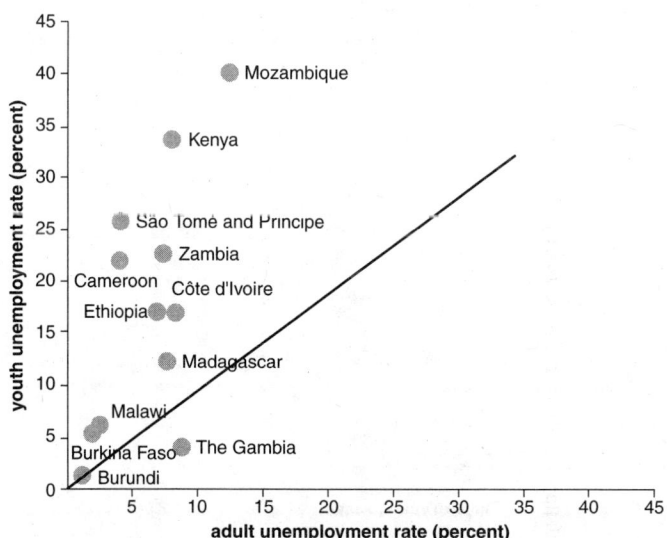

Source: Understanding Children's Work calculations based on World Bank Standard Files and Standard Indicators datasets.
Note: The diagonal line indicates that a country's adult and youth unemployment rates are similar. If the country is above the line, it indicates youth disadvantage, meaning higher youth unemployment rate compared to adults.

Figure 7.8. Ratio of Youth to Adult Unemployment Rates, Sub-Saharan African Countries and OECD Countries

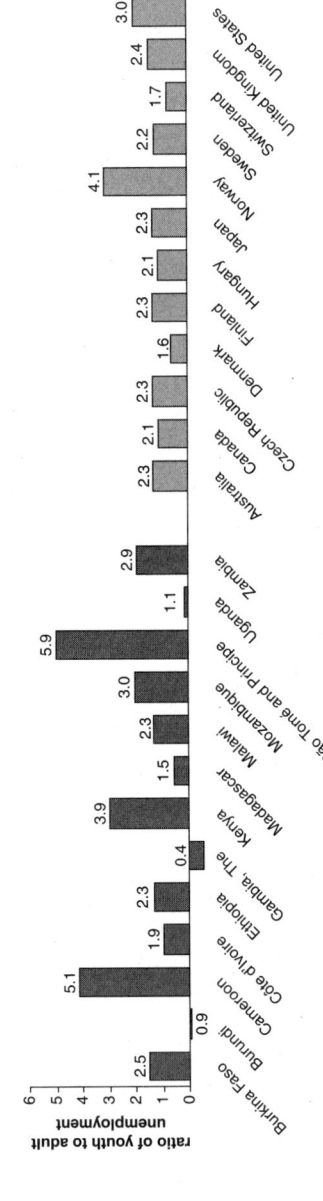

Source: Understanding Children's Work calculations based on World Bank Standard Files and Standard Indicators datasets and OECD (2000).
Note: 25–55 adult age cohort for OECD countries; 25–50 adult age cohort used for Sub-Saharan Africa countries. OECD data are for 1998.

Table 7.7. Youth versus Adult Employment Characteristics by Country

	Modality							
	Wage		Informal		Self		Other	
Country	Youth	Adult	Youth	Adult	Youth	Adult	Youth	Adult
Burkina Faso	3.24	7.55	90.85	59.29	5.82	32.49	0.09	0.68
Burundi	1.66	5.78	85.26	39.51	12.84	54.22	0.24	0.49
Cameroon	8.18	16.43	26.12	14.5	65.7	69.07	—	—
Côte d'Ivoire	—	—	—	—	—	—	—	—
Ethiopia	46.69	75.68	27.81	16.95	17.84	3.75	7.67	3.63
Gambia, The	10.07	19.22	46.07	13.83	42.73	65.82	1.13	1.12
Kenya	17.94	30.83	44.41	19.74	37.59	48.64	0.07	0.79
Madagascar	7.78	15.93	68.08	31.12	22.78	50.63	1.36	2.32
Malawi	18.82	26.68	7.12	5.11	70.28	64.89	3.77	3.33
Mozambique	15.13	16.61	—	—	53.45	69.56	1.19	0.47
São Tomé and Principe	63.21	57.79	28.8	41.53	—	—	7.99	0.68
Uganda	3.24	7.55	90.85	59.29	5.82	32.49	0.09	0.68
Zambia	9.54	23.85	51.76	16.85	37.79	58.3	0.91	1

Source: Understanding Children's Work calculations based on World Bank Standard Files and Standard Indicators datasets.
Note: — = unavailable data, because of survey instrument structure. Youth is 15–24 age group; adult is 25–50 age group.

job security and social protection and are less exposed to the instability and various risks associated with informal sector work. The fact that younger workers appear to be scarce among the self-employed suggests that they even find it difficult to start their own businesses, perhaps because of lack of capital.

The analysis in this section clearly indicates that young people, particularly urban young people, face a difficult labor market. Their unemployment and jobless rates are much higher than those of adults and of youth in more developed countries. They rely on informal work lacking basic job protections and benefits much more than do their adult counterparts. The disadvantaged position of youth in the labor market may be associated with, or even a result of, a difficult or inefficient transition from school to the labor market. The next section looks at this issue by constructing an indicator of the duration of the school-to-work transition, a first and necessary step to understanding the process by which young people transition to working life.

The Transition from School to Work

The transition from school to work is by no means a linear, well-defined process with a distinct end point. Individuals alternate between periods of employment and unemployment, change jobs, or even choose to remain out of work.

Young individuals might take up temporary jobs, work in the household farm or enterprise, or devote themselves to household chores for lack of better work opportunities or of the prospect of potential returns. These transition problems are particularly relevant in developing countries where women's labor force participation (at least in the market) is low; and, most important, underemployment, self-employment, home production, and casual employment are widespread. The process is made even more complex by the fact that the time of school leaving is endogenous and most likely influenced by expectations about the transition to work. A better understanding of this transition period would require integrating the analysis of optimal school-leaving age with the analysis of employment search and labor force participation.

Assessment of the Transition to Working Life

The transition to work in Sub-Saharan Africa can take two routes: through the schooling system, or from inactivity (or informal schooling[11]) to the labor force. This section examines both routes to identify vulnerable groups and targets for policies. It uses the synthetic indicator developed in annex 1 to provide an overview of the routes young people in Sub-Saharan Africa take from education to the labor force. For the group entering directly into the labor force, the average age of entry into the labor market is examined. A nonnegligible number of children drop out of school very early. While they are formally included in the youth transiting through school, their condition and the problems they face are likely to be closer to those of the children that never attended school.

School-to-Work Transitions

The timing and length of the transition depends to a considerable extent on the specific country of residence (table 7.8). The average school-leaving age varies from 15.9 years (São Tomé and Principe) to 19 years (Cameroon), and the average age at first job from 18.4 years (Côte d'Ivoire) to 24.4 years (Malawi). The total transition duration is just one year in Côte d'Ivoire, compared with almost seven years in Mozambique. The "vulnerability" of young people to unsuccessful transition, as reflected in beginning age and transition duration, varies greatly by country. The synthetic indicator can help to identify the age range upon which policy attention should be focused in each country.

Table 7.8. School-to-Work Transition Points by Residence and Country

| | Children ever in school | | | | | | Children never in school | |
| | Beginning point of transition | End point of transition | Transition duration | | | | | |
Country	Average age of school leaving	Average age of entering into work for the first time	Total	Urban	Rural		Average age of entering into work for the first time	Age reference group
Burkina Faso	17.1	18.6	1.5	2.9	1.6		8.4	5–24
Burundi	18.8	20.7	1.9	4.5	1.7		10.2	5–24
Cameroon	19.0	23.8	4.8	5.4	3.7		11.2	5–24
Côte d'Ivoire	17.4	18.4	1.0	0.3	3.0		11.5	5–24
Ethiopia	18.0	23.4	5.4	4.7	5.4		16.4	5–24
Gambia, The	17.4	23.2	5.8	6.8	3.5		11.3	5–24
Kenya	17.7	22.6	5.3	5.5	5.0		14.8	5–24
Madagascar	17.2	19.0	1.8	2.5	1.2		FEW OBS	10–24
Malawi	18.8	24.4	5.6	5.5	5.6		12.7	5–24
Mozambique	16.7	23.4	6.7	6.8	6.9		17.1	5–24
São Tomé and Príncipe	15.9	21.3	5.4	4.7	5.9		16.3	5–24
Uganda	18.0	21.3	3.3	3.8	3.2		13.8	5–24
Zambia	17.5	22.4	5.0	7.0	3.6		14.5	5–24

Source: Understanding Children's Work calculations based on World Bank Standard Files and Standard Indicators datasets.
Note: Table shows estimated probabilities calculated on the basis of the age at which work participation rate is at its maximum.

Looking first at the starting point of the transition, average school-leaving ages appear relatively high (table 7.8 and figure 7.9)[12]; however, two caveats apply to this conclusion. First, not all young people attend school, so this conclusion applies only to those who start school. Second, the same leaving age is likely to be associated with lower human capital accumulation in less developed countries because of frequent delayed entry into school, intermittent attendance, and grade repetition.

The relatively high school-leaving age in these 13 countries is noteworthy, particularly against a backdrop of low overall school enrollment rates in Sub-Saharan Africa. In Burkina Faso, for example, at 17.1 years, the average age of school leaving, overall educational involvement stands at just 15 percent (figure 7.10). The late average leaving age for students ever enrolled in school underscores the importance of the selection process associated with initial enrollment: those children with the opportunity to get into school in the first place tend to stay there well into their teens in all 13 countries examined.

The average age of entering the labor market shows a larger variation across countries than the age of leaving school, indicating that the transition from school to work is more affected by the characteristics of the process of finding a job than by time of school leaving. The length of the transition phase is strikingly different between urban and rural areas (see table 7.8). Gender differences are also likely to be important because of the lower participation rate of women, especially in urban areas.

Within countries, the characteristics of the transition appear to depend significantly on both residence and sex, and on the interaction between the two. Overall, females tend to leave school at an earlier age and transition to work more slowly than males, and rural youth tend to start the transition earlier and find employment more quickly than urban youth. There are four overall patterns:

- Male youth stay longer in education than female youth. Thus, male youth start the transition to work at a later age than females in both urban areas (except in Kenya) and rural areas (except in Kenya and Uganda).
- Urban youth are more advantaged than rural youth in educational attainment. The transition to work starts later in urban areas than in rural areas for both males (all countries) and females (except in São Tomé and Principe).
- Residence appears to affect transition duration for female youth but not male youth. Labor market entry takes longer for female youth in

Figure 7.9. Length and Timing of Transition from School to Work for Children Ever Attending School by Sex, Residence, and Country

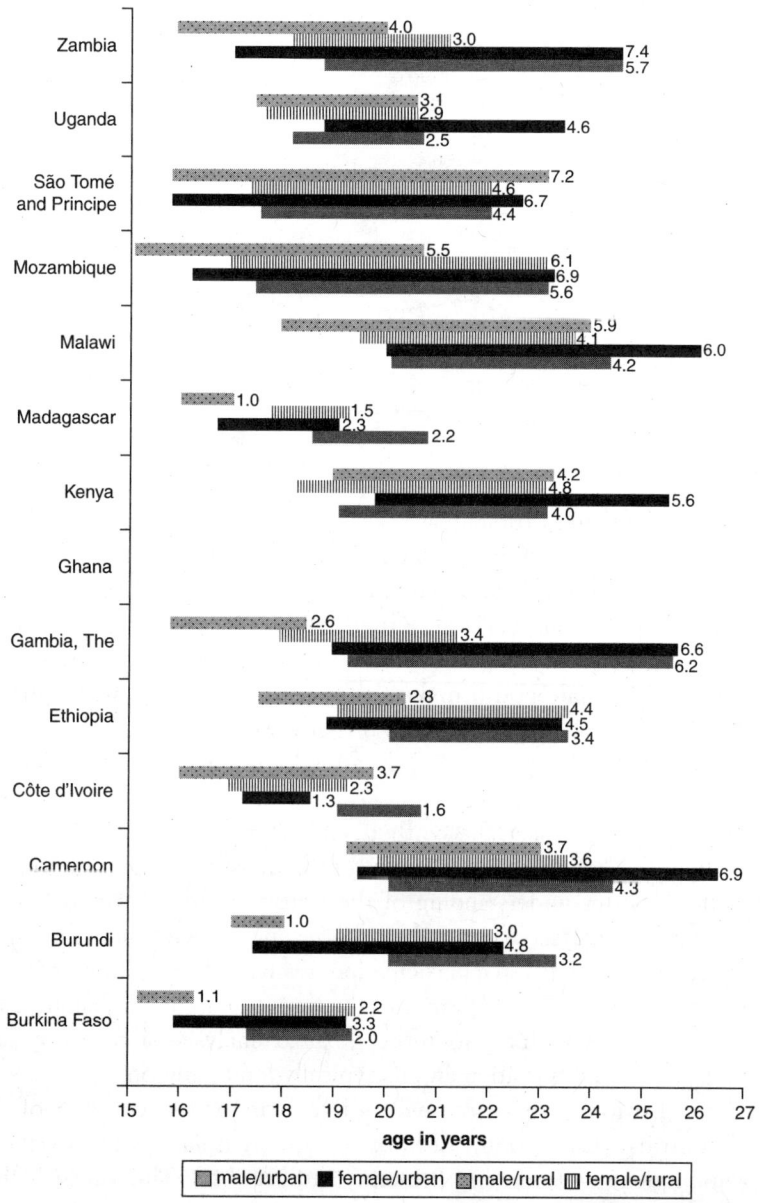

Source: Understanding Children's Work calculations based on World Bank Standard Files and Standard Indicators datasets.

Figure 7.10. School Enrollment by Age and School Attendance in Burkina Faso

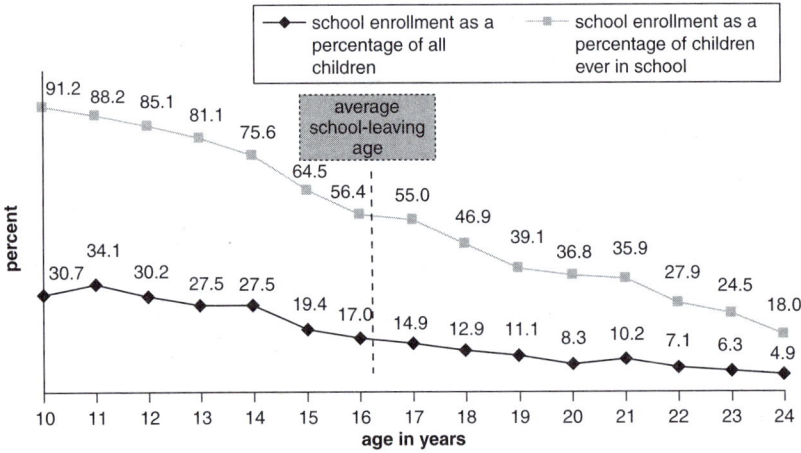

Source: Understanding Children's Work calculations based on World Bank Standard Files and Standard Indicators datasets.

urban areas than in rural areas (except in Côte d'Ivoire and São Tomé and Principe), but there is no consistent pattern in transition length by residence for male youth. The transition for female rural youth is particularly short in Burkina Faso, Burundi, and Madagascar, at only one year.

- Gender appears related to transition duration in urban but not in rural areas. Urban male youth make the transition to work more quickly than female urban youth (Côte d'Ivoire excepted), but there is no consistent pattern in transition duration by sex in rural areas.

As noted at the outset, the synthetic indicator does not permit conclusions about the "efficiency" or "success" of the transition in specific country contexts. A better understanding of the transition period would require integrating the analysis of optimal school-leaving age with that of employment search and labor force participation. Even so, the synthetic indicator does reveal two important features of the transition in Sub-Saharan Africa countries that fit within this more detailed analysis—a relatively late starting age for the transition and its typically long duration.

The transition is very prolonged—five years or longer—in 8 of the 13 countries (Cameroon, Ethiopia, The Gambia, Kenya, Malawi, Mozambique, São Tomé and Principe, and Zambia). This suggests that young people in these countries meet significant labor market entry problems on leaving the school system and must deal with a drawn out period of job search or inactivity. It is also interesting to observe that while the transition tends to be longer in urban areas in several countries, this is not a general pattern. The transition in rural areas can be equally long, indicating that problems of entry into the labor market are not an exclusively urban phenomenon. However, given that school attendance rates are generally substantially lower in rural areas, the phenomenon tends to be more relevant in absolute terms in urban areas.

An initial period of unemployment following schooling is not unusual as young people spend time looking for the best jobs, but the length of this jobless period in Sub-Saharan Africa extends well beyond what could plausibly be considered "wait" unemployment. As noted above, long periods of initial joblessness can translate into permanently reduced productive potential and job prospects. They therefore constitute a particular policy concern.

Factors Affecting the School-to-Work Transition

The duration of transition from school to work is characterized by large cross-country variation. It is beyond the scope of this report to identify the individual, household, and institutional characteristics that could help to explain this variation, but the extent to which characteristics of the economies considered could affect it are assessed.

GDP growth is an obvious candidate to control for differences in the ability of the economies to absorb school leavers in the labor market (figure 7.11). The school nonentrance rate and the share of youth in the total population proxy for cross-country differences in the size of the school leavers' cohort. Openness to trade (as proxied by the ratio of exports plus imports to GDP) and the share of industrial value added in total value added proxy for differences in the structure of the economies. Finally, a measure of income inequality controls for cross-country differences in access to labor markets resulting from wealth.

The data do not suggest any strong relationship between the duration of the school-to-work transition and the broader macroeconomic and demographic context (figure 7.11).[13] Cross-country variations in transition duration seem not to be explained on the basis of available information. This suggests that the factors specific to the youth labor market are more important in determining transitions than macroeconomic differences.

Transitions Directly to Working Life

To this point, only the group of children that has spent at least some time in formal education has been considered. However, youth entering the labor market do not necessarily pass through the schooling system.

A substantial group of young people in most Sub-Saharan African countries never enter school and thus transition directly from inactivity to the labor force.

This group of school nonentrants is also an important policy concern; with very little human capital, they are especially vulnerable to undesirable transition outcomes. As children, school nonentrants are among the groups most vulnerable to child labor (figure 7.12).

The size of the group of school nonentrants varies considerably across countries. For one broad group, most children (at least 90 percent) attend school for at least some period (for example, in Kenya, Mozambique, São Tomé and Principe, and Zambia), and the school-to-work transition framework is especially relevant for analyzing employment outcomes. For a

Figure 7.11. Correlation between Transition Duration and Selected Macroeconomic and Demographic Factors

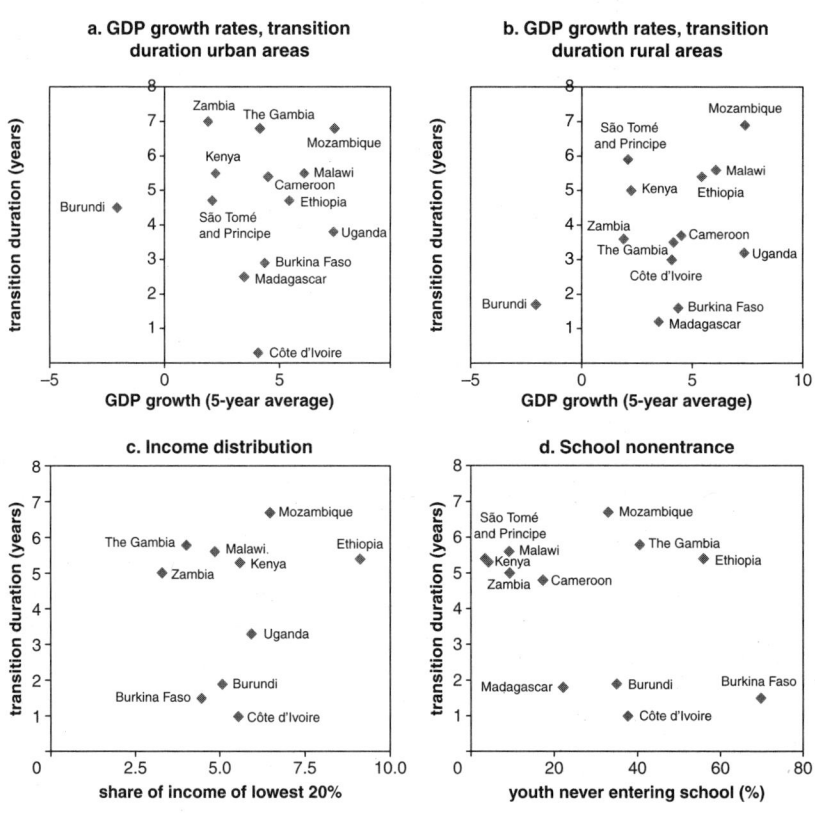

(continued)

Figure 7.11. *(continued)*

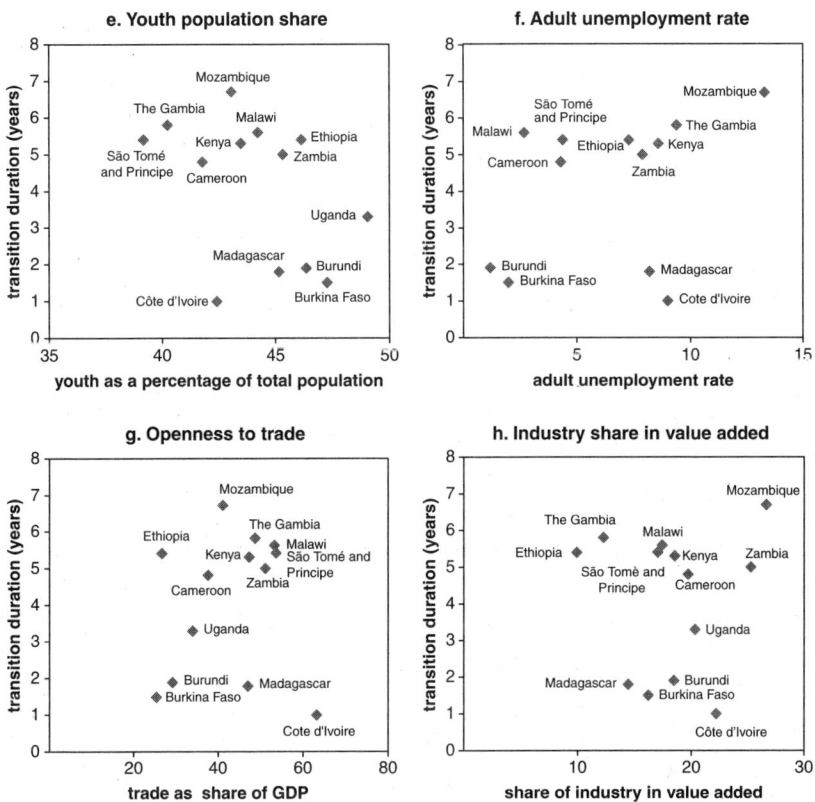

Source: Understanding Children's Work calculations based on World Bank Standard Files and Standard Indicators datasets; World Bank 2004.

second group, the percentage of youth that has not attended school is much higher, ranging from 17 percent in Cameroon to 70 percent in Burkina Faso. Differences exist by residence and sex within countries, and rural children, particularly rural female children, are consistently the least likely to have had the opportunity to enter school (for example, in Burkina Faso, Burundi, Cameroon, and Côte d'Ivoire).

No obvious benchmark allows us to establish at what age these children begin to look for employment. But the average age at first job for children never attending school is relatively high in several countries (figure 7.13). These children begin work in Kenya at 15 years old and in Ethiopia, Mozambique, and São Tomé and Principe at about 16 years old. Rural school nonentrants secure employment at the earliest age

Figure 7.12. The Proportion of Children Ages 8–12 Who Are Economically Active

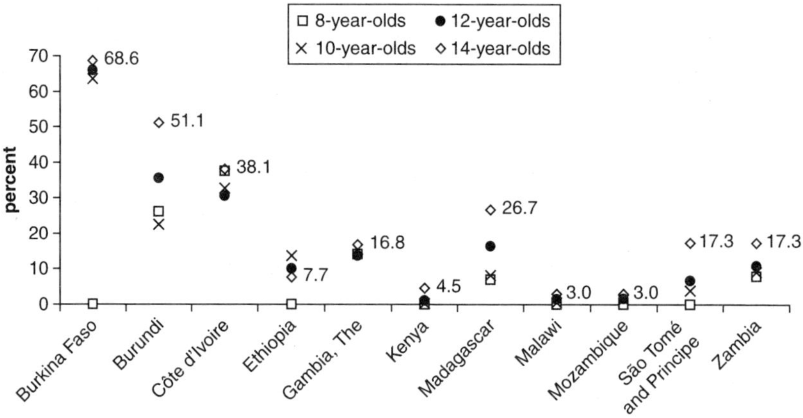

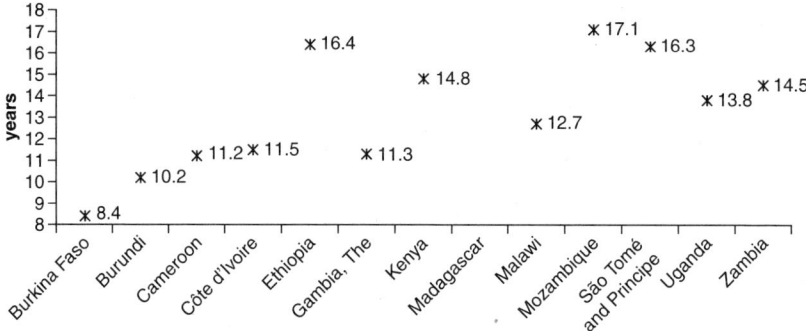

Source: Understanding Children's Work calculations based on World Bank Standard Files and Standard Indicators datasets.

Figure 7.13. Age at First Job for Children Never Attending School, by Country

Source: Understanding Children's Work calculations based on World Bank Standard Files and Standard Indicators datasets.

(Ethiopia and São Tomé and Principe excepted). Though it is reasonable to assume that because they are not involved in school, these children would start to look for employment rather early, progress in the labor market is not easy for them either.

The numbers of children who do not enter the school system are relatively large in several Sub-Saharan African countries.[14] These children are likely to enter the labor market in a particularly weak position and grow to be very vulnerable (employed or unemployed) youth. Children who never attended school tend to enter the labor market early, but they may still face difficulties in finding a job. An analysis of the situation of youth in the labor market cannot avoid focusing on these early labor market entrants. Child laborers of today will be the weakest youth tomorrow. The analysis of child labor should thus be integrated into labor market analysis to give a consistent picture of the condition of youth in the labor market.

Annex 7A.1

Building a Simple Indicator of the School-to-Work Transition

This annex develops a simple indicator of the transition from school to work that should be comparable across countries. To describe the transition from school to work, the distribution of school-leaving age and the distribution of age of entry into the first job must be derived. The difference between the average school-leaving age and the average age of first entry into work is computed as a synthetic indicator of this transition.

This is not the first attempt to describe the school-to-work transition process. For example, OECD (1998, 1999, 2000) uses the age at which 50 percent of individuals are in employment to determine the end point of the transition. Measures of transition based on this definition implicitly assume that the overall portion of individuals entering employment is above 50 percent (otherwise, no transition would ever be completed) and that the overall proportion of individuals who enter employment in all countries is roughly comparable (otherwise, this indicator would be biased by the overall differences in participation across countries). Neither of these assumptions is likely to be true, especially in developing countries. Similar problems occur when estimating the starting point of the transition. For example, OECD indicators implicitly assume that all children begin to attend school and that the vast majority of them stay in school at least until the end of the compulsory grade level, an assumption that can hardly be maintained in most developing countries.

We try to circumvent these problems by standardizing measures of school-to-work transition to the population in question: that is, those who eventually pass through school and participate in the labor force.

Modeling the transition process from school to work ideally requires longitudinal data with detailed job history information that follow individuals from childhood to adulthood, or alternatively, cross-sectional data with retrospective information to reconstruct work histories. In the absence of the longitudinal data (generally unavailable in developing countries), one can use cross-sectional data to measure the length of the transition. Under appropriate assumptions, the available cross-sectional data allow consistent identification of the parameters of interest. Because indicators and their interpretation depend on the underlying assumptions, it is necessary to describe the assumptions to allow comparability with other indicators.

Suppose there exists an age a_{min}, such that for $a > a_{min}$ individuals never transit into school and such that for $a \leq a_{min}$ individuals never transit out of school. In this case, at age a_{min} those who have ever entered school are all in school. Thus, if S denotes the event of being in school, the probability of leaving school at age a, denoted by SL_a is

$$SL_a = - [P(S_{a+1}) - P(S_a)] \quad \text{when } a > a_{min}. \tag{1}$$

Equation (1) is the change in enrollment across two consecutive ages, and simply states that if, say, 90 percent of children are in school at age 10 and 80 percent are in school at age 11, then 10 percent of children must have dropped out between age 10 and age 11.

Assume in addition that for any age $a < a_{max}$, individuals never leave work and for $a \geq a_{max}$ individuals have never entered work. This implies that at a_{max}, all who ever work are simultaneously in work. This assumption—admittedly more unrealistic than the previous one—rules out exit from employment before a_{max} and exit from inactivity after a_{max}. In this case, if W denotes work and EW_a denotes the probability of entry into work at age a,

$$EW_a = P(W_{a+1}) - P(W_a), \quad \text{when } a < a_{max}. \tag{2}$$

Equation (2) is the increase in participation from one year to another, and states that if, say, 10 percent of children are in work at age 14 and 15 percent are in work at age 15, then 5 percent of children must have started to work between age 14 and age 15.

One major difficulty with these indicators is that not all individuals make a transition through school (a relevant problem in developing countries) and, most important, that not all individuals transition into work. This is particularly true for women, especially if work is defined as participation in a market-oriented economic activity. Hence, these indexes are derived conditional on individuals ever transitioning into the relevant state; as for the others, there is no transition to be defined.

Under the foregoing assumptions, the average school-leaving age (conditional on having ever been in school) is expressed as

$$E(SL) = \Sigma_{a > a_{min}} a \times [SL_a / P(S_{a_{min}})] \tag{3}$$

and the distribution of age of entry into work is

$$E(EW) = \Sigma_{a > a_{max}} a \times [EW_a / P(W_{a_{max}})]. \tag{4}$$

Notice that $P(W_{a_{max}}) = \Sigma_{a < a_{max}} EW_a$ and hence $\Sigma_{a < a_{max}} [EW_a / P(W_{a_{max}})] = 1$. A similar reasoning applies to the weights in equation (3). We compute our synthetic index as

$$I = E(SL) - E(EW). \tag{5}$$

This index is the average gap between age of entry into work (conditional on ever entering work) and age of exit from school (conditional on ever entering school).

To the extent that the distribution of school-leaving rates (entry rates) is symmetrical, the indexes in equations (4) and (5) are also the median of the conditional distributions. In this case, our index differs from the one used by OECD (2000) in the adjustment factor for the population at risk, which seems necessary in the countries under study.

Empirical Implementation

This section describes the empirical implementation of the indicator when, as is the case here, only one cross-section is available. As a first step, we fit a probit model on the probability of being in school across all individuals in the sample separately for males and females in each country. We regress this on a polynomial in age. Fitting a probit model is useful for smoothing the age participation profiles in the presence of measurement errors and small sample sizes and allows sample predictions to be made, if necessary. The turning point in the estimated age participation profile is a_{min}. We repeat the same procedure for the probability of work. We fit a probit model on the probability of working across all individuals in the sample separately for males and females in each country. We regress this on a polynomial in age. We use these estimated probabilities to compute the indicators in equations (3) and (4) and, ultimately, equation (5).

There are several drawbacks to this procedure. First, although it is generally possible to ascertain whether individuals in work ever attended school, it is impossible to know whether those who attend school ever get a job. So, in computing the average age of exit from school we are unable to condition the average age of exit from school on those eventually transitioning to the labor market. The index in equation (5) is the average age gap for those who ever enter into work after school (hence, the true school-to-work transition age gap) only under the assumption that age of exit from school is uncorrelated with the probability of entering into work later in life, an assumption that some may not find compelling. If early school leavers are less likely to eventually find a job, the gap will be overestimated; if they are more likely to do so, the gap will be underestimated.

A second drawback of this procedure when applied to a single cross-section is that the index is derived from a comparison of individuals of different ages at a given time and hence from different birth cohorts. The bias is difficult to determine. If there is a secular increase in school-leaving age without relevant changes in the age of first employment across cohorts, it may result in an underestimation of the length of the transition period from school to work in each country. If the age of first employment shows a secular increase, the bias could go in either direction. However, if one is ready to assume that these biases are similar across countries, it is still possible to make a sensible inference about differences across countries.

Notes

1. The countries selected for inclusion in this book are Burkina Faso, Burundi, Cameroon, Côte d'Ivoire, Ethiopia, The Gambia, Kenya, Madagascar, Malawi, Mozambique, São Tomé and Principe, Uganda, and Zambia. As part of broader efforts toward durable solutions to child labor, the International Labour Organization, United Nations Children's Fund, and the World Bank initiated the interagency Understanding Children's Work (UCW) project in December 2000. The project is guided by the Oslo Agenda for Action, which laid out the priorities for the international community to fight child labor. Through a variety of data collection, research, and assessment activities, the UCW project is broadly directed toward improving understanding of child labor, its causes and effects, how it can be measured, and effective policies for addressing it. For further information, see the project Web site at www.ucw-project.org.

2. An *employed person* fits in any of the following categories: holding paid employment, at work, or with a job but not at work now. This includes persons waiting to rejoin employment and employers or persons in self-employment. This classification should include unpaid family laborers who hold jobs in

market-oriented establishments, irrespective of the number of hours worked during a reference period. However, some countries prefer for special reasons to set a minimum time criterion for the inclusion of unpaid family labor among the employed. Usually, if a person works for more than seven hours a day, they are considered employed.

An *unemployed person* is a person who fulfills any or all of the following criteria: without work and currently available for work or seeking work by taking necessary steps to seek paid employment (such steps include applying for jobs or registering with an agency).

An *inactive person* is a person who is neither in the labor force (employed or unemployed) nor in education.

3. As measured by the unemployment ratio (unemployed as a proportion of the population) rather than the unemployment rate (unemployed as a proportion of the labor force).

4. Joblessness, unlike unemployment, has the advantage of reflecting both unemployed and discouraged workers who have left or not entered the work force.

5. Inactivity among youth has important economic and social consequences and will require an in-depth analysis beyond the scope of the present report. Differences by residence in the composition of the inactive also merit investigation. In rural areas, where service coverage is typically less extensive, a larger proportion of inactive young people might in fact be performing chores such as water collection and fuelwood fetching. In urban areas, however, where the burden of household chores is typically lower, discouraged workers might constitute a larger proportion of the inactive.

6. Some forms of economic work, water fetching, for example, are also reflected in this category.

7. Teenagers refers to the 15–19 age group. Young adults refers to the 20–24 age group.

8. The unemployment rate (that is, unemployment as a proportion of the total labor force in the same age group; not shown in table) is actually higher for teenagers than for young adults. This is a reflection of the fact that teenagers are more likely to be in education and therefore outside the labor force.

9. See http://millenniumindicators.un.org/unsd/mi/mi_goals.asp.

10. *Wage employees* are all persons in paid employment remunerated by wages and salaries or commission from sales, price-rates, bonuses, or in-kind payments. Basic remuneration is not directly dependent on revenue of the unit worked for but on the explicit (written or oral) or implicit employment contract. Wage employees may be regular employees with fixed-term contracts or without limits of time, or casual workers without contracts.

Informal sector employees are those employed in a semiorganized unit, whether legally registered or not. At an operational level, the ILO informal sector surveys define informal sector employment to consist of all own-account workers, unpaid family workers who work for seven or more hours per day, and employers and employees in establishments with fewer than 5 or 10 persons engaged. Paid domestic workers are excluded.

Self-employed persons perform work for profit or family gain either in cash or in kind. The remuneration is dependent on profits derived from the goods and services produced (own consumption from enterprise is considered part of profits). The self-employed person makes operational decisions affecting the enterprise or may delegate decisions while retaining the responsibility for the welfare of the enterprise. This is a one-person business (meaning a business headed by a single person) and may include contributing family workers.

11. For example, Koranic schooling.

12. The calculation of average school-leaving age is, however, different in table 7.8 and figure 7.9; comparisons are therefore only indicative.

13. We also used different disaggregations of the duration of the transition by sex and by residence, but the results obtained are similar to those presented here.

14. To which should be added those children who drop out very early and who cannot be identified on the basis of the available information.

References

Bennell, P. S. 1996. "Rates of Return to Education: Does the Conventional Pattern Prevail in Sub-Saharan Africa?" *World Development* 24 (1): 183–200.

Betcherman, G., J. Fares, A. Luinstra, and R. Prouty. 2005. "Child Labor, Education and Children's Rights." *In Human Rights and Development: Towards Mutual Reinforcement*, ed. P. Alston and M. Robinson. Oxford, United Kingdom: Oxford University Press.

Collier, P., and J. W. Gunning. 1999. "Explaining African Economic Performance." *Journal of Economic Literature* 37 (1): 64–111.

Fluitman, F. 2001. "Working, But Not Well: Notes on the Nature and Extent of Employment Problems in Sub-Saharan Africa." International Training Centre of the International Labour Organization, Turin, Italy.

Freeman, R. B., and D. L. Lindauer. 1999. "Why Not Africa?" NBER Working Paper No. W6942, National Bureau of Economic Research, Cambridge, MA.

Glewwe, P. 1991. *Schooling, Skills and the Returns to Government Investment in Education: An Exploration Using Data from Ghana*. Washington, DC: World Bank.

ILO (International Labour Organization). 2003. "Key Indicators of the Labour Market." 3rd ed. Geneva.

———. 2004. "Global Employment Trends for Youth." Geneva.

————. 2006. *Global Employment Trends for Youth*. Geneva: ILO.

OECD (Organisation for Economic Co-operation and Development. 1998. "Getting Started, Settling In: The Transition from Education to the Labour Market." In OECD *Employment Outlook—Towards an Employment Centered Social Policy*. Paris.

————. 1999. *Preparing Youth for the 21st Century: The Transition from Education to the Labour Market*. Conference proceedings, "Preparing Youth for the 21st Century: The Policy Lessons from the Past Two Decades," Washington, DC, February 23–24.

————. 2000. *From Initial Education to Working Life: Making Transitions Work*. Paris.

Psacharopoulos, G. 1994. "Returns to Investment in Education: A Global Update." Policy Research Working Paper Series No. 1067, World Bank, Washington, DC.

World Bank. 2004. *World Development Indicators 2004*. Washington, DC.

CHAPTER 8

What Determines Labor Market Participation by Youth in Burkina Faso?

Daniel Parent

Many young people in Burkina Faso leave school very early in life. How do they perform in the labor force? How do their fortunes evolve over time? How do their labor market outcomes compare with those of more educated Burkinabes? How are household characteristics linked to youth outcomes?

Employment rates in Burkina Faso increased between 1993 and 2003, with nearly all of the increase generated by females. The female unemployment rate also increased, especially for younger, more educated individuals. The increase may reflect the fact that the higher employment rate encouraged more females to search for jobs. Unemployment also rose among males. Stagnant male employment rates across age groups may suggest that the labor market prospects of males in Burkina Faso deteriorated.

Urban adolescents, particularly those from poor families, tend to enter the labor force when their household economic conditions worsen. The evidence about what makes rural children and younger children enter the work force is more mixed. However, there is little evidence for any

Special thanks to workshop participants in Ouagadougou and at the World Bank in Washington, DC, especially Jean Fares, who provided very useful comments and suggestions.

age group that households take advantage of better economic conditions to pull their children out of school and make them work.

School proximity is a major determinant of school enrollment in Burkina Faso. Per capita household income is greater for households living relatively close to a school, especially secondary schools, even within narrowly defined geographical areas. These findings suggest that the rate of return to schooling is significant. The analysis yields several policy implications.

First, macroeconomic policies that reduce poverty (such as freer trade, which would enhance the demand for agricultural products) are not likely to increase child labor at the cost of basic schooling and literacy. Households value education and take advantage of education opportunities when they can afford to do so, particularly in urban areas. This suggests that they are likely to respond to conditional cash transfers to encourage them to keep (or put) their children in schools.

Second, households that have access to schools tend to take advantage of them. Improving access to schools—by building more schools or improving transportation infrastructure—therefore seems to represent a promising public investment.

Third, labor resources in Burkina Faso could be harnessed to participate in such infrastructure projects, particularly in rural areas, where a significant share of the population is underemployed.

Fourth, none of these policies will work well if the quality of education is not held at least constant. Sufficient numbers of additional teachers must be hired, teachers must be well qualified and motivated to work in largely rural areas, and related capital expenditures (books, basic instructional material) must be forthcoming.

Labor Market Indicators

The Household Living Standards Surveys, conducted in Burkina Faso every five years, provide data on individuals' main activities (school only, school and work, work only, unemployment, inactivity) the week preceding the interview. Although this chapter focuses on youth labor market and schooling outcomes, activities are reported for all age groups to be able to reveal changes in the relative outcomes of younger and older individuals not enrolled in school.

Five mutually exclusive categories of activities are defined for the three years with data (table 8.1): school only, combining school and work, work only, unemployed, and inactive. In general, the school enrollment rate among children and youth is very low in Burkina Faso. In 2003, only

Table 8.1. School and Work Status of Females and Males in Burkina Faso, by Age, 1993–2003

Age group	Activity	Female (percent)			Male (percent)		
		1993	1998	2003	1993	1998	2003
10–14	School only	27	22	26	35	29	33
	School and work	1	2	1	2	4	1
	Work only	57	66	59	57	62	56
	Unemployed	3	3	8	2	2	7
	Inactive	5	2	3	3	1	2
15–19	School only	11	11	13	16	16	17
	School and work	0	1	0	1	2	1
	Work only	70	75	73	78	77	77
	Unemployed	2	4	6	3	2	4
	Inactive	1	1	0	1	1	1
20–24	School only	3	5	5	8	9	8
	School and work	0	0	0	1	1	0
	Work only	71	77	77	84	84	85
	Unemployed	2	3	5	6	4	6
	Inactive	1	1	0	1	1	1
25–34	School only	0	0	0	1	1	1
	School and work	0	0	0	0	0	0
	Work only	79	85	83	94	95	95
	Unemployed	1	2	4	3	2	4
	Inactive	1	1	1	1	1	0
35–44	School only	0	0	0	0	0	0
	School and work	0	0	0	0	0	0
	Work only	84	89	88	96	98	97
	Unemployed	0	1	1	2	1	2
	Inactive	1	1	1	1	1	1
45 and older	School only	0	0	0	0	0	0
	School and work	0	0	0	0	0	0
	Work only	79	86	83	94	96	95
	Unemployed	0	1	1	1	1	2
	Inactive	7	6	6	3	1	2
All ages (10–64)	School only	7	7	8	12	11	12
	School and work	0	1	0	1	1	1
	Work only	73	79	77	81	83	82
	Unemployed	2	2	4	3	2	4
	Inactive	3	2	2	2	1	1

Source: Survey of Household Living Standards 1993, 1998, 2003.
Note: In 1993 and 1998, individuals were classified as unemployed if they reported not being occupied but having had a job at some point or not being occupied with no prior work experience. In 2003 a distinction among those with previous work experience was made by asking whether the reason the person did not work was due to seasonal factors. For females, being at home is the residual category. For this reason, the percentages for females sum to 100 percent (notwithstanding rounding errors), while the percentages for males do not.

33 percent of male children between the ages of 10 and 14 were in school. Among teenagers (ages 15 to 19) this share drops to 17 percent. For females, school incidence is even lower, at 26 percent for the 10–14 age group and 13 percent for teenage girls.

Among children ages 10–14, school enrollment appeared to decrease between 1993 and 1998 before rebounding to roughly the 1993 level in 2003 (table 8.1). Conditioning on the location of households relative to schools, however, enrollment did not drop at all over this period. The apparent decline in enrollment probably reflects the 1998 survey's use of a sampling frame that included more households located far away from schools.

Very few Burkinabe youth (2 percent or less) report being both enrolled in school and working as their main activity, suggesting that children leave school before going to work.[1] There is no evidence that many children move back and forth between school and the labor force: when they quit school, they do so for good.

A large fraction of children and youth start to work very early in Burkina Faso. More than half of children are already working between 10 and 14 years old. This fraction also rises very quickly with age among both males and females. Because of the high incidence of poverty and the lack of options outside the work force, most individuals work and cannot afford to be unemployed or inactive.

Employment rates among youth are high, and unemployment rates are low (table 8.2). There is evidence that the unemployment rate rose between 1993 and 2003 for every age group. Among males and females, however, the employment rate remained fairly constant, at very high levels.

Across all ages and education categories, the period between 1993 and 2003 witnessed a substantial increase in the fraction of females

Table 8.2. Employment and Unemployment Rates among Burkinabes Not Enrolled in School, by Age and Gender, 1993–2003

| | Employment rate (percent) | | | | | | Unemployment rate (percent) | | | | | |
| | Females | | | Males | | | Females | | | Males | | |
Age	1993	1998	2003	1993	1998	2003	1993	1998	2003	1993	1998	2003
15–19	79	85	84	94	95	94	3	4	7	4	3	5
20–24	74	82	81	92	93	92	3	3	5	6	5	7
25–34	78	85	83	94	96	95	1	2	4	4	3	5
35–44	81	87	84	96	97	97	0	2	3	2	2	2
45 and older	83	89	88	97	98	97	1	1	1	2	1	3
Total	78	86	83	94	95	93	2	3	6	4	3	6

Source: Survey of Household Living Standards 1993, 1998, 2003.

employed in the labor market and a proportionally larger increase in the fraction of females reported to be unemployed.[2] The vast majority of unemployed females were looking for a first job.

Labor market outcomes of the youngest and least educated boys deteriorated between 1993 and 2003 (table 8.3). For all other age groups and schooling levels, employment rates remained more or less constant. Surprisingly, the employment rate among males ages 20–29 declines with educational attainment. Individuals who have just completed a schooling period, such as secondary education, have higher unemployment rates than less educated individuals of the same age, but their employment rate increases sharply as they age. The key question then becomes whether the jobs the more educated individuals eventually get are better than the ones that less educated workers have. This chapter will return to this question when looking at the transition across occupations over time for a given birth cohort.

Employment rates increased for all age groups of urban males (table 8.4). They also increased among females in rural areas, while remaining unchanged among rural males. The decrease in employment is concentrated among young men with no education. Labor market indicators did not change dramatically for workers with any amount of schooling, almost all of whom work in rural areas.

Employment rates for females increased across all age groups, in both rural and urban areas. The increase was significantly larger in urban areas, where employment rates had been much lower than in rural areas in 1993. Female unemployment rates also increased substantially, probably reflecting the fact that women are more likely to search for jobs than to be inactive. An argument could even be made that because employment has increased for females, women may be more motivated to search for work, potentially raising the unemployment rate. Overall, the male labor market showed no sign of deterioration, at least with regard to employment incidence, except among young men ages 20–29. Two phenomena suggest that Burkina Faso's labor market expanded between 1993 and 2003. Much of the progress, however, occurred between 1993 and 1998, with the 1998–2003 period characterized by stagnation if not decline in employment.

Education appears to increase the chance of being employed, at least for boys in rural areas. This may seem somewhat of a paradox because the unemployment rate also increases with education. Because the cost of being unemployed is high in Burkina Faso given the absence of income support programs, the high unemployment rate probably reflects the fact that individuals believe it is worth waiting (or shopping) for better

Table 8.3. Employment and Unemployment Rates in Burkina Faso, by Age, Gender, and Education, 1993–2003

Educational attainment	Age	Employment rate (percent) Females			Males			Unemployment rate (percent) Females			Males		
		1993	1998	2003	1993	1998	2003	1993	1998	2003	1993	1998	2003
No schooling	15–19	83	88	87	96	97	96	1	2	4	2	1	3
	20–24	80	87	85	97	97	96	1	1	3	2	1	4
	25–29	81	89	86	96	98	97	0	1	2	2	1	3
	30–34	84	89	87	97	99	98	0	1	2	1	1	1
	35–39	85	90	90	97	99	97	0	0	1	1	1	2
	Total	82	89	86	96	97	94	1	1	4	2	1	5
Partial primary	15–19	63	69	70	92	92	90	10	18	17	7	6	8
	20–24	57	56	69	90	89	92	7	13	15	7	10	7
	25–29	69	53	71	94	98	93	1	6	16	5	2	7
	30–34	60	63	73	96	98	96	1	3	9	3	2	4
	35–39	73	68	73	98	99	91	1	3	13	1	1	6
	Total	65	63	72	92	93	91	6	13	15	6	6	7
Primary completed	15–19	39	51	43	79	66	76	5	19	28	7	5	10
	20–24	37	39	47	69	75	72	8	10	16	10	8	9
	25–29	48	52	56	80	87	89	2	5	11	7	5	8
	30–34	66	64	62	94	92	93	0	3	10	8	6	3

	35–39	61	78	65	94	96	97	3	2	0	5	1	4
	Total	48	52	54	80	84	85	5	11	16	7	6	8
Partial secondary	15–19	39	51	43	79	66	76	5	9	35	13	24	20
	20–24	37	39	47	69	75	72	14	25	26	29	23	26
	25–29	48	52	56	80	87	89	10	12	16	16	11	11
	30–34	66	64	62	94	92	93	4	13	15	6	7	7
	35–39	61	78	65	94	96	97	4	3	11	4	4	3
	Total	48	52	54	80	84	85	9	16	21	16	14	14
Secondary completed	20–24	64	49	100	82	73	87	22	25	0	18	20	13
	25–29	61	67	60	77	91	83	10	12	26	23	9	17
	30–34	87	68	90	98	92	98	5	5	10	2	5	2
	35–39	87	80	93	95	96	100	13	0	0	0	4	0
	Total	74	67	79	85	90	93	11	10	13	14	8	7
Postsecondary	20–24	21	54	—	73	50	34	25	0	—	27	50	66
	25–29	41	90	65	83	81	78	48	5	24	17	16	17
	30–34	87	100	94	97	88	95	8	0	0	3	12	1
	35–39	100	82	100	98	98	97	0	18	0	2	2	3
	Total	69	87	90	94	89	90	20	8	6	6	10	7

Source: Survey of Household Living Standards, 1993, 1998, 2003.

Note: — = Not available.

Table 8.4. Employment and Unemployment Rates in Urban and Rural Areas of Burkina Faso, 1993–2003

Item	Age	Female			Male		
		1993	1998	2003	1993	1998	2003
Employment rates							
Urban	15–19	34	42	45	68	72	73
	20–24	35	41	44	67	77	74
	25–29	42	51	53	80	87	85
	30–34	55	57	59	88	92	93
	35–39	54	65	68	90	96	93
	Total	41	49	52	76	83	81
Rural	15–19	87	92	91	98	98	97
	20–24	82	91	90	97	98	98
	25–29	85	92	90	98	99	98
	30–34	87	93	90	99	99	99
	35–39	88	94	92	99	99	98
	Total	85	92	89	97	98	95
Unemployment rates							
Urban	15–19	12	28	31	23	22	25
	20–24	10	17	24	28	21	24
	25–29	6	9	16	17	11	13
	30–34	2	6	12	8	7	7
	35–39	3	3	5	8	4	6
	Total	8	15	20	18	14	17
Rural	15–19	1	1	3	1	0	2
	20–24	1	0	1	1	0	1
	25–29	0	0	1	0	0	2
	30–34	0	1	1	1	0	1
	35–39	0	0	1	0	0	2
	Total	1	1	3	1	0	4

Source: Survey of Household Living Standards, 1993, 1998, 2003.

jobs, which will eventually materialize; or only those who can afford not to be employed wait for such jobs.

Occupational Transitions over Time

How do occupations at entry into the labor market vary across educational attainment categories? How does education affect progress over time from low-paying to high-paying occupations? To answer these questions, the study examines how occupations for people of varying education levels evolve over time, starting with 15 to 19 year olds in 1993 and tracing their occupations over 10 years, with follow-up samples in 1998 and 2003 (Parent 2006).[3]

For males with no schooling, the only meaningful transition is from a family helper to an independent worker, possibly as the head of a new household. The overwhelming majority of females stay employed as family helpers even after 10 years. The fraction of male independent workers begins to increase significantly after only five years. The picture is basically the same for illiterate individuals (as opposed to simply uneducated).

For male workers with a completed primary education, occupations are somewhat more diversified after 10 years, particularly for those in urban areas. However, even though these individuals are more educated, their entry occupation in 1993 is still clearly family helper. More or less the same holds for females with a completed primary education. Although early labor market outcomes indicate that upgrading the educational attainment of young Burkinabes has little impact (leaving aside the possibility that family helpers with primary education may earn more than uneducated family helpers), those who have completed primary schooling have more options as time goes on.

Males with partial secondary education start much at the same place as less educated youth, but transition across occupations much more quickly: after just five years the occupational composition of the sample of 20- to 24-year-olds is quite varied. Those 15- to 19-year-olds with partial secondary education are entering the labor market immediately, unlike individuals with just a primary or no education. Although there are not enough observations in 1993 to infer the occupation distribution for females at that point, the data from 1998 and 2003 show that the allocation of females with partial secondary education across occupations is more varied than for less educated females. Of interest is the fact that women are much more likely to be independent workers than men with similar education. Women are also more likely to be working in the trade industry (commerce) than men, whose sectors of activity are more diversified.[4]

The number of workers with a completed secondary education is small, but they tend to work as managers or skilled workers fairly early in their careers and clearly move into management after five years. This is true for both males and females. The small size of this category means that it is not a high priority group for policy development.

Given that workers with at least some partial secondary education tend to have high-paying occupations after 10 years, relative to the occupations held by less educated workers, it is not surprising that the unemployment rate tends to increase with the level of education. Quite simply, if no better-paying jobs exist in the economy than the ones they can have when they enter the labor force, there would be little point in being unemployed because the expected gain from attractive offers later would be small. The fact that more educated workers tend to report themselves as being unemployed than do less educated workers is evidence that education pays eventually, even if not immediately upon entry. It is also remarkable that, at least for people with up to a partial secondary education level, the occupation early in one's career is similar across all educational attainment groups for both genders.

Those with Multiple Jobs Are Underemployed

Human resources are underutilized in Burkina Faso, especially in rural areas. Many Burkinabes hold more than one job (table 8.5). Some 92 percent of these workers live in rural areas. Males are more likely than females to hold multiple jobs, although the difference is modest, and older workers are more likely to do so than younger workers.

Among the 16 percent of all Burkinabe workers who report being underemployed (that is, working fewer hours than they would like), the overwhelming majority hold multiple jobs. While only about 9 percent of people who hold single jobs wish they could work more, 47 percent of multiple job holders would like to do so. Males are more likely than females to want more work.

There is little evidence of a systematic relationship between income and holding multiple jobs (table 8.6). The relationship appears to have

Table 8.5. Percentage of Burkinabes Underemployed or Holding More Than One Job, 2003

		Female		Male	
Age group	Comments	Urban	Rural	Urban	Rural
10–14	Wants more work	11	8	6	8
	Holds more than one job	8	7	3	9
15–19	Wants more work	10	13	12	14
	Holds more than one job	8	14	7	13
20–24	Wants more work	12	16	13	20
	Holds more than one job	11	18	10	21
25–34	Wants more work	15	17	15	23
	Holds more than one job	9	21	11	28
35–44	Wants more work	15	18	15	26
	Holds more than one job	9	25	13	35
45 and older	Wants more work	18	16	16	22
	Holds more than one job	17	24	16	33

Source: Survey of Household Living Standards 2003.

Table 8.6. Percentage of Burkinabes Holding More Than One Job, by Household Income Quintile, 2003

Household income quintile	Females	Males
1	16	18
2	19	23
3	22	24
4	19	23
5	13	17

Source: Survey of Household Living Standards 2003.

an inverted U-shape, with people in the middle quintiles more likely to hold multiple jobs than people in the top or bottom quintiles.

Household Income, School Attendance, and Returns to Education

What factors are behind the low school enrollment rate among young people in Burkina Faso and the high incidence of child labor? Several explanations are put forward in the child labor literature and among policy makers. Most common among these are responses to adverse household income shocks, low returns to education, and the difficulty in accessing schools.

Household Income Shocks, Distance to School, and Child Labor Force Participation

One would expect that the labor force participation of children from poorer or more disadvantaged households would be more sensitive to deterioration in economic conditions. Is this indeed the case? Table 8.7 looks at changes in a household's most important source of income (as a proxy for changes in total household income during the year). This may be a suspect proxy if households derive income from equally important sources.[5] To make the distinction as sharp and as easy to interpret as possible, a dummy variable is constructed equal to 1 if income decreased from the previous year and 0 if it increased or stayed the same. Table 8.8 examines respondents' perceptions of their general economic situation, with a second dummy variable equal to 1 if the respondent reports that their situation is worse than or as bad as the previous year.

Table 8.7. Household Income Shocks and Labor Force Participation in Burkina Faso, 2003

Independent variable	Males				Females			
	(1)	(2)	(3)	(4)	(5)	(6)	(7)	(8)
12- to 14-year-olds living in urban areas								
Household income decreased in past year	0.045	0.049	0.037	0.121	0.053	0.062	0.026	0.060
	(0.028)	(0.029)	(0.029)	(0.046)	(0.027)	(0.032)	(0.028)	(0.044)
Decrease in income × household head's education		−0.005				−0.016		
		(0.003)				(0.022)		
Decrease in income × income in bottom quintile			0.077				0.275	
			(0.086)				(0.116)	
Decrease in income × household size				−0.007				−0.001
				(0.003)				(0.003)
30–59 minutes away from primary school	0.031	0.031	0.031	0.033	−0.024	−0.024	−0.020	−0.024
	(0.042)	(0.042)	(0.042)	(0.042)	(0.040)	(0.040)	(0.040)	(0.040)
60+ minutes away from primary school	0.008	0.007	0.006	0.000	0.446	0.446	0.458	0.446
	(0.143)	(0.144)	(0.139)	(0.141)	(0.172)	(0.172)	(0.168)	(0.172)
30–59 minutes away from secondary school	0.031	0.031	0.032	0.030	0.015	0.015	0.015	0.015
	(0.031)	(0.031)	(0.031)	(0.031)	(0.030)	(0.030)	(0.030)	(0.030)
60+ minutes away from secondary school	0.061	0.061	0.054	0.065	0.049	0.049	0.037	0.050
	(0.061)	(0.061)	(0.061)	(0.061)	(0.063)	(0.063)	(0.061)	(0.063)
Number of observations	1,575	1,575	1,575	1,575	1,692	1,692	1,692	1,692
12- to 14-year-olds living in rural areas								
Household income decreased in past year	0.007	0.005	0.002	0.019	−0.010	−0.011	−0.005	−0.016
	(0.016)	(0.016)	(0.018)	(0.024)	(0.016)	(0.016)	(0.018)	(0.022)
Decrease in income × household head's education		0.011				0.005		
		(0.004)				(0.003)		

	(1)	(2)	(3)	(4)	(5)	(6)	(7)
Decrease in income × income in bottom quintile			0.020 (0.031)			-0.001 (0.024)	-0.022 (0.038)
Decrease in income × household size							0.000 (0.001)
30–59 minutes away from primary school	0.060 (0.017)	0.060 (0.017)	0.060 (0.017)	0.060 (0.017)	0.033 (0.017)	0.033 (0.017)	0.033 (0.017)
60+ minutes away from primary school	0.170 (0.017)	0.170 (0.017)	0.170 (0.017)	0.170 (0.017)	0.091 (0.021)	0.091 (0.021)	0.091 (0.021)
30–59 minutes away from secondary school	0.097 (0.027)	0.098 (0.027)	0.096 (0.027)	0.097 (0.027)	0.067 (0.025)	0.067 (0.025)	0.067 (0.025)
60+ minutes away from secondary school	0.165 (0.033)	0.166 (0.033)	0.164 (0.033)	0.165 (0.033)	0.151 (0.032)	0.151 (0.032)	0.151 (0.032)
Number of observations	5,033	5,033	5,033	5,033	4,643	4,643	4,643
8- to 11-year-olds living in urban areas							
Household income decreased in past year	-0.010 (0.011)	-0.020 (0.011)	-0.014 (0.012)	0.016 (0.018)	-0.012 (0.013)	-0.005 (0.014)	-0.011 (0.013)
Decrease in income × household head's education		0.024 (0.011)			-0.021 (0.013)		
Decrease in income × income in bottom quintile			0.028 (0.035)			-0.002 (0.001)	-0.005 (0.039)
Decrease in income × household size							0.004 (0.002)
30–59 minutes away from primary school	0.037 (0.021)	0.037 (0.020)	0.037 (0.020)	0.036 (0.020)	0.033 (0.017)	0.032 (0.017)	0.033 (0.017)
60+ minutes away from primary school	0.046 (0.119)	0.039 (0.113)	0.051 (0.122)	0.044 (0.117)	0.091 (0.021)	0.091 (0.021)	0.091 (0.021)
30–59 minutes away from secondary school	0.004 (0.012)	0.004 (0.012)	0.004 (0.012)	0.005 (0.012)	0.067 (0.025)	0.067 (0.025)	0.067 (0.025)

(continued)

Table 8.7. Household Income Shocks and Labor Force Participation in Burkina Faso, 2003 *(continued)*

Independent variable	Males				Females			
	(1)	(2)	(3)	(4)	(5)	(6)	(7)	(8)
60+ minutes away from secondary school	−0.010	−0.010	−0.012	−0.010	0.151	0.151	0.151	0.151
	(0.021)	(0.020)	(0.020)	(0.021)	(0.032)	(0.032)	(0.032)	(0.032)
Number of observations	2,191	2,191	2,191	2,191	2,156	2,156	2,156	2,156
8- to 11-year-olds living in rural areas								
Household income decreased in past year	−0.023	−0.031	−0.022	−0.005	−0.015	−0.014	−0.005	−0.012
	(0.013)	(0.013)	(0.015)	(0.018)	(0.013)	(0.013)	(0.016)	(0.018)
Decrease in income × household head's education		0.083				−0.006		
		(0.030)				(0.006)		
Decrease in income × income in bottom quintile			−0.004				−0.035	
			(0.015)				(0.027)	
Decrease in income × household size				−0.001				0.000
				(0.001)				(0.001)
30–59 minutes away from primary school	0.078	0.077	0.078	0.078	0.027	0.027	0.027	0.027
	(0.015)	(0.015)	(0.015)	(0.015)	(0.016)	(0.016)	(0.016)	(0.016)
60+ minutes away from primary school	0.095	0.094	0.095	0.095	0.053	0.053	0.053	0.053
	(0.020)	(0.020)	(0.020)	(0.020)	(0.018)	(0.018)	(0.018)	(0.018)
30–59 minutes away from secondary school	−0.044	−0.047	−0.044	−0.044	0.053	0.053	0.054	0.053
	(0.029)	(0.029)	(0.029)	(0.029)	(0.031)	(0.031)	(0.031)	(0.031)
60+ minutes away from secondary school	−0.010	−0.013	−0.010	−0.010	0.079	0.079	0.079	0.079
	(0.027)	(0.027)	(0.027)	(0.027)	(0.025)	(0.025)	(0.025)	(0.025)
Number of observations	8,084	8,084	8,084	8,084	7,470	7,470	7,470	7,470

Source: Survey of Household Living Standards, 2003.
Note: Robust standard errors in parentheses.

Table 8.8. Changes in Household's Economic Conditions and Labor Force Participation

	Males				Females			
Independent variable	(1)	(2)	(3)	(4)	(5)	(6)	(7)	(8)
12- to 14-year-olds living in urban areas								
Economic conditions of household deteriorated over last calendar year	0.080 (0.045)	0.132 (0.057)	0.067 (0.046)	−0.019 (0.103)	0.070 (0.045)	0.108 (0.057)	0.023 (0.045)	0.105 (0.091)
Conditions deteriorated × household head's education		−0.073 (0.044)				−0.035 (0.029)		
Decrease in income × income in bottom quintile			0.029 (0.122)				0.643 (0.154)	
Conditions deteriorated × household size				0.010 (0.010)				−0.004 (0.009)
30–59 minutes away from primary school	−0.023 (0.071)	−0.023 (0.068)	−0.016 (0.070)	−0.027 (0.070)				
60+ minutes away from primary school	−0.190 (0.057)	−0.140 (0.053)	−0.191 (0.061)	−0.190 (0.056)	−0.067 (0.086)	−0.065 (0.086)	−0.054 (0.085)	−0.069 (0.086)
30–59 minutes away from secondary school	0.093 (0.058)	0.105 (0.057)	0.091 (0.059)	0.102 (0.060)	−0.080 (0.053)	−0.075 (0.055)	−0.106 (0.053)	−0.081 (0.054)
60+ minutes away from secondary school	0.228 (0.129)	0.236 (0.132)	0.228 (0.125)	0.237 (0.132)	−0.119 (0.070)	−0.115 (0.072)	−0.131 (0.062)	−0.120 (0.071)
Number of observations	486	486	486	486	508	508	508	508
12- to 14-year-olds living in rural areas								
Economic conditions of household deteriorated over last calendar year	0.008 (0.026)	0.006 (0.027)	0.012 (0.030)	−0.060 (0.055)	0.003 (0.025)	0.012 (0.025)	−0.002 (0.027)	−0.060 (0.057)
Conditions deteriorated × household head's education		0.001 (0.051)				−0.087 (0.062)		

(continued)

Table 8.8. Changes in Household's Economic Conditions and Labor Force Participation (continued)

Independent variable	Males				Females			
	(1)	(2)	(3)	(4)	(5)	(6)	(7)	(8)
Decrease in income × income in bottom quintile			-0.021 (0.052)				0.019 (0.058)	
Conditions deteriorated × household size				0.006 (0.005)				0.006 (0.005)
30–59 minutes away from primary school	0.089 (0.031)	0.090 (0.031)	0.089 (0.032)	0.088 (0.031)	0.040 (0.032)	0.040 (0.032)	0.039 (0.032)	0.039 (0.032)
60+ minutes away from primary school	0.203 (0.028)	0.202 (0.028)	0.201 (0.028)	0.201 (0.028)	0.058 (0.038)	0.062 (0.038)	0.058 (0.037)	0.055 (0.038)
30–59 minutes away from secondary school	0.093 (0.049)	0.093 (0.049)	0.094 (0.050)	0.093 (0.049)	0.032 (0.046)	0.031 (0.047)	0.032 (0.046)	0.036 (0.046)
60+ minutes away from secondary school	0.122 (0.060)	0.122 (0.060)	0.121 (0.062)	0.110 (0.061)	0.032 (0.046)	0.031 (0.053)	0.032 (0.053)	0.038 (0.054)
Number of observations	1,564	1,564	1,564	1,564	1,425	1,425	1,425	1,425
8- to 11-year-olds living in urban areas								
Economic conditions of household deteriorated over last calendar year	0.051 (0.035)	0.038 (0.037)	0.056 (0.035)	0.052 (0.073)	0.036 (0.026)	0.032 (0.031)	0.022 (0.026)	0.079 (0.051)
Conditions deteriorated × household head's education		0.036 (0.044)				0.004 (0.017)		
Decrease in income × income in bottom quintile			-0.046 (0.044)				0.248 (0.246)	
Conditions deteriorated × household size				-0.001 (0.006)				-0.004 (0.004)
30–59 minutes away from primary school	0.001 (0.045)	0.001 (0.045)	0.001 (0.044)	0.001 (0.045)	-0.016 (0.032)	-0.016 (0.032)	-0.020 (0.031)	-0.017 (0.032)

	(1)	(2)	(3)	(4)	(5)	(6)	(7)	(8)
60+ minutes away from primary school	0.076 (0.202)	0.073 (0.202)	0.096 (0.220)	0.076 (0.202)	0.116 (0.105)	0.117 (0.106)	0.102 (0.098)	0.118 (0.108)
30–59 minutes away from secondary school	0.035 (0.032)	0.032 (0.033)	0.040 (0.032)	0.035 (0.033)	0.019 (0.029)	0.018 (0.028)	0.020 (0.028)	0.018 (0.028)
60+ minutes away from secondary school	0.113 (0.106)	0.105 (0.107)	0.076 (0.095)	0.113 (0.106)	-0.020 (0.019)	-0.021 (0.019)	-0.130 (0.023)	-0.020 (0.020)
Number of observations	469	469	469	469	643	643	643	643
8- to 11-year-olds living in rural areas								
Economic conditions of household deteriorated over last calendar year	-0.009 (0.023)	-0.008 (0.023)	-0.015 (0.025)	-0.042 (0.048)	-0.009 (0.023)	-0.002 (0.024)	-0.018 (0.028)	-0.001 (0.051)
Conditions deteriorated × household head's education		-0.007 (0.056)				-0.098 (0.078)		
Decrease in income × income in bottom quintile			0.027 (0.046)				0.026 (0.050)	
Conditions deteriorated × household size				0.003 (0.004)				-0.001 (0.004)
30–59 minutes away from primary school	0.092 (0.032)	0.092 (0.032)	0.091 (0.032)	0.092 (0.032)	0.052 (0.026)	0.052 (0.026)	0.052 (0.026)	0.052 (0.026)
60+ minutes away from primary school	0.101 (0.039)	0.101 (0.039)	0.101 (0.039)	0.099 (0.039)	0.017 (0.036)	0.017 (0.036)	0.017 (0.036)	0.017 (0.036)
30–59 minutes away from secondary school	-0.052 (0.045)	-0.052 (0.045)	-0.051 (0.045)	-0.051 (0.045)	-0.015 (0.049)	-0.014 (0.049)	-0.014 (0.049)	-0.015 (0.049)
60+ minutes away from secondary school	-0.030 (0.045)	-0.029 (0.045)	-0.028 (0.045)	-0.029 (0.045)	0.019 (0.041)	0.020 (0.041)	0.020 (0.042)	0.019 (0.042)
Number of observations	2,418	2,418	2,418	2,418	2,314	2,314	2,314	2,314

Source: Survey of Household Living Standards 2003.

Note: Robust standard errors in parentheses.

For the youngest age group (8–11 years old), household income has at best a modest effect on labor force participation. Although the results for boys ages 8–11 living in rural areas suggest that child labor force participation decreases when household income decreases, one should be cautious in interpreting the measured negative effect because of possible reverse causality: income may have increased over the previous year because the child quit school to contribute to household farming activities.

In urban areas, higher household income reduces the chance that older children (ages 12–14) participate in the labor force (by 4.5 percent for boys and 5.3 percent for girls). These results are supportive of the hypothesis that Burkinabe households do not pull their adolescent children out of school to make them work to take advantage of good economic conditions.[6] The results support the notion that macroeconomic policy favoring growth would reduce child work in urban areas and ultimately help create a more educated labor force.

Child labor force participation is less sensitive to changes in income in households where the head is more educated while it is more sensitive in households in the bottom quintile of the income distribution. In fact, the effect is quite large for females: their labor force participation increases by 27.5 percentage points if the household income drops from one year to the next. So, whether 12- to 14-year-old girls attend school instead of working depends more on changes in the economic fortunes of the poorest households than it does for males.

Looking at the relationship between the self-reported indicators of whether general economic conditions improved over the previous year (table 8.8), much the same overall conclusions emerge, with the exception of the youngest age group in urban areas. As in table 8.7, the labor force participation of individuals ages 12–14 increases when urban households report being economically better off relative to the year before. In addition, the impact is more pronounced in households in which the head is less educated or is poor, especially for females. The evidence suggests that boys' labor force participation behavior responds more to shifts in households' economic conditions when the head is relatively less educated than is the case for females. But the labor force participation of young females is more responsive to changes in households located in the bottom quintile of the income distribution. The evidence for ages 8–11 in urban areas is similar to what is reported for the 12- to 14-year-olds living in urban areas: deterioration in household economic conditions is associated with an increase in child work.[7]

In rural areas, school proximity is a more important factor in determining labor force participation, at least for males. Distance to school increases the likelihood of participating in the labor force. This effect is not as significant in urban areas. For females, the results for the impact of school proximity are somewhat different. Although the results for females living in rural areas are very similar to the ones for males, they diverge from the results for males in urban areas: school proximity is a major determinant of labor force participation (see panel A [12- to 14-year-olds living in urban areas] of table 8.7). So, labor force participation clearly contains a gender-specific component in its relationship with the time it takes to reach the closest school.

Multivariate Analysis of Enrollment Decisions

To formally assess the role of various household, individual, and institutional characteristics in determining school enrollment, a series of probits by age group and gender are estimated (table 8.9). The education of the head of the household is significant across all categories, strongly suggesting that educational attainment is highly correlated across generations within households, a sign of low intergenerational mobility.

To check this conjecture in a slightly different way, a subsample of sons and fathers in 2003 was created and used to compute the correlation coefficient between their educational attainment for different age groups. The correlation is 0.42 for sons ages 20–29 and 0.53 for sons ages 30–39. In the United States, the correlation is about 0.30; the correlation is lower in European countries. Repeating the same exercise with the 1993 data yields lower correlation coefficients, about 0.30 for both age groups, suggesting that intergenerational mobility in educational attainment decreased in Burkina Faso between 1993 and 2003. Although this is rather impressionistic evidence, it should be cause for concern if it is indeed the case.

Controlling for the educational attainment of the household head, the position of the household in the income distribution does not appear to be a major driving force behind enrollment. While there is some evidence of an income gradient, the magnitude is modest relative to the head's education, and most of the coefficients are not statistically significant. The effect of being in the lowest income quintile becomes much more significant if the household experiences a decrease in income from one year to the next.

One key factor influencing (or at least associated with) school enrollment is the time it takes to get to school. Although similar variables have

Table 8.9. School Enrollment Probits for Burkina Faso, 1993–2003

	Males			Females		
Item	1993	1998	2003	1993	1998	2003
7- to 11-year-olds						
Household head's education: some primary	0.039	0.141	0.133	0.112	0.092	0.145
	(0.042)	(0.046)	(0.045)	(0.049)	(0.037)	(0.043)
Household head's education: primary completed	0.284	0.130	0.202	0.206	0.163	0.248
	(0.055)	(0.047)	(0.077)	(0.043)	(0.048)	(0.072)
Household head's education: some secondary	0.272	0.329	0.409	0.212	0.284	0.179
	(0.060)	(0.068)	(0.072)	(0.064)	(0.065)	(0.067)
Household head's education: secondary completed	0.500	0.375	0.275	0.176	0.586	0.366
	(0.076)	(0.136)	(0.217)	(0.160)	(0.152)	(0.178)
Household head's education: postsecondary	—	0.375	—	0.097	0.104	0.214
		(0.136)		(0.095)	(0.071)	(0.142)
Household head handicapped	0.055	-0.018	0.109	0.022	-0.004	-0.072
	(0.056)	(0.034)	(0.053)	(0.051)	(0.028)	(0.043)
30–59 minutes away from primary school	-0.089	-0.075	-0.017	-0.062	-0.055	-0.063
	(0.029)	(0.020)	(0.022)	(0.028)	(0.014)	(0.021)
60+ minutes away from primary school	-0.226	-0.205	-0.178	-0.177	-0.181	-0.101
	(0.048)	(0.022)	(0.029)	(0.027)	(0.017)	(0.025)
30–59 minutes away from secondary school	-0.023	-0.067	0.030	-0.056	-0.041	-0.044
	(0.033)	(0.028)	(0.035)	(0.021)	(0.019)	(0.023)
60+ minutes away from secondary school	-0.149	-0.144	0.007	-0.110	-0.128	-0.087
	(0.029)	(0.032)	(0.033)	(0.026)	(0.025)	(0.029)
Household size	-0.011	-0.003	-0.016	-0.013	-0.002	-0.018
	(0.002)	(0.001)	(0.002)	(0.002)	(0.001)	(0.002)
Household income in second quintile	0.008	-0.004	-0.006	-0.018	0.006	0.069
	(0.030)	(0.029)	(0.029)	(0.032)	(0.023)	(0.030)

Household income in third quintile	-0.022	0.050	0.054	0.005	0.072
	(0.030)	(0.028)	(0.029)	(0.036)	(0.030)
Household income in fourth quintile	0.038	0.040	0.040	0.038	0.109
	(0.033)	(0.028)	(0.030)	(0.036)	(0.032)
Household income in fifth quintile	0.022	0.048	0.039	0.097	0.111
	(0.032)	(0.033)	(0.038)	(0.038)	(0.037)
Pseudo R^2	0.347	0.348	0.349	0.406	0.413
Number of observations	5,254	5,095	3,733	4,803	3,676
12- to 14-year-olds					
Household head's education: some primary	0.120	0.066	0.148	0.046	0.074
	(0.104)	(0.058)	(0.065)	(0.057)	(0.049)
Household head's education: primary completed	0.053	0.146	0.162	0.105	0.170
	(0.066)	(0.070)	(0.106)	(0.049)	(0.088)
Household head's education: some secondary	0.290	0.344	0.246	0.114	0.200
	(0.092)	(0.083)	(0.091)	(0.048)	(0.072)
Household head's education: secondary completed	—	0.525	0.300	0.277	0.104
		(0.199)	(0.224)	(0.124)	(0.128)
Household head's education: postsecondary	—	0.583	0.598	0.065	0.026
		(0.113)	(0.156)	(0.082)	(0.080)
Household head handicapped	-0.053	-0.021	-0.012	-0.032	0.104
	(0.065)	(0.045)	(0.066)	(0.043)	(0.071)
30–59 minutes away from primary school	-0.017	0.038	-0.038	-0.026	-0.036
	(0.038)	(0.031)	(0.032)	(0.026)	(0.029)
60+ minutes away from primary school	-0.014	-0.019	-0.185	-0.026	-0.065
	(0.050)	(0.038)	(0.040)	(0.048)	(0.038)
30–59 minutes away from secondary school	-0.070	-0.074	-0.110	-0.049	-0.068
	(0.039)	(0.033)	(0.034)	(0.021)	(0.029)

(continued)

Table 8.9. School Enrollment Probits for Burkina Faso, 1993–2003 *(continued)*

Item	Males			Females		
	1993	1998	2003	1993	1998	2003
60+ minutes away from secondary school	-0.115	-0.177	-0.138	-0.090	-0.176	-0.013
	(0.038)	(0.037)	(0.041)	(0.025)	(0.033)	(0.033)
Household size	-0.011	-0.001	-0.009	-0.006	-0.002	-0.010
	(0.002)	(0.001)	(0.002)	(0.001)	(0.001)	(0.003)
Household income in second quintile	0.054	0.042	-0.012	-0.029	-0.039	0.007
	(0.042)	(0.036)	(0.041)	(0.028)	(0.026)	(0.034)
Household income in third quintile	0.001	0.070	0.045	-0.033	-0.004	0.042
	(0.041)	(0.040)	(0.043)	(0.026)	(0.027)	(0.039)
Household income in fourth quintile	0.042	0.025	0.032	0.036	-0.001	0.025
	(0.065)	(0.044)	(0.045)	(0.040)	(0.027)	(0.036)
Household income in fifth quintile	-0.003	0.001	0.064	0.018	-0.030	-0.029
	(0.042)	(0.042)	(0.047)	(0.032)	(0.028)	(0.038)
Pseudo R^2	0.345	0.350	0.390	0.400	0.403	0.421
Number of observations	2,489	2,539	2,023	2,454	2,330	1,879
15- to 18-year-olds						
Household head's education: some primary	0.034	0.021	0.027	0.036	0.050	0.002
	(0.022)	(0.035)	(0.035)	(0.022)	(0.042)	(0.016)
Household head's education: primary completed	0.019	0.083	0.057	0.043	0.107	0.081
	(0.029)	(0.033)	(0.040)	(0.021)	(0.037)	(0.038)
Household head's education: some secondary	0.097	0.217	0.074	0.103	0.114	0.033
	(0.038)	(0.046)	(0.035)	(0.036)	(0.034)	(0.036)
Household head's education: secondary completed	0.133	0.384	0.486	0.089	0.147	0.010
	(0.108)	(0.147)	(0.182)	(0.076)	(0.089)	(0.032)

	(1)	(2)	(3)	(4)	(5)	(6)
Household head's education: postsecondary	0.212	0.325	0.327	0.069	0.114	-0.007
	(0.110)	(0.099)	(0.126)	(0.039)	(0.054)	(0.016)
Household head handicapped	-0.003	-0.016	-0.041	0.003	-0.010	-0.018
	(0.039)	(0.026)	(0.029)	(0.015)	(0.017)	(0.034)
30–59 minutes away from primary school	0.052	0.036	-0.009	0.024	-0.004	-0.016
	(0.021)	(0.025)	(0.019)	(0.017)	(0.012)	(0.012)
60+ minutes away from primary school	-0.072	0.027	-0.080	0.035	-0.020	-0.024
	(0.019)	(0.027)	(0.018)	(0.045)	(0.018)	(0.017)
30–59 minutes away from secondary school	-0.072	-0.043	-0.023	-0.027	-0.018	-0.005
	(0.01)	(0.015)	(0.017)	(0.006)	(0.010)	(0.010)
60+ minutes away from secondary school	-0.172	-0.147	-0.076	-0.088	-0.077	-0.071
	(0.024)	(0.025)	(0.021)	(0.014)	(0.019)	(0.018)
Household size	-0.006	-0.002	-0.006	-0.002	-0.001	-0.003
	(0.001)	(0.001)	(0.002)	(0.001)	(0.001)	(0.001)
Household income in second quintile	-0.002	0.004	-0.051	0.002	-0.017	-0.011
	(0.027)	(0.024)	(0.031)	(0.019)	(0.015)	(0.020)
Household income in third quintile	0.039	0.008	0.080	0.031	-0.005	0.022
	(0.028)	(0.025)	(0.033)	(0.020)	(0.016)	(0.022)
Household income in fourth quintile	-0.012	0.021	0.068	0.033	-0.003	0.030
	(0.021)	(0.026)	(0.032)	(0.018)	(0.015)	(0.026)
Household income in fifth quintile	0.057	0.018	0.127	0.066	0.009	0.061
	(0.029)	(0.025)	(0.040)	(0.022)	(0.017)	(0.029)
Pseudo R^2	0.389	0.397	0.378	0.423	0.387	0.433
Number of observations	2,860	2,865	2,321	2,629	2,774	2,260

Source: Survey of Household Living Standards.

Note: Standard errors are in parentheses. All individuals for whom the head of household had the indicated level of education were enrolled in school, hence those observations were dropped. Other regressors include region of residence, whether the head of household is handicapped, the time it takes to reach the food market, and whether other siblings are also enrolled.

been used in the economics of education literature (Card 1995; Laszlo 2005), the variable is usually the distance from the home to the school. It is plausible that time matters more in developing countries, where the main modes of transportation to school are more varied.

In Burkina Faso, enrollment is associated with having a school nearby. Although one would expect that older individuals' decisions to enroll in secondary school would be primarily affected by the time it takes to get to a secondary school, the time to primary school is a significant determinant of enrollment for secondary school–age individuals. Similarly, the time it takes to reach a secondary school is negatively associated with the enrollment of primary school–age children. It seems unlikely that some households would not enroll their children in primary schools because secondary schools are far away, so these variables must be picking up many things other than just the time-to-school dimension. Note also that the time-to-school factor affects males slightly more than females.

Economic Returns to Education

The estimated annual return to one year of additional education in Burkina Faso is 11.5 percent (table 8.10).[8] This estimate is at the high end of the range of returns estimated in developed countries but in line with estimates for developing countries (Psacharopoulos and Patrinos 2002).

Inclusion of the head of household's educational attainment in the regression makes a substantial difference: the estimated return per category of schooling drops by more than 35 percent when the head of household's education is included in the regression. This strongly suggests that household and family background factors are important joint determinants of educational attainment.[9]

Having a literate household head has a very large effect on household income (not shown). Limiting the sample to households in which the head has some primary education yields an even larger effect of head literacy on household income, suggesting that the basic skills learned in school play an important role in the welfare of the household.

The relationship between schooling and earnings is roughly linear in urban areas. In contrast, in rural areas the return to education increases markedly for people with some secondary education.

Many unmeasured confounding factors could be driving the estimated positive relationship between schooling and household income. For example, it is likely that unmeasured household and institutional characteristics exhibit considerable heterogeneity across geographic areas and that this variation is systematically related to both schooling and

Table 8.10. Rate of Return to Schooling in Burkina Faso, 2003

Dependent variable: Log of total per capita household income in 2003

Variable	Ordinary least squares (1)	Ordinary least squares (2)	Census-zone fixed effects (3)	Census-zone fixed effects (4)
Average educational	0.350	0.211	0.285	0.175
attainment in household	(0.019)	(0.028)	(0.018)	(0.029)
Number of household	0.085	0.102	0.050	0.057
members enrolled in school	(0.045)	(0.044)	(0.041)	(0.041)
Educational attainment of	—	0.125	—	0.101
head of household		(0.019)		(0.021)
Fraction of females	−0.113	−0.143	−0.066	−0.089
in household	(0.065)	(0.065)	(0.063)	(0.063)
Household size	0.059	0.060	0.058	0.059
	(0.005)	(0.005)	(0.004)	(0.004)
Lives in rural area	−0.521	−0.528	—	—
	(0.071)	(0.007)		
Average age of	0.043	0.039	0.031	0.028
household members	(0.010)	(0.010)	(0.009)	(0.009)
Average age squared × 100	−0.060	−0.050	−0.042	−0.037
	(0.010)	(0.015)	(0.013)	(0.013)

Source: Survey of Household Living Standards 2003.

Note: — indicates that the variable is not included in the regression. Results are based on a sample of 7,125 individuals ages 10–60 not enrolled in school. Regional dummies are included in all specifications. Ordinary least squares standard errors are adjusted for the clustering at the census-zone level. Individual educational attainment is aggregated into six categories: none, partial primary, primary completed, partial secondary, secondary completed, and postsecondary.

household income. Although the regressions include dummy variables to control for region of residence, more refined regional variation—driven in part by ethnic differences—could have an impact on the results.

Columns 3 and 4 of table 8.10 show the results when unrestricted census-zone dummy variables are added to the model. These surveys are conducted in more than 400 such zones. With census-zone fixed effects, the estimated returns are obtained by exploiting only the variation in household income and schooling within census zones. The resulting decline is modest.

Controlling for unmeasured heterogeneity within census zones does not control for the joint endogeneity of educational attainment and household income. This problem stems from two main sources. The first has to do with unmeasured household ability, which could be positively correlated with both schooling and income. The second is associated with the marginal cost of acquiring extra education. Households with little taste for education and households with financial constraints are observationally the same, in that both are likely to have fairly high discount rates. Larger returns to education are needed to induce such households to send their children to school. This line of argument comes from Becker's classic schooling model, in which individuals face constraints and have preferences and abilities related to acquiring education. If the (individual-specific) marginal rate of return to education is decreasing and the (individual-specific) marginal cost of acquiring education is increasing, there should be a distribution of educational attainment in any given population as long as there is some heterogeneity on either the cost or the ability side.

To identify the true average marginal return to education, the measures of access to schooling (primary or secondary) are used as exclusion restrictions in a simultaneous equation system. To provide for an extra source of variation, the measures of access to secondary schooling are interacted with the educational attainment of the head of the household. The idea behind such an interaction is that one would expect the educational attainment decisions of poorer households to be more sensitive to the proximity of a primary or secondary school.

The results indicate that the instruments are very good predictors of household educational attainment (table 8.11). The estimated instrumental variable returns are at least as large as the ordinary least squares estimates and substantially larger than the fixed-effects estimates, suggesting that if ability is biasing the ordinary least squares estimates upward, other, empirically more important factors are biasing them downward. These other factors could be measurement error or constraints on access to school. One can think of the instrumental variable results as representing the marginal return to schooling for those whose levels of educational attainment were affected by the instruments (Imbens and Angrist 1994).[10]

To see whether the cross-sectional heterogeneity in returns to education is at least partly attributable to geographical differences, the longitudinal structure (along census regions lines) of the data is exploited to estimate fixed-effects instrumental variable models (table 8.12). Whether one allows for the time-to-school measures to have a direct effect on household income does not make any substantial difference, in large part because those main effects are both modest and not statistically significant. The evidence suggests that much of the heterogeneity across households in the returns to education that could have been the source of the test rejecting the same overidentifying restrictions in table 8.11 were driven

Table 8.11. Instrumental Variables Estimates of Rate of Return to Schooling

Dependent variable: Log of household total income per head in 2003

Variables	Model [1] First-stage	Model [1] IV-estimate	Model [2] First-stage	Model [2] IV-estimate	Model [3] First-stage	Model [3] IV-estimate
Household average educational attainment		0.369		0.385		1.497
		(0.030)		(0.028)		(0.624)
Number of household members enrolled in school	0.292	0.080	0.292	0.104	0.256	-0.185
	(0.020)	(0.045)	(0.020)	(0.047)	(0.017)	(0.171)
Head of household's educational attainment	—	—	—	—	0.642	-0.642
					(0.011)	(0.367)
Fraction of females in household	-0.284	-0.115	-0.284	-0.109	-0.286	-0.209
	(0.032)	(0.070)	(0.032)	(0.070)	(0.026)	(0.193)
Household size	-0.009	0.045	-0.009	0.045	-0.005	0.051
	(0.002)	(0.006)	(0.002)	(0.005)	(0.002)	(0.006)
Lives in rural area	-0.389	-0.600	-0.389	-0.613	-0.295	-0.274
	(0.020)	(0.071)	(0.020)	(0.080)	(0.017)	(0.199)
Time to primary school	0.014	—	0.014	0.171	-0.032	0.201
	(0.011)		(0.011)	(0.046)	(0.009)	(0.051)
Time to secondary school	-0.263	—	-0.263	-0.043	-0.063	0.049
	(0.011)		(0.011)	(0.040)	(0.010)	(0.068)
Head's education × time to second. school	0.322	—	0.322	—	-0.036	—
	(0.004)		(0.004)		(0.007)	
First-stage F	2430.9		6731.9		28.24	
Overidentification test statistic [P-Value]		12.597 0.002		Just identified		Just identified
Number of observations: 7,125						

Source: Survey of Household Living Standards.
Note: Standard errors are in parentheses.

Table 8.12. Panel Data IV Estimates

Dependent variable: Log of household total income per head in 2003

Variables	Model [1] First-stage	Model [1] IV-estimate	Model [2] First-stage	Model [2] IV-estimate	Model [3] First-stage	Model [3] IV-estimate
Household average educ. attainment	—	0.354 (0.027)	—	0.350 (0.027)	0.598 (0.012)	0.793 (0.603)
Head of household's educ. attainment	—	—	—	—	—	-0.241 (0.336)
Time to primary school	0.001 (0.014)	—	0.001 (0.014)	0.019 (0.029)	-0.024 (0.012)	0.009 (0.032)
Time to secondary school	-0.232 (0.016)	—	-0.232 (0.016)	-0.030 (0.031)	-0.020 (0.014)	0.013 (0.040)
Head's educ. × time to second. school	0.296 (0.004)	—	0.296 (0.004)	—	-0.029 (0.007)	—
First-stage F	1437.29		4286.15		14.95	
Overidentification test statistic [P-Value]		2.191 0.334		Just identified		Just identified
Number of observations: 7,125						

Source: Survey of Household Living Standards.
Note: Standard errors are in parentheses.

by variation across census regions.[11] This cross-region variation is absorbed with the fixed effects and the models in table 8.12 use only the within-census-region variation to estimate the return to education.

Finally, the returns estimated with model 3 in table 8.12 are suspiciously large, although they are smaller than in table 8.11. Again, the direct effect of the head of household's education, controlling for the predicted schooling, is negative. This does not appear realistic. As explained above, the likely problem is that there is simply insufficient variation in the head's educational attainment variable, with such a large fraction having no schooling at all.

The analysis of the economic returns to education suggests that the returns to education are large, and there is no indication that the simple cross-sectional estimates overstate the true effect of education on household income. One possible explanation for the result is that rural households with more education use better farming technology (for an analysis along these lines, see Laszlo [2005] for Peru and Jolliffe [2002] for Ghana).

Notes

1. The school enrollment question is distinct from the one on the main activity during the survey week. This allows the construction of a school and work indicator, a combination that is not one of the choices among the main activities.

2. Because of the small number of girls going beyond primary schooling, conclusions for females with more education are based on very imprecise estimates, especially for older age groups.

3. For the underlying data, see Parent (2006). The approach used in the background paper relies on the assumption that the group of individuals under study is statistically the same in 1993, 1998, and 2003. That is, even though the samples are made up of different individuals, the assumption is that individuals in all three surveys are drawn from the same underlying population, so that 25- to 29-year-olds in 2003 are on average the same as the 15- to 19-year-olds in 1993. The main threat to the validity of this assumption is emigration. Even migration within the country poses problems if occupation and industry structures differ significantly across regions.

4. Educated people's sectors of activity are also much more diversified than are those for uneducated workers, who are virtually all employed in primary industries (agriculture, fishing, and hunting).

5. The less-than-ideal quality of this measure would be expected to bias toward zero whatever impact there might be, thus likely providing a lower bound estimate of the true impact.

6. The theoretical impact of increased income on child work is a priori ambiguous, as Edmonds and Pavcnik (2005) note. On the one hand, favorable labor market conditions raise the pure price effect of sending one's child to school, making labor force participation procyclical. On the other hand, the wealth effect of economic growth may allow households to consume more education.

7. It is interesting to speculate as to why we can detect it with the self-reported indicator of changes in the overall household economic conditions but not with the constructed income change measure. One possibility is that the bias-inducing mechanical relationship between child work and household income by which income should increase if children are asked to leave school to contribute is less of a factor with the reported change in overall economic conditions. It could be, for example, that even if income increased somewhat, households might still report that they were better off the year before if increases in living costs outstripped the increase in income.

8. This estimate is based on the assumption that partial primary education corresponds to 3 years of education, primary completed to 6 years, partial secondary to 9 years, secondary completed to 12 years, and postsecondary to 14 years.

9. The same regressions run on the subsample of individuals living in rural areas (not shown) produced similar, albeit slightly weaker, results. The estimated returns were higher for people living in urban areas.

10. Even with this type of underlying mechanism in mind, the very large return estimated in model 3 in table 8.11, in which the household head's education has a direct effect on income, appears unrealistically high. One likely reason is that the variation in the education of heads of households is relatively small. Model 3 attempts to use the variation in the household head's education interacted with the time it takes to reach a secondary school to predict average household education at the same time it is used to predict income conditional on predicted education. This is asking quite a lot from that variable, and in fact the household head's education has a large and negative effect on income (conditional on predicted education), which does not make much sense.

11. Excluding the time-to-school variables along with the interaction of the time it takes to get to a secondary school with the educational attainment of the head allows testing of the overidentification restrictions. Contrary to the analogous model in table 8.11, the overidentifying restrictions easily pass the test.

References

Card, David. 1995. "Using Geographic Variation in College Proximity to Estimate the Return to Schooling." In *Aspects of Labor Market Behaviour: Essays in Honour of John Vanderkamp*, ed. L. N. Christofides, E. K. Grant, and R. Swidinsky. Toronto: University of Toronto Press.

Edmonds, Eric, and Nina Pavcnik. 2005. "Child Labor in the Global Economy." *Journal of Economic Perspectives* 19 (1): 199–220.

Imbens, Guido W., and Joshua D. Angrist. 1994. "Identification and Estimation of Local Average Treatment Effects." *Econometrica* 62 (2): 467–75.

Jolliffe, Dean. 2002. "Whose Education Matters in the Determination of Household Income? Evidence from a Developing Country." *Economic Development and Cultural Change* 50 (2): 287–312.

Laszlo, Sonia. 2005. "Self-Employment Earnings and Returns to Education in Rural Peru." *Journal of Development Studies* 41 (7): 1247–87.

Parent, Daniel. 2006. "Youth Labor Market in Burkina Faso: Recent Trends." Social Protection Discussion Paper No. 0607, World Bank, Washington, DC.

Psacharopoulos, George, and Harry Anthony Patrinos. 2002. "Returns to Investment in Education: A Further Update." Policy Research Working Paper No. WPS2881, World Bank, Washington, DC.

CHAPTER 9

Child Labor and Youth Employment in Ethiopia

Lorenzo Guarcello, Scott Lyon, and Furio Rosati

Youth unemployment and underemployment represent growing concerns worldwide. In 2002, some 88 million young people (those ages 15–24) were unemployed, representing about 41 percent of the world's unemployed, according to the International Labour Organization (ILO 2004). Young workers everywhere have much higher rates of joblessness and much lower earnings than older workers. In many countries young people are also concentrated in low-skill informal work or in hazardous forms of work that are ill-suited to their age and experience. Employment outcomes are typically worst for former child laborers and other early school leavers, groups with the least opportunity to accumulate the human capital needed for gainful employment.[1]

The challenge of youth employment is especially great in Sub-Saharan Africa, where people ages 15–24 account for 36 percent of the working-age population. The number of young people looking for work is expected to increase by 28 percent—an additional 30 million people—over the next 15 years. Failure to address youth employment issues will have ominous consequences for the economy and society. Without opportunities for young people to earn a living, intergenerational cycles of poverty will persist, exacerbating problems in societies already made vulnerable by HIV/AIDS, food insecurity, and violence.

The problem of youth unemployment is particularly acute in Ethiopia, home to one of the largest youth populations in Sub-Saharan Africa. The lack of employment opportunities for young people is among the critical development challenges facing Ethiopia and a key barrier to national efforts toward meeting the Millennium Development Goals. Only about 40 percent of Ethiopian children complete primary education, and just 13 percent are enrolled in secondary education, meaning that most young people enter the labor market with low levels of human capital (see chapter 7 of this volume).

The specific factors affecting youth employment in Ethiopia have received little research attention. There is, therefore, limited empirical basis for formulating policies and programs promoting youth employment and successful school-to-work transitions in Ethiopia. This chapter aims to begin to fill this gap, by analyzing a set of youth employment indicators drawn primarily from the 2001 Ethiopia Labour Force Survey. The chapter looks at the labor market outcomes of young people and key factors influencing these outcomes, including early labor market entry and human capital accumulation. It also examines the process of labor market entry and the duration of the transition from school to work.

National Context

This section describes the main features of Ethiopia as background for understanding both child labor and youth employment in the country.

Macroeconomic Trends

Ethiopia has witnessed high but erratic output growth since the end of the civil war in 1991. Growth has averaged about 6 percent a year, one of the most rapid rates in Africa. Year-to-year fluctuations in economic performance, however, have been large (table 9.1). Annual growth ranged from 1 percent to 10 percent between 1991–92 and 1997–98 (Easterly 2002, as cited in World Bank 2005).

Despite the government's commitment to agriculture-led development, the main sources of growth have been nonagricultural, led by the service and industrial sectors. Annual growth in the agriculture sector averaged about 3.6 percent a year between 1992 and 1996, and then decreased to 2.3 percent a year between 1997 and 2000, while services grew about 9 percent a year. Though much smaller, industry contributed as much to growth as agriculture between 1992 and 2000 (Easterly 2002, as cited in World Bank 2005).

Table 9.1. Macroeconomic Indicators for Ethiopia, 1982–2001

Sector or indicator	1982–86	1987–91	1992–96	1997–2001
Average annual percentage change				
Real GDP	−0.4	3.9	4.6	4.7
Real GDP per capita	−3.0	0.9	1.8	2.0
Agriculture	−1.5	5.5	3.6	2.3
Industry	6.2	−5.3	8.4	6.1
Percentage of GDP				
Gross domestic investment	13.5	13.8	14.4	16.3
Gross domestic savings	5.7	7.1	5.8	3.1

Source: Data on agriculture and industry are from ECA (2002) and MEDaC (1999, 2000). All other data are from World Bank (2002), as cited in Denu, Tekeste, and van der Deijl (2005).

Levels of poverty are very high in Ethiopia, with annual per capita income in 2003 standing at just US$102 (about US$800 in purchasing power parity; MOFED [2002], as cited in Denu, Tekeste, and van der Deijl [2005]). In 1999, about 44 percent of the population lived below the poverty line ($1.50 in 1993 purchasing power parity; *World Development Indicators* 2000 data, as cited in Getachew and Kallaur [2005]). World Bank poverty assessments point to a rise in urban poverty over the past decade and to only a marginal decline in rural poverty (MOFED [2002], as cited in Getachew and Kallaur [2005]).

Demographic Trends
Ethiopia has undergone rapid population growth in recent decades. The population was estimated at 73 million people in 2005, making Ethiopia the second most populous country in Sub-Saharan Africa after Nigeria. Ethiopia's population is heavily concentrated in the young age cohorts, with more than half the population under age 25. People 65 and older represent just 3 percent of the total population, a reflection of Ethiopia's life expectancy of just 44 years (UN population data for 2001, as cited in Getachew and Kallaur [2005]).

The proportion of people ages 15–24 increased over the past two decades, rising from 14 percent of the population in 1984 to about 20 percent in 2005. The youth population is projected to grow in absolute terms, from about 15 million in 2005 to 26 million in 2030, but it will remain at about one-fifth of the population (Central Statistical Authority, as cited in Getachew and Kallaur [2005]).

Labor Market Characteristics
Rapid population growth during recent decades has resulted in a large increase in the labor force (figure 9.1). The national labor force included

Figure 9.1. Ethiopia's Labor Force Tripled between 1960 and 2002

Source: Central Statistical Authority (various years), as cited in Denu, Tekeste, and van der Deijl (2005).

an estimated 32.2 million people in 2005, up from 12.9 million people in 1984. The labor force is projected to double again over the next 25 years, placing a huge strain on the labor market even under the most optimistic growth scenario.

More than 80 percent of the labor force is employed in subsistence agriculture, with little difference in labor force composition between young people and adults. Most people with jobs cannot read or write and work in the informal sector as casual workers (Central Statistical Authority, as cited in Denu, Tekeste, and van der Deijl [2005]).

The activity rate of the working-age population was 72 percent in 1999, one of the highest in the world. Underemployment is prevalent, however, because economic necessity dictates that individuals secure some form of work when no full-time jobs are available. Informal sector work is therefore important, with the sector employing some 4.8 million people in 1999 (Denu, Tekeste, and van der Deijl 2005). Open unemployment is confined largely to the middle class, with people awaiting positions in the public sector accounting for a significant share (Woldehanna, Guta, and Ferede 2005).

Education Trends

Educational attainment in Ethiopia is very low: in 2004 the average male adult had completed 1.8 grades, the average female had completed just 0.9 grades, and only 5 percent of the population had some secondary or higher education (Getachew and Kallaur 2005).

Figure 9.2. Gross Primary School Enrollment in Ethiopia More Than Doubled between 1995 and 2003

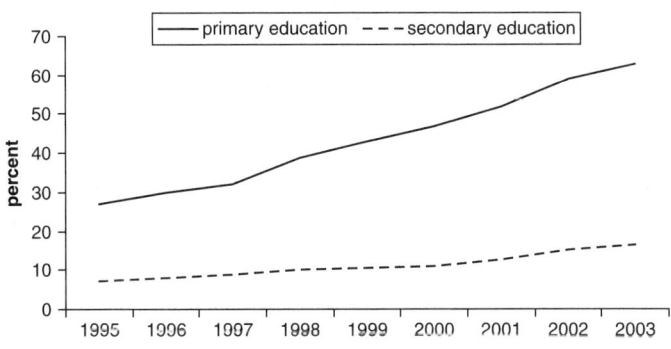

Source: Ministry of Education 2003.

A major government effort in recent years has led to significant progress in expanding access to education (figure 9.2). Between 1995 and 2003 the primary gross enrollment ratio more than doubled (from 26 percent to 64 percent) and secondary gross enrollment almost tripled (from 7 percent to 19 percent). Primary school enrollment rose from 2.64 million students in 1994 to 8.74 million students in 2003, while enrollment in secondary school increased from about 357,000 students in 1994 to more than 586,000 in 2003 (Ministry of Education 1999, 2003).

Despite such improvement, universal primary enrollment remains a distant target, especially in rural areas, where primary enrollment is less than half that in cities and towns. Disparities between girls and boys are also significant. The primary gross enrollment ratio was 75 percent and the secondary gross enrollment ratio 24 percent for boys in 2003, while the corresponding figures for females were 54 percent and 14 percent. Rural girls are particularly disadvantaged with regard to education opportunities (Ministry of Education 2003).

Child Labor

In Ethiopia, as in several other Sub-Saharan Africa countries, a large proportion of the labor force enters the labor market before age 15, with little or no formal education. For better or worse, children's work represents an important avenue of access to the labor market. An analysis of youth in the labor market would therefore not be complete without considering early labor market entry and the consequences of early entry for labor market outcomes.

Child Involvement in Economic Activity

Ethiopia has one of the highest rates of child labor in the world. Half of all 5- to 14-year-olds—more than 7.5 million children—were involved in economic activity in 2001.[2] Child labor is closely related to youth labor market outcomes because early experiences in the labor market can significantly influence lifetime patterns of employment, earnings, and unemployment. With low levels of human capital, former child laborers are at a particular disadvantage in finding and maintaining a place in the adult labor force.

Child economic activity rises sharply with age (figure 9.3), but 40 percent of even the youngest children (those ages 5–9) are involved in economic activity. Rural children and boys face the greatest risk of involvement in child labor: 54 percent of rural children ages 5–14 are involved in economic activity, compared with only 15 percent of their urban counterparts (table 9.2). The economic activity rate of boys exceeds that of girls by 20 percentage points, although this difference does not take into account the performance of household chores, such as water and fuelwood collection, which are typically the domain of girls.

Household demand for labor has been identified as the most important reason for not sending children to school in Ethiopia (Yamano 2000). Indeed, children's productivity often constitutes a vital component of household survival strategies. Although the marginal productivity of a child worker is about one-third to one-half that of a working adult man (Cockburn 2002), each working child contributes 4–7 percent of a household's income in rural areas (and the contribution can reach as high as 50 percent).

Figure 9.3. Rural Residents and Boys in Ethiopia Are More Likely to Work as Children Than Urban Residents and Girls

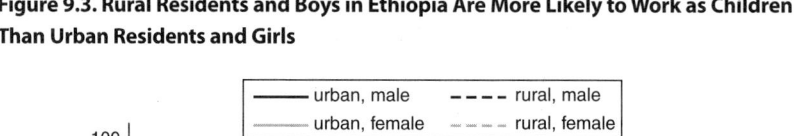
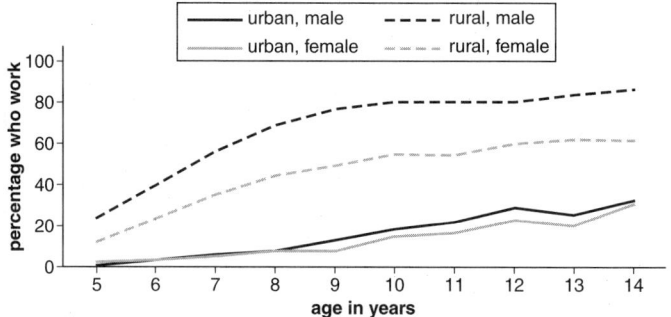

Source: Understanding Children's Work calculations based on Ethiopia Labour Force Survey 2001.

Table 9.2. Work and School Activity of Ethiopian Children, by Age, Gender, and Urban-Rural Location

Age group	Gender and location	Only in work (1)	Only in school (2)	Combining work and school (3)	Neither in school nor working (4)	In work (1) + (3)	In school (2) + (3)
5–9	Male	36.2	15.0	12.4	36.4	48.6	27.4
	Female	24.3	16.8	5.7	53.3	30.0	22.5
	Urban	2.0	67.4	3.1	27.5	5.1	70.5
	Rural	33.4	10.2	9.7	46.6	43.1	19.9
	Total	30.3	15.9	9.1	44.7	39.4	25.0
10–14	Male	37.6	22.0	36.2	4.2	73.8	58.2
	Female	34.8	29.1	17.5	18.5	52.4	46.7
	Urban	5.7	72.9	17.2	4.2	22.9	90.1
	Rural	41.5	17.3	28.8	12.4	70.4	46 1
	Total	36.3	25.5	27.1	11.1	63.4	52.6
5–14	Male	36.8	18.1	22.7	22.4	59.5	40.8
	Female	28.8	22.0	10.8	38.5	39.5	32.8
	Urban	3.9	70.3	10.6	15.2	14.5	80.9
	Rural	36.8	13.2	17.7	32.3	54.5	30.9
	Total	32.9	20.0	16.8	30.3	49.7	36.8

Source: Understanding Children's Work calculations based on Ethiopia Labour Force Survey 2001.

Very high levels of child labor translate into very low levels of school enrollment. Only 28 percent of 6- to 9-year-olds, and a little more than half of 10- to 14-year-olds, are enrolled in school. Nonentrance and late entrance in school are both important concerns; 63 percent of children ages 10–14 have no formal schooling, and many more from this age group enter school after the official starting age of six. Those managing to enroll in school, however, tend to remain well into their teens. Indeed, children entering school do not leave, on average, until after their 19th birthdays.

Low enrollment is primarily a rural problem: enrollment for 6- to 14-year-olds in urban areas exceeds 80 percent, but only 30 percent of rural children 6–14 are enrolled in school. Some 71 percent of rural 10- to 14-year-olds have never entered school, compared with only 17 percent of their urban counterparts. Girls are disadvantaged compared with boys, with rural girls least likely to benefit from schooling opportunities.

What Kinds of Work Do Children Perform?

The agriculture sector absorbs 80 percent of children involved in economic activity. Just 12 percent work in services and 4 percent in manufacturing. More than 90 percent of working children work for their families without wages; just 2 percent work outside the family for wages.

The composition of children's work changes somewhat as they age and are able to take on more complex tasks. Older children are slightly less likely to work in agriculture and more likely to work in manufacturing and services. They are also slightly more likely to take on wage work and self-employment outside the family unit.

The composition of children's work in urban and rural areas differs significantly, a reflection of underlying differences in rural and urban labor markets. Virtually all rural child workers work in family-based agriculture. In contrast, in urban areas the service sector is the most important source of child work, accounting for 42 percent of urban child workers; agriculture ranks second, accounting for 30 percent of urban child workers. Construction (including mining and quarrying; and electricity, gas, and water) and manufacturing are also important in urban areas, with 17 percent of urban children working in construction and 11 percent working in manufacturing. More than a third of child laborers work outside the family in urban areas, compared with only 4 percent of their rural counterparts.

Labor Market Status of Young People in Ethiopia

This section describes the labor situation of young people in Ethiopia.

Time Use

Most Ethiopians between the ages of 15 and 24 are working. Almost three-fourths of them are employed, while less than one-fifth are involved in some form of education or training. Another 5 percent are actively seeking work but unable to find it.[3] Some 13 percent of young people are "inactive," that is, neither in the labor force nor in education, a category that also includes discouraged workers and disabled people.[4]

These aggregates mask large variations in time use by age. This is not surprising because the 15–24 age range is a period of transition from adolescence to adulthood and from education to working life. Relatively few Ethiopians remain in school past their teens. Young adults (ages 20–24) are more likely than teenagers (ages 15–19) to be in the labor force (both employed and unemployed), although the labor force participation rate of teenagers is also very high (more than 70 percent).[5] Young adults are more likely than teenagers to be inactive, owing in part to the fact that young adulthood coincides with the beginning of childbearing for most Ethiopian women.

The time-use profiles of young Ethiopians are also strongly affected by underlying differences in the rural and urban labor markets. Compared with rural youth, urban youth stay in school longer and join the labor force later. Involvement in education is more than three times higher for urban youth than for rural youth, while the employment rate of rural youth is almost twice that of their urban counterparts. Measured unemployment is much higher among urban youth, while underemployment may be more of a problem among rural youth.

Unemployment

Unemployment is the most important measure of the labor market difficulties of young people. Prolonged unemployment early in life may permanently impair a person's productive potential (and therefore employment opportunities), leading to serious social adjustment difficulties. In Sub-Saharan Africa, whether a young person has a job can often determine on which side of the poverty line his or her household lays.[6]

Levels of measured unemployment are relatively low among young people in Ethiopia: almost 5 percent of all 15- to 24-year-olds and over 6 percent of those in the labor force are unemployed (see table 9.3). Levels of joblessness (the sum of unemployed and inactive), arguably

Table 9.3. Youth Unemployment, Inactivity, and Joblessness Indicators in Ethiopia, by Age Group, Gender, and Urban–Rural Location

Item	Unemployment ratio[a] (percent)	Unemployment rate[b] (percent)	Inactivity[c] (percent)	Joblessness[d] (percent)
Age range				
10–14	1.2	1.9	9.9	11.2
15–17	2.2	3.1	8.5	10.7
18–19	5.8	7.8	14.0	19.8
20 24	6.0	7.4	15.1	21.0
15–24	4.9	6.4	13.0	17.8
Gender				
Male	3.4	4.0	3.2	6.7
Female	6.1	8.9	21.5	27.6
Location				
Urban	9.7	18.6	11.7	21.4
Rural	3.7	4.6	13.2	17.0

Source: Understanding Children's Work calculations based on Ethiopia Labour Force Survey 2001.
a. Unemployment ratio refers to total unemployed expressed as a proportion of total population in same age range.
b. Unemployment rate refers to total unemployed as a proportion of total work force in the same age range.
c. Inactivity rate refers to people who neither attend school nor work nor are classified as unemployed, as a proportion of total population in same age range.
d. Joblessness refers to total number of jobless people as a proportion of total population in same age range.

a better measure of youth employment disadvantage because it also captures discouraged workers, are higher.[7] Some 18 percent of all 15- to 24-year-olds and 28 percent of 15- to 24-year-old females are jobless. Unemployment and joblessness are lower for the 10–17 age group, perhaps indicating that youth who enter the labor market with higher levels of human capital face more difficulties finding employment. These levels place Ethiopia in the middle range of countries in Sub-Saharan Africa (figure 9.4).

Young people in urban Ethiopia are much more likely to be unemployed than their rural counterparts, underscoring the different nature of the urban and rural economies, in particular the important role that the agriculture sector plays in absorbing young rural workers. High public sector wages are a possible cause of unemployment among urban young people. Differences in urban unemployment levels begin to emerge at age 17 and peak at age 23, when 20 percent of urban youth are unable to find work, compared with 3 percent of their rural counterparts (figure 9.5). For the 15–24 age group as a whole, urban residents are three times as likely as rural residents to be unemployed.

While measured youth unemployment appears to be primarily an urban phenomenon, data on hours worked suggest that youth underemployment may be more prevalent in rural areas.[8] Urban workers work more hours per week than rural workers for all age cohorts beyond age 15 (though seasonality may explain some of the difference; figure 9.6).[9]

Figure 9.4. The Unemployment Ratio and Rate of Joblessness among 15-to 24-Year-Olds in Ethiopia Are About Average for Sub-Saharan Africa

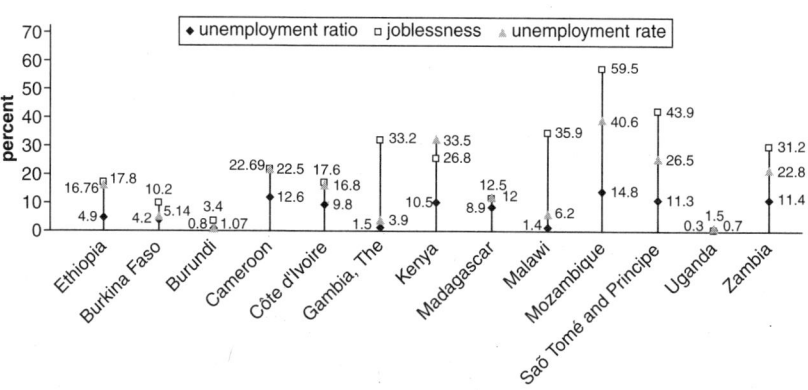

Source: Understanding Children's Work calculations based on World Bank Standard Files and Standard Indicators (SFSI) Database.

Figure 9.5. Youth Unemployment Ratios in Ethiopia Are Much Higher in Urban Than in Rural Areas

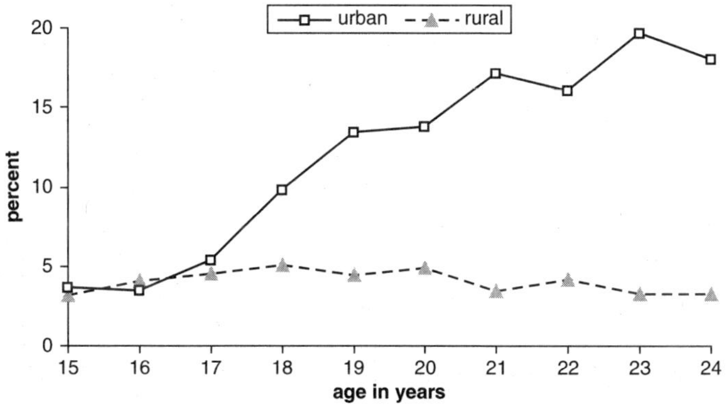

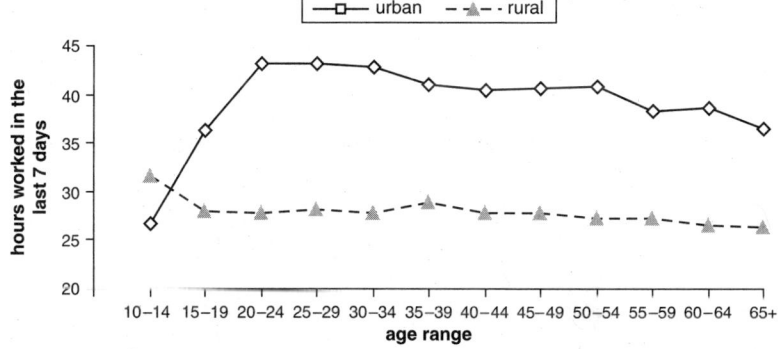

Source: Understanding Children's Work calculations based on Ethiopia Labour Force Survey 2001.

Figure 9.6. Urban Workers in Ethiopia Work Many More Hours per Week Than Rural Workers

Source: Understanding Children's Work calculations based on Ethiopia Labour Force Survey 2001.

The correlation between age and employment appears to depend on location. In cities and towns the risk of unemployment rises sharply as youth grow older, while in rural areas unemployment varies little by age.

Unemployment indicators differ by gender. Across all ages, female youth are more likely to be unemployed and much more likely to be jobless than male youth (table 9.3). Females are also significantly overrepresented among inactive young people, a category that includes people performing household chores and other forms of noneconomic work typically assigned to females.[10]

The 2001 Ethiopia Labour Force Survey does not provide data on the duration of unemployment. Evidence from the 2003 Urban Biannual Employment Unemployment Survey (CSA 2003) suggests that much of urban youth unemployment is structural rather than transitory. About one-third of unemployed teenagers and almost half of unemployed young adults had been without a job for at least a year at the time of the 2003 survey (figure 9.7). Even more worrisome is that the share of youth with very long spells of unemployment (more than two years) increases with age.

Unemployment and jobless rates do not fully capture youth difficulties in the labor market. In fact, in countries such as Ethiopia, where poverty is widespread, the unemployment rate may be misleading because many youth are simply too poor to be unemployed and must take up work regardless of its quality, decency, or level of remuneration. Obtaining employment itself is therefore an insufficient condition for successful entry into the labor market; indicators reflecting the conditions of the employed are also critical to assessing the labor market success of young people.

Nonwage labor performed within the household is by far the most important form of youth work: more than two of every three employed young people work without monetary wages for their families (table 9.4).

Figure 9.7. The Duration of Urban Unemployment in Ethiopia Is a Cause for Concern

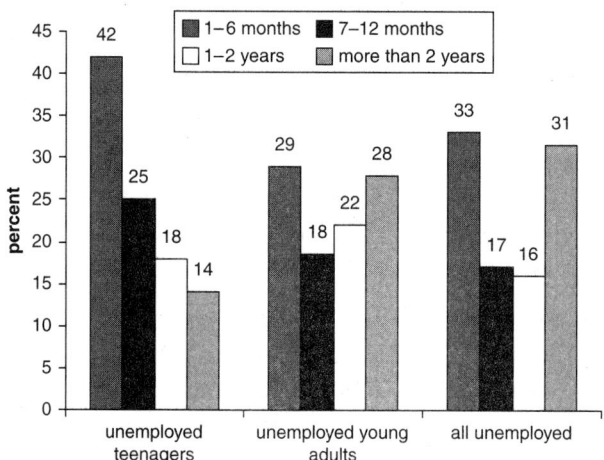

Source: 2003 Urban Biannual Employment Unemployment Survey, as cited in Denu, Tekeste, and van der Deijl (2005).

Table 9.4. Work Modality, Sector of Employment, and Average Weekly Hours of Employed Ethiopian Youth

Age group	Sex and residence	Work modality[a]					Sector[b]				Average weekly working hours
		Domestic employee	Wage employee	Self-employed	Unpaid family worker	Other employment	Agriculture	Manufacturing	Services[c]	Other[d]	
5–14	Male	0.3	3.2	1.4	94.8	0.3	96.8	0.4	2.3	0.5	36.1
	Female	1.0	0.9	2.4	95.2	0.6	89.6	2.6	5.7	2.1	29.4
	Urban	9.6	5.3	14.5	63.9	6.6	30.2	10.5	42.3	17.0	26.7
	Rural	0.3	2.2	1.3	96.0	0.2	96.2	0.9	2.3	0.6	33.8
15–19	Male	0.7	8.7	8.6	81.0	0.9	89.9	1.7	6.6	1.7	31.6
	Female	4.6	3.8	12.5	78.2	0.9	72.4	6.6	15.7	5.4	25.0
	Urban	17.8	15.8	26.9	34.7	4.7	15.4	15.4	46.4	22.7	36.0
	Rural	0.7	5.4	8.4	85.0	0.5	89.8	2.6	6.5	1.1	27.8
	Total	2.5	6.5	10.3	79.8	0.9	82.0	3.9	10.7	3.4	28.6
20–24	Male	0.5	11.7	38.9	48.4	0.4	86.5	2.2	9.0	2.3	32.6
	Female	2.7	6.3	23.6	67.0	0.4	74.1	5.6	16.8	3.5	25.8
	Urban	11.4	35.2	35.8	16.0	1.6	8.9	16.8	56.8	17.5	27.6
	Rural	0.3	5.7	31.0	62.8	0.2	90.3	2.1	6.8	0.9	43.0
	Total	1.6	9.2	31.6	57.3	0.4	80.6	3.8	12.7	2.9	29.3
15–24	Male	0.6	10.1	22.7	65.9	0.7	88.3	1.9	7.7	2.0	32.0
	Female	3.7	5.0	17.9	72.7	0.6	73.3	6.1	16.2	4.4	25.4
	Urban	14.6	25.7	31.4	25.1	3.1	12.0	16.1	51.8	20.1	39.5
	Rural	0.5	5.5	19.1	74.5	0.3	90.0	2.3	6.7	1.0	27.7
	Total	2.1	7.8	20.5	69.1	0.7	81.4	3.8	11.7	3.1	29.0

Source: Understanding Children's Work calculations based on Ethiopia Labour Force Survey 2001.

a. Percentage distribution of employed population in each age group.

b. Percentage distribution of employed population in each age group. Sector breakdown based on ISIC Revision 3 if information is available.

c. Services include wholesale and retail trade, hotels and restaurants, transport, financial intermediation, real estate, public administration, education, health and social work, other community services, and private household services.

d. Other includes mining and quarrying; electricity, gas, and water; construction; and extraterritorial organization.

Of the remaining working youth, 21 percent are self-employed[11]; just 8 percent work for wages.[12] Hence, most youth seem to be engaged in nonpaying (or low-paying) activities. These aggregates mask large differences between the rural and urban youth labor markets. Unpaid family work is preponderate in rural areas, while domestic employment, wage employment, self-employment, and unpaid family work prevail in urban areas. The agricultural sector absorbs most of Ethiopia's labor force, including workers ages 15–24. About 81 percent of employed youth are engaged in agriculture, followed by 12 percent in services and 4 percent in manufacturing. Differences by location are large (table 9.4). While agriculture predominates in rural areas, the services sector is the most important source of youth employment in cities and towns, accounting for half of all employed youth. The construction and manufacturing sectors are also important in urban areas, accounting for 20 percent and 16 percent, respectively, of total employed youth. The modality and composition of employment vary somewhat by the age and gender of the worker. With age, there is a shift away from family-based nonwage work toward wage work and self-employment outside the family. Nonwage family work nonetheless still accounts for more than half of total employment for the 20–24 age group. The sectoral composition of work changes little moving across the 15–24 age spectrum. There appears to be a significant degree of employment specialization by gender. Compared with male youth, female youth are less likely to be in wage work and more likely to be in unpaid family work; they are less concentrated in the agricultural sector and more concentrated in the services and manufacturing sectors.

What do these breakdowns by employment modality and composition say about employment quality? The generally low level of wage employment is significant, given that wage employment is typically the most sought after form of work among young people and is most likely to offer a measure of job stability and provide some form of benefits. Informal farm work, by contrast, is typically low paid and seasonal, and it does not constitute a reliable route out of poverty. In urban areas, informal work frequently means insecure, nonfamily work in settings where labor and safety regulations do not apply, leaving workers susceptible to work place exploitation. According to the 2003 Urban Biannual Employment Unemployment Survey, more than half of employed urban youth are in the informal sector.[13]

Labor Market Disadvantage

Comparing youth and adult unemployment rates provides some indication of the extent to which young workers are disadvantaged relative to adults in securing jobs. Youth are more likely than adults to be unemployed, but unemployment (expressed as a percentage of either the population or the labor force) is relatively low for both groups (figure 9.8). The difference between youth and adult unemployment levels is not large in comparison with other countries in Sub-Saharan Africa (table 9.5).

The picture changes somewhat when rural and urban labor markets are examined separately (figure 9.9). Rural youth appear to encounter little difficulty in securing employment; rural unemployment is very low and varies little across the 15–55 age spectrum. This is not the case for youth living in cities and towns. The urban unemployment ratio peaks among 20- to 24-year-olds but remains very high among the next population cohort

Figure 9.8. Youth Have Weaker Labor Indicators Than Adults in Ethiopia, but Unemployment among Both Groups Is Low

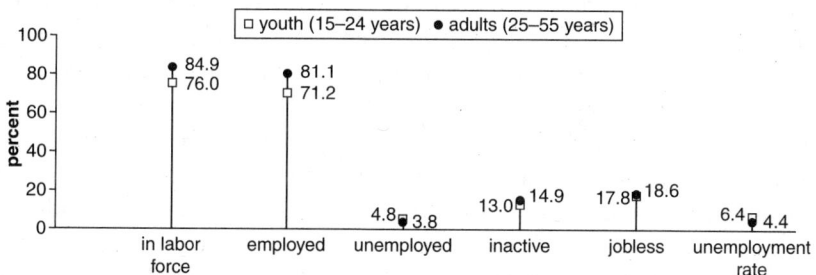

Source: Understanding Children's Work calculations based on Ethiopia Labour Force Survey 2001.

Table 9.5. Ratio of Youth to Adult Unemployment Rates in Selected Sub-Saharan African Countries

Country	Total	Urban	Rural
Ethiopia	1.4	1.7	1.4
Burkina Faso	2.5	3.4	1.9
Burundi	0.9	3.3	0.3
Cameroon	5.1	4.0	15.7
Côte d'Ivoire	1.9	1.6	4.6
Gambia, The	0.4	0.7	0.5
Kenya	3.9	3.7	3.9
Madagascar	1.5	2.2	1.3
Malawi	2.3	5.0	2.1
Mozambique	3.0	2.4	3.6
São Tomé and Principe	5.9	5.0	6.9
Uganda	1.1	2.2	2.1
Zambia	2.9	3.7	2.5

Source: Understanding Children's Work calculations based on Ethiopia Labour Force Survey 2001 and World Bank Standard Files and Standard Indicators data sets.

Figure 9.9. The Unemployment Ratio among Ethiopian Adults of All Ages Is Higher in Urban Than in Rural Areas

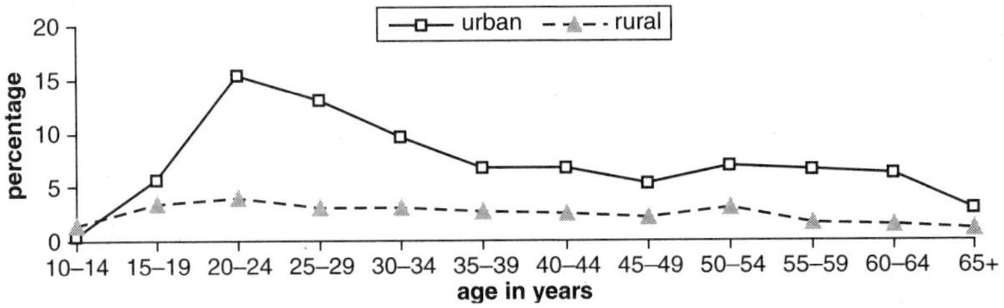

Source: Understanding Children's Work calculations based on Ethiopia Labour Force Survey 2001.

(ages 25–29) before falling sharply thereafter. In many cases the period required to settle into work extends well into adulthood.

Differences in youth and adult work characteristics also provide an indication of youth labor market disadvantage. The sectoral composition of youth and adult employment differs in urban but not in rural areas. In urban areas, compared to youth, adult workers are more likely to work in family farming and construction and less likely to work in services. In both rural and urban areas, young workers are much more concentrated in unpaid work and less concentrated in self-employment than adults. Urban young people are much less likely to secure wage employment than adults; about the same proportion of adults and youth work in the informal sector (CSA 2003).

Young people in urban areas of Ethiopia face a significant labor market disadvantage. Their unemployment and jobless rates are much higher than those of adults, and they are only half as likely as adult workers to be in wage employment. The disadvantaged position of youth in the labor market can be associated with, or even the result of, a difficult or inefficient transition from school to the labor market.

The next section looks at this issue by constructing an indicator of the duration of the school-to-work transition. As will be apparent later, such a measure is not able to indicate precisely where the problem lays, but it is a first and necessary step toward understanding the process by which young people make the transition to working life.

Transition to Working Life

The transition to work can take two routes: through the schooling system or directly from inactivity (or informal schooling) to the labor force. This section examines both routes to identify vulnerable groups and targets for policies. It uses a synthetic indicator to provide an overview of the routes young people take from education to the labor force.[14] For the group transitioning directly to the labor force, it examines the average age of entry into the labor market.

A substantial number of children drop out of school very early. While they are formally included in the youth transitioning through school, their condition and the problems they face are likely to be closer to those of children who never attended school.

The School-to-Work Transition

The average school-leaving age (that is, the starting point of the transition) in Ethiopia is high compared with other countries in Sub-Saharan Africa (figure 9.10). Most children entering school stay there well beyond the basic cycle. To the extent that schooling is an indicator of human capital levels and labor market preparedness, Ethiopians leave the schooling system seemingly well-equipped for the transition to working life.[15]

A number of caveats apply to this conclusion. First, as emphasized below, not all young people transition through school. Second, a given school-leaving age is likely to be associated with lower human capital accumulation in less developed countries, as a result of frequent delayed

Figure 9.10. Ethiopian Youth Begin the Transition from School to Work Later Than Youth in Other Countries in Sub-Saharan Africa

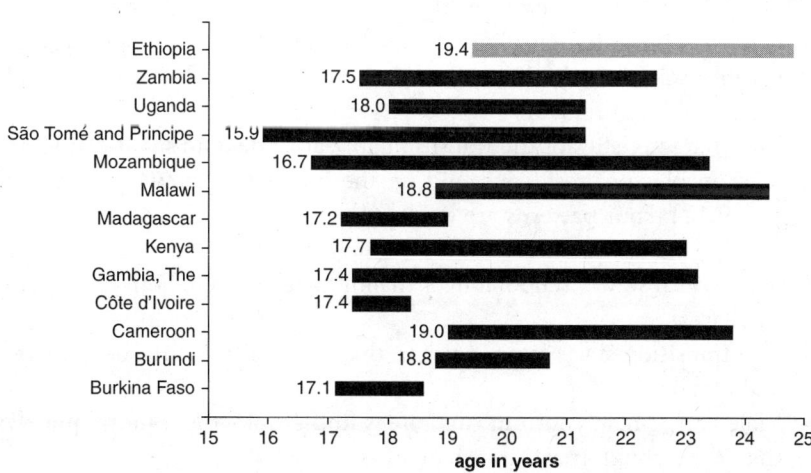

Source: Understanding Children's Work calculations based on Ethiopia Labour Force Survey 2001 and World Bank Standard Files and Standard Indicators data sets.

Table 9.6. School-to-Work Transition Points in Ethiopia, by Gender and Urban-Rural Location

| Item | Beginning point of transition (average age of school leaving) | Children ever in school | Transition duration (years) | Children never in school |
		End point of transition average age of (entering into work for the first time)		Average age of entering into work for the first time
Total	19.4	23.4	4.0	8.0
Male	19.6	23.9	4.3	8.1
Female	19.1	21.5	2.4	7.5
Location				
Urban	19.3	23.4	4.1	9.5
Rural	18.9	23.6	4.7	8.0
Male urban	20.0	23.8	3.8	9.5
Female urban	18.8	23.8	5.0	9.5
Male rural	19.0	21.8	2.8	8.2
Female rural	17.5	19.5	2.0	7.0

Source: Understanding Children's Work calculations based on Ethiopia Labour Force Survey 2000, except "Children never in school" data are from Ethiopia Labour Force Survey 2000.

entry into school, intermittent attendance, grade repetition, and poor school quality and relevance.

The relatively high school-leaving age in Ethiopia is noteworthy, particularly against the backdrop of a low overall school enrollment rate (table 9.6). The late average leaving age among youth who ever attended school (19.4 years) underscores the importance of the selection process associated with initial enrollment: those children with the opportunity to get into school in the first place tend to stay there almost to the end of their teens (figure 9.11).

The characteristics of the transition appear to depend significantly on gender, on place of residence, and on the interaction between the two (figure 9.12). Four patterns are evident:

- Male youth stay in school longer than female youth in both urban and rural areas.
- The transition starts later in urban than in rural areas for both males and females.
- Male and female youth in rural areas find employment more quickly than their counterparts in urban areas.
- Female youth find employment more quickly than male youth in rural areas. In urban areas the opposite holds true.

Figure 9.11. Ethiopian Children Who Start School Tend to Remain in School through Their Teens

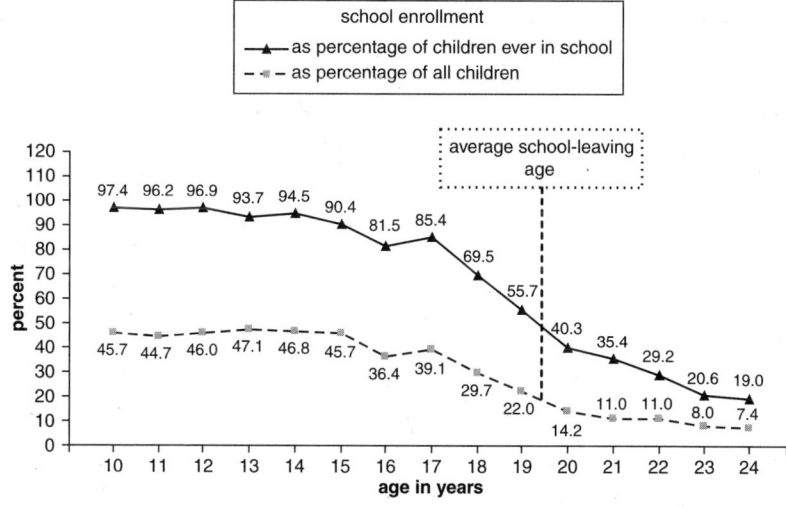

Source: Understanding Children's Work calculations based on Ethiopia Labour Force Survey 2001.

Figure 9.12. Gender and Location Affect the Duration and Timing of the Transition from School to Work in Ethiopia

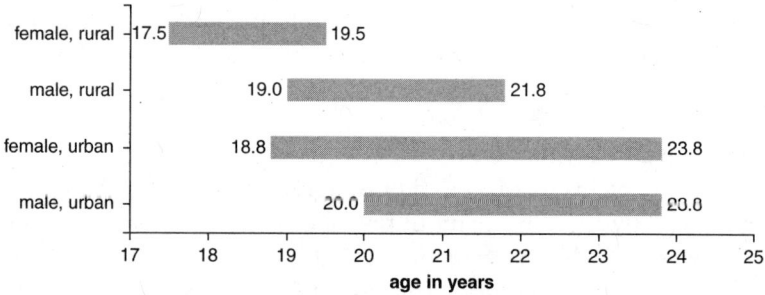

Source: Understanding Children's Work calculations based on Ethiopia Labour Force Survey 2000.

The synthetic indicator does not permit conclusions to be drawn about the "efficiency" or "success" of the transition in specific country contexts. A better understanding of the transition period would require integrating the analysis of optimal school-leaving age with the analysis of employment search and labor force participation. Nonetheless, the synthetic indicator does reveal two important features of the transition in

Figure 9.13. Ethiopian Children Begin Work Much Earlier Than Children in Other Countries in Sub-Saharan Africa

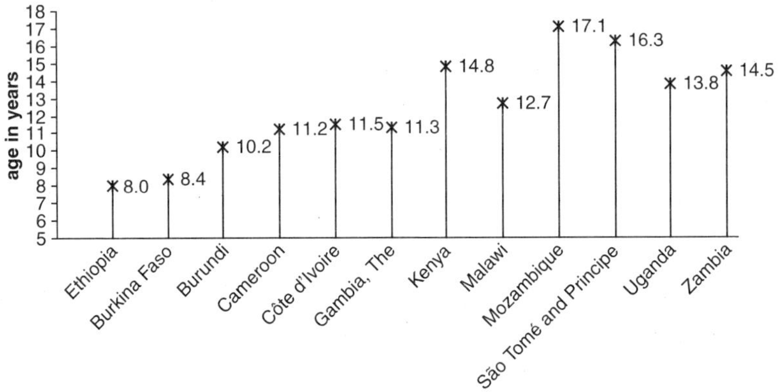

Source: Understanding Children's Work calculations based on World Bank Standard Files and Standard Indicators (SFSI) datasets.

Ethiopia that fit within this more detailed analysis: the relatively late starting age of the transition and its long average duration (four years).

An initial period of unemployment following schooling is not unusual, because young people spend time looking for the best job match. In Ethiopia, however, the length of this jobless period extends well beyond what could plausibly be considered "wait" unemployment. Because long periods of initial joblessness can translate into permanently reduced productive potential and job prospects, this problem constitutes an important policy concern.

Transitions Directly to Work

The majority of 15- to 24-year-old Ethiopians never enter school, transitioning directly from inactivity to the labor force. Among these people, the average child begins work at age eight, much earlier than in other Sub-Saharan Africa countries (figure 9.13). Rural school nonentrants secure employment earliest, though rural-urban differences in starting age are not large (see table 9.6).

Child Labor, Human Capital, and Youth Labor Market Outcomes

This section examines the consequences of child labor for human capital—and thus for the labor market.

Educational Attainment

Most young people in Ethiopia have had very little opportunity to acquire human capital. More than 8.3 million 15- to 24-year-olds (three-quarters of this age group) possess only a primary education or less; 6.6 million of these people possess no formal education at all. Limited formal education is much more common in rural areas than in urban areas, and it is more common among young adults (ages 20–24) than among teenagers (ages 15–19), indicating progress over time in expanding access to basic level schooling.

These school nonentrants and early leavers are a serious policy concern, because they are especially vulnerable to undesirable transition outcomes. As children, school nonentrants are among the groups most vulnerable to child labor, underscoring that the issue of finding satisfactory employment as adults cannot be separated from the issue of child labor.[16]

Human Capital Levels and Labor Force Status: Descriptive Evidence

The rate of unemployment increases with education level, peaking among those with higher education (figure 9.14). This partially reflects the fact that less-educated young people begin their transition to work at an earlier age and therefore have had longer exposure to the labor market and more time to secure employment. In addition, because the reservation wage is likely to rise with skill level, search time may increase with the

Figure 9.14. Employment Rates among Ethiopians Ages 20–24 Decrease with Education, and Unemployment Rates Increase

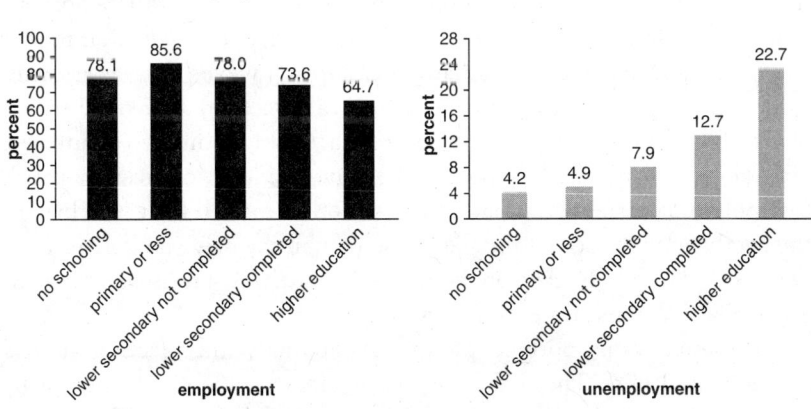

Source: Understanding Children's Work calculations based on Ethiopia Labour Force Survey 2001.

level of human capital. This finding itself, therefore, says little about links between human capital levels and success in the labor market.

Educational attainment appears to have a positive influence on the type of employment (table 9.7). More-educated workers are much more likely to be in wage employment and much less likely to be in unpaid work than their less-educated counterparts (figure 9.15).

Human Capital Levels and Labor Force Status: Econometric Analysis

This section examines the determinants of youth employment, paying special attention to the role of the stock of human capital with which youth enter the labor market and to local labor market conditions. Youth who enter the labor market with little or no education are more likely to be employed than youth with more education. Whether this is due to human capital or earlier entry in the labor market is impossible to determine, however. In view of this problem, we try to identify whether the effects of the explanatory variables considered vary with the level of education. While this approach does not directly indicate the possible effect of human capital on employability, it may provide some indirect evidence.

The sample is divided into five groups: never attended school, primary school or less, some lower secondary school, completed lower secondary school, and at least some higher education (including higher secondary). Separate regressions are run on the employment probability on each of these subsamples, using the explanatory variables described below. The obvious problem of sample selection is exacerbated here by the fact that the choice subsuming the selection is not generated by a bivariate normal. One way to deal with this issue would be to estimate a selection model and follow a generalized Heckman procedure. However, there is growing evidence (consistent with current empirical practice) that once major observable characteristics are taken into account, estimates of interest often do not change with respect to the naive model. Moreover, there are two potential costs to estimating the selection model. First, the bias in the coefficients can sometimes be worse than in the naive model. Second, the coefficients in the selection model can be much less precisely estimated, especially if the instruments are weak.

For these reasons, both simple probit equations and selection models are estimated here. The data sets do not offer a wide choice of instruments, so household structure (number of adults and of siblings) was used to identify the selection (school grade) equation.[17] The focus is on

Table 9.7. Employment Status and Employment Modality of Ethiopians Not in School, by Educational Attainment and Age Group
(percent)

Age group and highest education level attained	Employment status[a]			Employment modality[b]				
	Employed	Unemployed	Inactive	Domestic employee	Wage employee	Self-employed	Unpaid family worker	Other
20–24								
No schooling	78.1	4.2	17.7	1.4	5.1	30.1	63.2	0.2
Primary or less	85.6	4.9	9.5	2.1	7.8	36.3	53.3	0.5
Lower secondary not completed	78.0	7.9	14.0	2.2	10.0	38.5	49.0	0.3
Lower secondary completed	73.6	12.7	13.7	1.4	18.9	34.8	43.2	1.7
Higher education	64.7	22.7	12.6	1.5	51.8	25.6	19.2	1.9
25–55								
No schooling	79.6	3.3	17.1	0.5	4.0	60.4	35.0	0.2
Primary or less	89.4	2.3	8.2	0.8	7.7	77.8	13.4	0.4
Lower secondary not completed	86.0	4.6	9.5	1.0	13.5	73.8	11.1	0.6
Lower secondary completed	83.8	6.6	9.6	0.7	16.4	67.7	14.4	0.9
Higher education	82.5	9.5	8.0	0.9	61.3	32.2	5.1	0.6

Source: Understanding Children's Work calculations based on Ethiopia Labour Force Survey 2001.
a. Percentage distribution of employed population in each age group.
b. Percentage distribution of employed population in each age group. Sector breakdown is based on UN International Standard Industrial Classification Revision 3 if information is available.

Figure 9.15. The Higher Their Level of Education, the More Likely Ethiopians Ages 20–24 Are to Work in Wage Employment

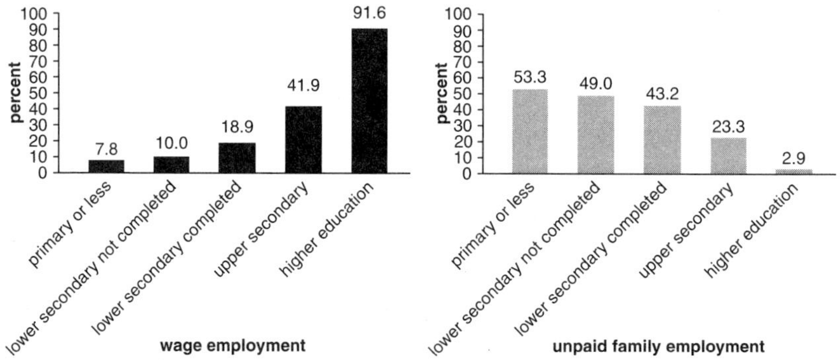

Source: Understanding Children's Work calculations based on Ethiopia Labour Force Survey 2001.

the probit estimates, for reasons mentioned above and because the selection terms in the generalized Heckman model are not significant.

The 2000 Ethiopia Labour Force Survey does not contain a large amount of information. In fact, only a few variables relevant to the analysis of employment are included. The level of expenditure of the household, household size, and home ownership (as a proxy for household wealth) are used here. Because the data for household expenditures are available only in categories and do not allow per capita expenditures to be computed, household size is used to control for the number of household members. The information is obviously very scant, so these results must be interpreted with caution.

To eliminate possible biases in the results from the fact that some youth do not live with their parent (or extended family), models were estimated including and excluding youth who do not live at home. The results do not show any significant difference.

To better reflect the large differences between rural and urban settings in Ethiopia, all equations are estimated separately for rural and urban areas. The effects of local labor market conditions on the probability of being employed are proxied by two variables that should be related to the supply and demand sides of the market. As an indicator of the condition of demand, we used the adult (ages 25–55) employment-to-population ratio. To proxy the supply side, we used the proportion of youth (ages 15–24) in the working-age population.

Defining the relevant local labor market is difficult empirically. Several different approaches were followed. First, the local labor market as defined at the administrative regional level was identified, computing all indicators for the 11 regions of Ethiopia. Anecdotal evidence of migration and labor market flows and discussion with labor market experts led to the conclusion that the smaller administrative unit (that is, the zone) covers too limited an area to define a local labor market. However, if it is reasonable to assume that flows of work can occur within the rural and urban areas of the same region, it is also true that the integration of rural and urban labor markets may be far from perfect, especially in the short to medium run (as a result of the cost of migration, difficulties commuting, lack of information, and the like). For this reason, the indicators for local labor markets were also computed separately for rural and urban areas of each region.

We tried to exploit the information available on internal migration to identify local labor markets. Obviously, administrative boundaries are not adequate confines for an area's economy. A local economy and its labor market should be defined on the basis of the interrelationships between buyers and sellers of labor. The only information available in this respect is the flow of migrants across administrative zones. Using this information, a two-way flow matrix was built, and normalized and made symmetric. Each cell of the matrix reflects the gross flow of migration between (to and from) a few zones.[18] The application to this matrix of hierarchical cluster analysis helped identify groups of zones that are clustered together and hence can be defined as constituting a local labor market. This kind of methodology involves a substantial degree of value judgment because there are no general criteria for fixing the threshold for the intensity of exchanges that define the local labor markets.

Estimation Results

This section presents the results for the probit estimates of the probability of employment by level of education, with the standard errors corrected for clustering. As expected, the results show large differences between urban and rural areas and across levels of education (tables 9.8 and 9.9). In urban areas, the probability of being employed increases with age only for youth with no education or less than primary education. This could indicate that less-educated youth face fewer difficulties finding employment, although the result may be biased by the fact that there is too little variation in exposure to job searching for youth with more than primary education.

Gender effects are large: the probability of a female being employed is 14–22 percent lower than that of a male. The gender bias in employment is weaker for the less-educated and for the most-educated youth.

Table 9.8. Probability of Employment among Ethiopians Ages 10–24: Probit Estimates Using Regionwide Definition of Local Labor Market

Variable	Never attended school		Primary or less		Not completed lower secondary		Lower secondary completed		Higher education	
	dy/dx	z	dy/dx	z	dy/dx	z	dy/dx	z	dy/dx	z
Urban										
Age	0.1409	6.51	0.0622	1.97	-0.0184	-0.38	0.1632	1.39	-0.0791	-0.64
Age squared	-0.0038	-6.08	-0.0018	-1.9	0.0003	0.25	-0.0041	-1.45	0.0022	0.75
Female*	-0.1493	-3.62	-0.2036	-4.08	-0.2224	-5.8	-0.1818	-4.21	-0.1411	-10.73
Household size	-0.0040	-0.93	-0.0105	-1.73	-0.0103	-1.94	0.0069	1.04	-0.0097	-2.85
Homeowner*	-0.0049	-0.19	0.0476	0.91	0.0025	0.09	0.0227	0.91	0.0065	0.39
Expenditure quintile 1*	-0.3834	-4.51	-0.4583	-7.17	-0.2693	-3.56	-0.0785	-0.97	-0.1377	-1.78
Expenditure quintile 2*	-0.3801	-5.49	-0.3963	-8.32	-0.2207	-3.92	-0.0041	-0.05	-0.0727	-1.62
Expenditure quintile 3*	-0.1945	-2.11	-0.3244	-5.63	-0.2357	-3.73	-0.0533	-0.6	-0.0672	-1.87
Expenditure quintile 4*	-0.0671	-0.91	-0.2178	-4.35	-0.0987	-1.4	0.1010	1.13	-0.0711	-1.14
Local labor market indicator										
Adult employment ratio	2.3418	2.71	1.3490	5.4	1.3697	7.26	1.7341	4.69	1.0234	2.83
Share of population	-5.2088	-2.53	-3.0692	-5.24	-1.6528	-2.28	-1.9929	-2.43	0.4631	0.48

Rural

Age	0.0314	2.74	0.0290	2.38	0.0649	1.57	-0.2079	-1.3	0.0697	0.26
Age squared	-0.0008	-2.65	-0.0007	-2.13	-0.0017	-1.6	0.0052	1.25	-0.0009	-0.14
Female*	-0.2513	-15.32	-0.2041	-7.54	-0.1783	-5.3	-0.1284	-2.63	-0.1642	-2.56
Household size	0.0006	0.29	0.0003	0.11	0.0005	0.16	0.0044	0.58	-0.0016	-0.26
Homeowner*	0.0636	1.63	0.0282	0.82	0.1345	2.45	0.1457	2.19	-0.0515	-0.65
Household expenditure quintile (reference group: top quintile)										
Expenditure quintile 1*	-0.0349	-0.22	-0.0829	-0.99	-0.0650	-1.08	-0.1814	-2.4	0.1865	11.2
Expenditure quintile 2*	-0.0331	-0.22	-0.0766	-1.23	-0.0893	-1.55	-0.0206	-0.69	0.3717	7.94
Expenditure quintile 3*	0.0003	0	-0.0528	-0.63	-0.1340	-1.17	-0.0358	-0.87	0.1606	4.53
Expenditure quintile 4*	0.0060	0.05							0.1689	5.8
Local labor market indicator										
Adult employment ratio	0.6400	2.14	0.3376	2.33	0.4533	2.53	1.4439	4.88	0.2242	0.52
Share of population	0.8467	1.25	0.4590	1.12	-0.2614	-0.79	-1.7349	-2.16	0.8189	0.61

Source: Understanding Children's Work calculations based on Ethiopia Labour Force Survey 2001.

*dy/dx is for discrete change of dummy variable from 0 to 1.

Table 9.9. Probability of Employment among Rural and Urban Ethiopians Ages 10–24, by Level of Education: Probit Estimates Obtained Using Indicators of Local Labor Market Separated for Rural and Urban Areas

Variable	Never attended school		Primary or less		Not completed lower secondary		Lower secondary completed		Higher education	
	dy/dx	z	dy/dx	z	dy/dx	z	dy/dx	z	dy/dx	z
Urban										
Age	0.141	6.5	0.061	1.89	-0.021	-0.44	0.158	1.33	-0.075	-0.6
Age squared	-0.004	-6.05	-0.002	-1.81	0.000	0.3	-0.004	-1.4	0.002	0.72
Female*	-0.155	-3.88	-0.205	-4.08	-0.225	-5.83	-0.182	-4.24	-0.142	-11.02
Household size	-0.001	-0.3	-0.009	-1.53	-0.010	-2.07	0.007	1.03	-0.011	-2.65
Homeowner*	-0.009	-0.43	0.044	0.83	-0.001	-0.03	0.023	0.88	0.007	0.4
Household expenditure quintile (reference group: top quintile)										
Expenditure quintile 1*	-0.401	-4.31	-0.457	-7.1	-0.274	-3.58	-0.066	-0.79	-0.144	-1.83
Expenditure quintile 2*	-0.396	-5.21	-0.395	-8.19	-0.223	-3.96	0.006	0.07	-0.080	-1.78
Expenditure quintile 3*	-0.215	-2.13	-0.329	-5.49	-0.239	-3.84	-0.046	-0.53	-0.072	-1.96
Expenditure quintile 4*	-0.084	-1.05	-0.219	-4.43	-0.100	-1.45	0.103	1.15	-0.074	-1.21
Local labor market indicator										
Adult employment ratio	1.918	2.85	0.993	3.91	1.312	10.35	1.503	3.63	1.436	3.32
Share of population	-1.896	-2.54	-1.292	-2.89	-0.126	-0.41	-0.104	-0.25	0.994	1.28

Rural

Age	-0.075	-0.60	0.029	2.30	0.060	1.43	-0.199	-1.03	0.070	0.26
Age²	0.002	0.72	-0.001	-2.06	-0.002	-1.46	0.005	1.00	-0.001	-0.14
Female*	-0.142	-11.02	-0.205	-8.05	-0.179	-6.08	-0.105	-2.73	-0.164	-2.51
Household size	-0.011	-2.65	0.001	0.17	0.000	0.15	0.006	0.72	-0.002	-0.27
Homeowner*	0.007	0.40	0.030	0.87	0.134	2.34	0.227	2.36	-0.053	-0.68
Household expenditure quintile (reference group: top quintile)										
Expenditure quintile 1*	-0.144	-1.83	-0.085	-1.04	-0.058	-0.97	-0.108	-1.80	0.187	10.81
Expenditure quintile 2*	-0.080	-1.78	-0.078	-1.29	-0.084	-1.45	0.011	0.27	0.373	7.36
Expenditure quintile 3*	-0.072	-1.96	-0.054	-0.65	-0.127	-1.11	-0.007	-0.13	0.162	4.54
Expenditure quintile 4*	-0.074	-1.21							0.169	5.68
Local labor market indicator										
Adult employment ratio	1.436	3.32	0.441	4.73	0.866	8.05	0.398	0.65	0.257	0.48
Share of population	0.994	1.28	0.353	2.57	-0.848	-6.06	1.305	1.05	0.600	0.76

Source: Understanding Children's Work calculations based on Ethiopia Labour Force Survey 2001.

*dy/dx is for discrete change of dummy variable from 0 to 1.

The level of income or wealth, as proxied by the expenditure dummy variables, is significant for less-educated youth; the effects of expenditures on the probability of employment lose size and significance as the level of education increases. If household resources are important for finding a job, credit rationing or social networking might be important elements in determining youth employment. However, this interpretation should be taken with care because the data do not allow the exclusion from household income of the income generated by possibly employed youth (the data on expenditures are ranked in categories), hence reverse causation cannot be ruled out. Especially in poor households, where we expect to find relatively less-educated youth, the additional employment of one household member might substantially alter the expenditure level of the household.

Local labor market conditions appear to substantially influence the probability of finding employment. The regional adult employment ratio is significant for all groups considered and indicates that an increase of 10 percentage points in the adult employment ratio increases the probability of youth finding employment by 10–25 percentage points. This effect is stronger for youth who never attended school and substantially weaker for other groups, especially youth with at least some higher education. The supply of youth labor, as proxied by the share of young people in the population, seems to negatively affect the possibility of finding employment. The effect is larger for youth who never attended school and smaller for other groups. It is not significant for people with some higher education. Similar results are obtained when the labor market conditions are computed only for the urban areas of each region (see table 9.9). Local labor market conditions are hence important for determining youth employment, especially for youth with little or no education. Not surprisingly, supply and demand conditions are most relevant for the less-qualified work force, which is more exposed to the phases of the economic cycle, because all the factors that put a wedge between the economic cycle and firm employment behavior (labor hoarding, hiring and firing costs, and the like) are far less relevant for these groups.

In rural areas, the results are similar but much more attenuated because of the dominance of agricultural self-employment and underemployment. The effect of age is present for the less-qualified work force but is much smaller than that observed in urban areas.

Gender biases are large and somewhat more pronounced than in urban areas, especially for youth with little or no formal education. The link between household income and employment is weak and not well-defined, possibly because of the lack of employment opportunities or the prevalence of underemployment in the agriculture sector.

The adult employment ratio appears to have a positive effect on the employment probability of youth. The effect is stronger for youth who never attended school but overall much smaller than that observed in urban areas. The relative size of the youth cohort is not significant for any of the groups considered.

In short, there appears to be much less of a market for labor in rural areas than in urban areas. The prevalence in agriculture of self-employment, often subsistence employment—and hence underemployment—insulates this part of the economy from the workings of a competitive labor market.

Policies and Programs for Youth Employment in Ethiopia

The government ministries in Ethiopia most directly concerned with youth and the labor force are the Ministry of Youth, Sports, and Culture; the Ministry of Education; the Ministry of Labour and Social Affairs (MOLSA); and the Ministry of Trade and Industry.[19] The policies with arguably the most significant impact on youth labor force employment opportunities are the education policy and the set of policies governing micro- and small enterprises.

National Youth Policy

The Ministry of Youth, Sports, and Culture formulated Ethiopia's first National Youth Policy in March 2004, with the broad objectives of encouraging the active participation of youth (defined as those ages 15–29) in the economic, social, and cultural life of the country and supporting democratization and good governance. The policy was officially launched in September 2004. Both the strategic plan and action plan are still under preparation. The ministry and its regional bureaus (Bureaus for Labour and Social Affairs—BOLSAs) are responsible for coordinating, integrating, and evaluating implementation of the policy.

The basic principles of the policy are to ensure that youth are active participants in and beneficiaries of democratization and economic development activities, to bring about unity, to allow youth to organize themselves to protect their rights and interests, and to build capacity (through skills training, for example). The policy addresses a wide range of issues, ranging from HIV/AIDS to environmental protection and social services.

The youth and economic development policy sets out to facilitate the participation of youth in the formulation, implementation, and evaluation of national development polices, strategies, and programs. It also promises to facilitate growth of self-employment and formal and informal employment opportunities and to create favorable conditions for rural youth to acquire farming plots and grazing lands on the basis of existing laws.

The youth, education, and training policy outlines a vision for creating an enabling environment for youth to benefit from education and training and for out-of-school youth to develop their reading and writing skills through adult education services. It acknowledges rural-urban, gender, and interregional disparities in education participation and aims to work toward reducing them.

Labor Proclamation 377/2003

Ethiopia's Labor Law was proclaimed in 2003 to ensure that worker-employer relations are governed by certain basic principles, to guarantee the rights of workers and employers to form associations, and to strengthen and define labor administration.[20] The law applies to the entire labor force, though some provisions may be more relevant for youth than others. Article 29 states that in the event of a reduction in the size of an organization's work force, the employer, in consultation with trade unions, shall give priority based on workers' skills and productivity. In the case of equal skills and productivity, the workers to be affected first by reduction should be those with the shortest length of service and those with the fewest dependents.

Article 48 discusses apprenticeships and allows for contracts to be formed with people at least 14 years old. The article covers the contents of the contract, obligations of the parties, termination of a contract, and certification. Article 110 includes provisions for the payment of benefits to dependents and payment of funeral expenses (equal to at least two months' wages) in the case of work-related injuries. Because regulations on formal and informal apprenticeships are the responsibility of MOLSA, apprenticeship training centers are required to have a contract agreement with relevant BOLSAs to ensure that they are in conformity with the Labor Law.

Part of the Labor Law is devoted to 14- to 18-year-olds. The proclamation prohibits employment of people under age 14 and prohibits employment of young workers for activities that endanger their lives and health. Prohibited activities include the following:

- Work involving the transport of passengers and goods (by road, railway, air, internal waterway, and docksides) or heavy lifting, pulling, pushing, or any other related type of labor

- Work connected with electric power generation plants, transformers, or transmission lines
- Underground work (such as mining or quarrying)
- Work in sewers or tunnels

Article 90 states that the normal workday for young workers should not exceed seven hours (one hour less than for other workers). In addition, employers are prohibited from hiring young workers for overtime work or work performed at night (between 10 p.m. and 6 a.m.), on weekly rest days, or on public holidays.

Education Policy

In 1994, a new education policy that dramatically changed the education system was introduced. The policy included a major supply-side push on technical and vocational education and training (TVET) to facilitate the school-to-work transition. Before 1994, primary school included grades 1–6, junior secondary included grades 7–8, and secondary school included grades 9–12. In grade 12, students took a school-leaving exam that determined their eligibility to pursue higher education. Only a small percentage of students could enroll in higher education. The majority of students left school without any readily marketable professional or technical skills.

The new education policy aimed to change this picture by focusing on producing a skilled labor force rather than a large cohort of relatively unskilled secondary school graduates. Grades 1–8 are now considered primary school and grades 9–10 the first cycle of secondary school. Both levels provide general academic education. A national exam is given upon completion of grade 10, with those who score well promoted to the second cycle of secondary school (grades 11 and 12), which is considered college or university preparatory. Those who do not score well enough to continue in secondary school have the opportunity to pursue formal TVET, which takes one to three years. One- and two-year training programs (known as "10 + 1" and "10 + 2") are considered certificate level, while three years of training ("10 + 3") is considered diploma level.

A pilot tracer study of TVET is currently under way to gather information on graduates, including their employment status, to see if the new system is effective. The Ministry of Education is also working on a study, in cooperation with Deutsche Gesellschaft für Technische Zusammenarbeit, of the projected demand for mid-level human resources to better understand current skill gaps in the labor force and thus to inform education policy. The Ministry of Education has formed a stakeholder network, which includes employers, to help prepare the TVET curriculum. Since 1999, the Ministry of Education has offered summer training for teachers of technical and vocational education to improve the quality and practical relevance of its programs. It continues to face the challenge of making its programs responsive to the changing needs of the market.

Education Sector Development Program III

The main objectives of the education sector in Ethiopia are to ensure access to a good-quality primary school education for all children by 2015 and to create a skilled labor force at all levels. The government developed its Third Education Sector Development Program (ESDPIII), covering 2005/06–2010/11, to continue implementation of its education policy. TVET, along with general tertiary education, is a major element of the ESDPIII, reflecting the government's belief that encouraging and equipping youth (through a strong skills-based training program) to become self-employed is an important way to reduce youth unemployment.

According to the action plan, the government will

- provide relevant and demand-driven education and training by monitoring the labor market and reorienting and refocusing the TVET system;
- provide education and training for basic- and junior-level trainees;
- ensure the quality of TVET by establishing a testing system throughout the country in all trades;
- regard income-generating activities as a source of income and a component of training to reduce government allocations to the TVET sector;
- develop demand-oriented curricula based on occupational standards by involving experts from the work world;
- completely revise the curricula of technical teacher training institutions at universities and institutes to improve instruction; and
- use aptitude tests to avoid rigid trainee selection placement procedures.

To increase the efficiency of TVET, the Ministry of Education issued a proclamation in March 2004 providing procedural guidelines on preaccreditation, accreditation, internships, certification, board and council establishments, vocational guidance and counseling, cost sharing, and production centers. It also issued a handbook on the development of occupational standards.

Micro- and Small Enterprises Development Strategy

In recognition of the economic and social role of micro- and small enterprises in providing goods and services, creating employment opportunities, and generating income, the Ministry of Trade and Industry formulated the micro- and small enterprises development strategy in 2004. The strategy defines microenterprises as formal or informal enterprises with paid-up capital not exceeding Ethiopian birr (Br) 20,000 (US$2,300). Small enterprises are defined as firms other than high-tech firms with paid-up capital of Br20,000–50,000 (US$2,300–$5,750). The objectives of the strategy are to

- strengthen micro- and small enterprises to facilitate economic growth and bring about equitable development;
- create long-term jobs;
- strengthen cooperation among micro- and small enterprises;
- provide a basis for medium- and large-scale enterprises;
- promote exports; and
- balance preferential treatment between micro- and small enterprises and medium- and large-scale enterprises.

The strategy gives priority to enterprises operated by women. It also favors enterprises operated by school dropouts, people with disabilities, and previously unemployed youth. It outlines key limitations faced by micro- and small enterprises and sets out the goal of providing the following kinds of support: credit services, entrepreneurship and business management training, appropriate technology research, market support, information and counseling, business development services, and infrastructure provision, including roads, electricity, and water and access to land and work places.

Industrial Development Strategy

The Ethiopian industrial development strategy, formulated in 2001, recognizes the private investor as the engine for industrial development and encourages the development of labor-intensive industries. The strategy underlines the importance of micro- and small enterprises, recognizing the role these enterprises play in youth employment. It acknowledges micro- and small enterprises as important vehicles in ameliorating unemployment and boosting investment and savings. These enterprises are second only to the agriculture sector for employment generation.

Licensing and Supervision of Microfinance Institutions

The National Bank of Ethiopia has the authority to license and supervise microfinance institutions, which must adhere to its regulations. To operate legally, microfinance institutions must be licensed, which requires minimum paid-up capital of Br200,000 (US$23,000). This amount was set fairly low to attract investors to the microbanking sector. Some microfinance institutions were originally founded by nongovernmental organizations, but a change in the law means that a minimum of five shareholders is required to operate a microfinance institution, so many are jointly owned by a mixture of public, nongovernmental organization, and private shareholders. The National Bank of Ethiopia's loan policy requires that microfinance institutions give preference to poor rural farmers and microeconomic activities of rural and urban communities with small cash requirements.

Until the law was amended, the minimum annual interest rate paid on savings and time deposits of microfinance institutions was 7 percent, and individual microfinance institutions could set their own interest rates on loans, up to a maximum of 15.5 percent a year. Since the change in the law in 1998, each institution's board of directors can set interest rates on loans and advances. The minimum interest rate payable on savings and time deposits was also amended and lowered to 6 percent. The cap of Br5,000 (US$575) per loan was relaxed to accommodate borrowers who needed medium-size loans—more than microfinance institutions could offer but not enough to access credit from commercial banks. Currently, microfinance institutions can offer up to 20 percent of their annual lending amount in loans larger than Br5,000.

HIV/AIDS Policy

Ethiopia's HIV/AIDS policy was crafted in 1998—more than a decade after the first reported AIDS cases—in response to the alarming spread of HIV/AIDS. It contains several provisions relevant to employment. Article 3, subarticle 3.3, states that no person should be forced to undergo HIV screening for job recruitment purposes unless the nature of the occupation requires such testing. Article 8, subarticle 8.2, outlines the rights of people with HIV/AIDS for access to employment and associated privileges, education and training facilities, and public facilities. Subarticle 8.4 strengthens this provision by stating that people should not be subjected to discriminatory practices on the basis of HIV/AIDS.

In 2003, the HIV/AIDS Prevention and Control Office developed a mainstreaming guideline to provide both conceptual and practical guidance and information on how government sectors should respond to the threat of the epidemic in the work place. The guideline empha-sized mainstreaming HIV/AIDS awareness into routine operations of all federal ministries and organizations to encourage prevention. MOLSA was requested to incorporate HIV/AIDS awareness in its development plan, strategies, and policies; to undertake studies on the impact of HIV/AIDS on women, youth, and children; and to coordinate and assist relevant organizations in eliminating HIV/AIDS.

Through MOLSA's Labour Affairs Department, the ministry is sup-posed to provide guidance on employment procedures and the labor law to prevent mandatory preemployment and periodic medical checkups for HIV/AIDS. It is supposed to develop and disseminate a national HIV/AIDS code of conduct for the work place. Through its Children and Family Affairs Department, MOLSA is required to establish and strengthen youth anti-AIDS clubs and peer-to-peer leadership forums to combat the epidemic.

Conclusions and Policy Recommendations

Despite recent increases in enrollment rates, young people in Ethiopia enter the labor market with very low levels of human capital. This is especially true in rural areas, where more than 70 percent of 15- to 24-year-olds have never attended school and only 17 percent have attended primary school. In urban areas the situation is less dramatic, but even there about 30 percent of young people have no more than a primary education, while another 24 percent have not completed lower secondary school.

These low levels of educational attainment result in a large number of youth who enter the labor market at an early age. By age 18, about 80 percent of rural residents and 40 percent of urban residents are working. Gender differences are large, especially in rural areas, where females are much less likely than their male counterparts to be in formal employment.

Strong rural-urban differences also characterize the status of young people in the labor market. In rural areas, youth unemployment is low (about 4 percent), transition from school to work for the few who attend school is about two years, and youth workers are not disadvan-taged with respect to adult workers in either employment type or unem-ployment. However, employment is overwhelmingly in the agriculture sector (largely subsistence), labor income is low, and underemployment is widespread.

In urban areas, youth unemployment is high (almost 20 percent), and the transition from school to work is more than twice as long as in rural areas. Urban youth are at a disadvantage with respect to the adult population in employment and type of occupation. In particular, they face more difficulty finding wage jobs and employment in the formal sector.

Education appears to help young people secure better jobs, but difficulties in finding a job increase with the level of human capital. Unemployment rates are also higher for better-educated prime-age adults. These findings need to be interpreted with caution, however, because not enough information is available to assess how much of the higher unemployment rate of the more educated may be "wait" unemployment.

The econometric analysis confirms most of the descriptive findings and adds some insights on the effects of household background and local labor markets. The estimates indicate that rural employment is less influenced than urban employment by household characteristics and by the status of the local labor market.

Household background characteristics, in particular the level of expenditures, seem to affect the probability of employment, especially for youth entering the labor market with low levels of human capital. Although this result should be interpreted with care, it seems to indicate that credit rationing and parental support are important determinants of employment probability.

Local labor market conditions influence the probability of employment, especially but not exclusively for youth with low levels of human capital. Youth employment appears to respond to the demand for labor and to the relative supply of young people. Macroeconomic improvement is thus likely to help reduce the labor disadvantage of youth.

Several policy issues emerge from this research:

- The very high levels of child labor and associated very low levels of school attainment affect patterns of employment (unemployment), job quality, and remuneration later in life. Developments in the education sector have resulted in some progress in raising attendance, but addressing the access and quality issues influencing parents' decisions to enroll their children in school remains a major challenge in rural areas. Developing and expanding policies designed to offset or minimize the opportunity costs of rural children's time in school—such as flexible school scheduling designed around the agricultural seasons or school attendance incentive schemes—may hold promise.

- A large number of youth in the labor market have very low levels of human capital. Even if the general enrollment situation improves, the current generation of young people will have few chances to see real changes in their circumstances. More investment in special training and skill formation activities is therefore needed in parallel with broader education expansion efforts to improve the employment prospects of this stock of low-educated or uneducated youth.

- Unemployment is higher among the minority of youth (primarily urban) with higher levels of human capital. More information is needed to identify the causes of this phenomenon and to distinguish voluntary from involuntary unemployment. Distinguishing between wait unemployment and an employability problem is important in formulating policy, especially because successful education policies will substantially increase the relative number of educated youth in the labor market in the near future. An assessment of the determinants of excess unemployment and of the education-specific unemployment of youth will be essential to designing appropriate policies.

- Although a number of labor market surveys have been carried out in Ethiopia, especially in urban areas, information gaps persist, preventing a complete picture of the youth labor market situation from being drawn. It would be useful to introduce minor changes in the current survey instruments to fill these gaps. The addition of a few retrospective questions could go a long way in compensating for the absence of panel data.

- Low skill levels and the likely impact of credit rationing have negative effects on youth labor force outcomes. These results underscore the relevance of the government's micro- and small enterprise development and microfinance strategies. Unfortunately, no information is available for an assessment of the impact of such strategies. Filling these gaps should be a priority.

- The strong role that labor market conditions play in determining the probability of employment indicates that macroeconomic growth is crucial to youth employment and that youth employment hinges to a large extent on the success of national development policies. The fact that labor market effects are particularly strong for the less-educated labor force points to the special vulnerability of these groups and to the need to introduce risk-reduction policies.

Notes

1. A longer version of this chapter is available as "Child Labor and Youth Employment: Ethiopia Country Study," (Guarcello and Rosati 2007). Data tables supporting the assertions in this chapter can be found in the longer version.

2. "Child economic activity" is used as a proxy for child labor in this chapter. Technically, child labor is a narrower concept than child economic activity, referring only to those forms of work that are injurious, negative, or undesirable for children and that should be targeted for elimination in accordance with International Labour Organization Conventions 138 (minimum age) and 182 (worst forms). Economically active children include all children performing at least one hour of economic activity during the reference week. Economic activity is defined in the sense of the System of National Accounts and corresponds to the international definition of employment adopted by the 13th International Conference of Labour Statisticians in 1982. Economic activity covers all market production (paid work) and certain types of nonmarket production (unpaid work), including production of goods for own use. It excludes household chores performed by children in their own household.

3. The data do not allow us to unambiguously identify youth who are both working and attending school. An employed person is someone who is involved in paid employment, at work, or has a job but is not currently at work. This includes people waiting to rejoin employment and employers or people in self-employment. This category should include unpaid family laborers who hold jobs in a market-oriented establishment irrespective of the number of hours worked during a reference period. However, some countries set a minimum time criterion for including unpaid family laborers among the employed. Usually, if a person works more than seven hours a day, he or she is considered employed. An unemployed person is a person who is without work, currently available for work, or seeking work by taking necessary steps to seek paid employment, such as applying for jobs or registering with an agency.

4. The data do not allow us to clearly identify people with disabilities. Even looking at the main reason for not attending school, we could identify only 2 percent of idle youth in the 15–24 age range as ill or disabled.

5. The unemployment rate (unemployment as a proportion of the total labor force in the same age group) is actually higher for teenagers, because teenagers are more likely to be in school and therefore outside the labor force.

6. Youth unemployment is included as an indicator for monitoring Millennium Development Goal Target 16, to "develop and implement strategies for decent and productive work for youth." See http://millenniumindicators.un.org/unsd/mi/mi_goals.asp.

7. Unlike unemployment, joblessness has the advantage of reflecting both unemployed and discouraged workers (workers who have left or did not enter the work force).

8. According to the very broad definition of employment used in generating estimates of employment, anyone who is undertaking economic activity for one hour or more during the reference week is considered employed, even if he or she is actively looking for additional work.

9. In the 1999 Labour Force Survey, rural youth respondents did not indicate a greater willingness or availability to work extra hours than their urban counterparts, raising the possibility that rural youth may be working more hours than reported.

10. Some forms of economic work, such as fetching water, are also included in this category.

11. A self-employed person is one who performs some work for profit or family gain, in cash or in kind. The remuneration is dependent on the profits derived from the goods and services produced (own consumption from enterprise is considered part of profits). The incumbent makes operational decisions affecting the enterprise or may delegate decisions while retaining the responsibility for the welfare of the enterprise. Self-employed people work in one-person businesses that may include contributing family workers.

12. Wage employees are people who are remunerated by wages or salaries. Wage employees may also receive remuneration in the form of commissions from sales, price rates, bonuses, or in-kind payments. Basic remuneration is not directly dependent on revenue of the unit one works for but on the explicit (written or oral) or implicit employment contract. A wage employee may be a regular employee with or without a fixed-term contract or a casual worker without a contract.

13. The Ethiopia Labour Force Survey 2001 did not collect information on informal sector work.

14. See chapter 7 of this book for development of the indicator.

15. This, of course, is a strong assumption because school quality, the relevance of schooling to labor market demands, and student characteristics, among other factors, also affect labor market preparedness.

16. In the absence of retrospective information on work involvement, it is not possible to estimate the proportion of young people who worked as children.

17. The method used is that suggested in Bourguignon, Fournier, and Gurgand (2001), who generalize the approach originally proposed by Lee (1983).

18. For a detailed description of the methodology followed, see Tolbert and Killian (1987).

19. This section draws on Getachew and Kallaur (2005).

20. Ethiopia does not have an official employment policy or a minimum wage law.

References

Bourguignon, F., M. Fournier, and M. Gurgand. 2001 "Selection Bias Correction Based on the Multinomial Logit Model." CREST Working Paper, Center for Research in Economics and Statistics, Paris, France.

CSA (Central Statistical Authority of Ethiopia). 2003. Urban Biannual Employment Unemployment Survey 2003 data set. Addis Ababa.

Cockburn, J. 2002. "Income Contribution of Child Work in Rural Ethiopia." Working Paper 2002-12, Oxford University, Centre for the Study of African Economies, Oxford, United Kingdom.

Denu, B., A. Tekeste, and H. van der Deijl. 2005. "Employment Strategy Papers: Characteristics and Determinants of Youth Unemployment, Under-employment and Inadequate Employment in Ethiopia." International Labour Organization, Employment Policies Unit Employment Strategy Department, Geneva.

Easterly, W. 2002. "Growth in Ethiopia: Retrospect and Prospect." Center for Global Development, Institute of International Studies, Washington, DC.

ECA (Economic Commission for Africa). 2002. "Economic Report on Africa 2002: Tracking Performance and Progress." ECA, Addis Ababa, Ethiopia.

Getachew, M., and E. Kallaur. 2005. "Youth Employment in Ethiopia: Overview and Inventory of Existing Policies and Programs." World Bank, Washington, DC.

Guarcello, L., and F. Rosati. 2007. "Child Labor and Youth Employment: Ethiopia Country Study." Social Protection Discussion Paper No. 0704, World Bank, Washington, DC.

ILO (International Labour Office). 2004. "Global Employment Trends for Youth." ILO, Geneva.

Lee, Lung-Fei. 1983. "Generalized Econometric Models with Selectivity." Econometrica 51(2): 507–12.

MEDaC (Ministry of Economic Development and Cooperation). 1999. "Survey of the Ethiopian Economy: Review of the Post Reform Developments." Addis Ababa.

———. 2000. "Ethiopian Economy in Figures: Selected Indicators." Department of Macroeconomic Planning and Policy Analysis, MEDaC, Addis Ababa, Ethiopia.

MOE (Ministry of Education). 1999. *Educational Statistics Annual Abstract 1991 E.C. (1998–99)*. Education Management Information Systems, Addis Ababa.

———. 2003. *Educational Statistics Annual Abstract 1995 E.C (2002–03)*. Education Management Information Systems, Addis Ababa.

MOFED (Ministry of Finance and Economic Development). 2002. "Sustainable Development and Poverty Reduction Program." Addis Ababa.

Tolbert, C. M., and M. S. Killian. 1987. "Labor Market Areas for the United States." U.S. Department of Agriculture, Washington, DC.

Woldehanna T., F. Guta, and T. Ferede. 2005. "Labour Market Flexibility and Employment Security in Ethiopia: Economic Part." International Labour Office, Employment Strategy Department, Geneva.

World Bank. 2002. "The Federal Democratic Republic of Ethiopia: Developing Exports to Promote Growth." Sector Report 23294-ET, Washington, DC.

———. 2005. "Ethiopia Risk and Vulnerability Assessment." Report No. 26275-ET, Africa Region, Human Development Group III, Washington, DC.

Yamano, T. 2000. "Does Food Aid Reduce Child Farm Labor Supply in Ethiopia?" World Bank, Washington, DC.

CHAPTER 10

Youth in the Labor Market and the Transition from School to Work in Tanzania

Florence Kondylis and Marco Manacorda

Like many Sub-Saharan African countries, Tanzania suffered from severe youth unemployment and inactivity in urban areas in the 1990s (Mjema 1997). Despite sustained growth in the second half of the last decade, labor market outcomes have deteriorated (Government of Tanzania 2003).

Unemployment is largely an urban phenomenon in Tanzania, but labor market outcomes of rural youth are also weak. Rural children begin to work very early in life, with little or no schooling or sometimes in combination with school (Beegle and Burke 2004; Beegle, Dehejia, and Gatti 2006). Most end up in low-productivity jobs on household farms. Poor employment prospects may be a major reason behind increasing migration from the countryside to urban areas (U.S. Census Bureau 1995), even in the face of poor and deteriorating urban labor market prospects.

This chapter aims to shed some light on youth unemployment in Tanzania. It provides evidence on different dimensions of youth labor

The authors are grateful to Jean Fares, Marito Garcia, and seminar participants at the workshop "Youth in Africa's Labor Market," held February 7, 2006, in Washington, DC, for comments and suggestions.

market performance from the 2000/01 Tanzanian Integrated Labour Force Survey (NBS 2003). This large household survey, covering more than 11,000 households, provides a rich array of information on employment, job search, schooling, training, and migration, together with basic information on individual and household characteristics. This chapter attempts to identify the determinants of youth labor market outcomes and to tease out significant predictors of labor market success and failure using simple regression tools.

The first section of this chapter presents an overview of the youth unemployment problem. The second section presents the data as well as detailed descriptive statistics on youth labor market performance. The third section presents the regression results. The last section draws conclusions.

Why Is Unemployment Higher among Youth?

An extensive literature analyzes youth labor market outcomes and the transition to adulthood in developed countries, especially the United States (OECD 1996, 1998, 1999, 2000; Ryan 2001). Youth typically display lower labor market attachment and have lower employment rates than older workers (Rees 1986). Some of them are in school full time or combine education with work; others devote time to job searching or move from one job to another as part of their investment in human capital or as a process of mutual information gathering with employers. From this perspective, youth joblessness reflects a potentially efficient mechanism of allocating workers to jobs. Lack of dependents and the possibility of relying on parental support often make joblessness a less painful alternative for young workers and less of a problem from the viewpoint of social planners. Lower wages associated with lower experience levels or stronger preferences for leisure may also imply lower disutility of not working.

Young people not only display higher rates of joblessness and unemployment than adults due to frictional reasons at any given time, they also appear to be more sensitive to the state of the economic cycle. The youth unemployment problem in most developed countries (in particular, the Organisation for Economic Co-operation and Development countries following the oil shocks of the 1970s) has been attributed largely to the weakness of the economy and to overall lack of labor demand (Rees 1986; Freeman and Wise 1982; Blanchflower and Freeman 2000a, 2000b; ILO 2000; Card and Lemieux 2000). Disadvantaged youth in particular appear to bear a disproportionate share of the cost of economic downturns or weak labor demand (Freeman 1991; Freeman and Rodgers 1999). The vulnerability of youth to economic downturns results largely from their lower levels of labor market skills (experience and sometimes education) and lower labor market attachment (including lower job search), their lack of employment protections, and hiring and firing rules that often penalize recently hired workers.

Aggregate supply matters, too. For a given level of labor demand, an increase in the proportion of youth in the labor market disproportionately hurts youth. This is consistent with a world in which youth and adults are only imperfect substitutes in production. Excess supply relative to demand affects wages, employment, or both (Welch 1979; Card and Lemieux 2001; Koreman and Neumark 2000). As young workers see their employment prospects deteriorate, not only do they tend to work less, they also respond with adjustments by staying in school, residing with parents (Card and Lemieux 2000), and possibly committing crime (Freeman 1996, 1999).

Much less is known about the behavior of youth in developing countries. Rosenzweig (1988) and O'Higgins (2003) show that unemployment and joblessness are higher among youth in many developing countries. Guarcello and others (2005) document very high inactivity rates among youth in 13 Sub-Saharan African countries. Other researchers present similar pictures from other parts of the developing world (see, for example, Rama [2003] for Sri Lanka).

A commonly held view about urban labor markets in developing countries is that youth joblessness is a luxury accessible only to those from more advantaged backgrounds, often proxied by their education. Unemployment is often regarded as an option pursued by youth queuing for jobs in the public sector or waiting to fill vacancies in the formal private sector. In the presence of widespread poverty and the absence of public provision of welfare, nonemployment is a not a viable option for the poor, who have no choice but to make ends meet through informal and casual work. From this perspective, the youth unemployment problem should not on its face be a source of major policy concern, because it is largely a voluntary phenomenon.

The rest of this chapter documents youth labor market outcomes in Tanzania. It attempts to determine what role, if any, market forces play in shaping these outcomes and how individuals respond to changing economic incentives. It argues that youth joblessness is by no means a voluntary phenomenon in Tanzania and suggests potential roles for policy makers.

Descriptive Evidence

This section presents data on individuals' labor force status and school attendance. It then examines the characteristics of youth who work before focusing on youth who are out of work.

The Tanzanian Integrated Labour Force Survey

The Integrated Labour Force Survey is a large sample survey (43,558 individual observations in 11,158 households) collecting a rich array of information on work activity, schooling, and job search. This section draws on this survey to present evidence on teenagers (ages 15–19) and young adults (ages 20–24)—collectively termed "youth"—relative to prime-age adults (35–49). Separate results are presented for men and women and for the main geographical areas of the country—Dar es Salaam, other urban areas, and rural areas.

Differences between groups of workers are exploited to uncover the determinants of youth labor market outcomes. While this strategy has the advantage of generating sufficient variation in the data to credibly identify the impact of the variables of interests, it implies that we remain largely indifferent to the macro determinants (that is, determinants common to everyone in the labor market) of the state of the labor market in Tanzania.

School Enrollment and Labor Force Participation

The data illustrate that school attendance is about 58 percent for male teenagers in Dar es Salaam and tends to be lower in other urban areas and lower still in rural areas, where school attendance is about 39 percent (table 10.1). A similar pattern can be identified for male young adults, with about 14 percent of them in school in Dar es Salaam and only 2 percent in rural areas. Among youth out of school, some drop out at an earlier age while others never attend. School attendance at some point in life is almost universal in Dar es Salaam (about 97 percent for men). A similar picture emerges in other urban areas where the proportion of males who never attended school is about 4 percent, irrespective of age. School attendance, though, is far from universal in rural areas: 15 percent of male young adults there have never attended school. This proportion rises to 19 percent for prime-age adult men, suggesting an improvement in education outcomes across subsequent cohorts of men.

Patterns of work participation illustrated in column table 10.1 are, to a large extent and in all areas, the mirror image of patterns of school attendance. Work refers to any work activity in the week before the

Table 10.1. Labor Force and Schooling Status in Tanzania, 2000/01

(percent)

Item	School	Never attended school	Work	Work and school	No work and no school
Males					
Dar es Salaam					
Teens	58.1	2.6	20.6	3.6	24.9
Young adults	14.2	4.2	47.2	2.0	40.7
Prime-age adults	0	2.1	97.4	0	2.6
Other urban					
Teens	50.8	4.0	43.5	12.2	17.8
Young adults	7.8	3.8	76.0	1.6	17.7
Prime-age adults	0	4.2	94.9	0	5.1
Rural					
Teens	39.1	14.6	76.1	21.9	6.7
Young adults	2.3	15.4	92.2	0.9	6.5
Prime-age adults	0	19.2	96.8	0	3.2
Females					
Dar es Salaam					
Teens	44.2	3.6	26.5	2.7	31.9
Young adults	5.4	4.3	37.4	0.9	58.0
Prime-age adults	0	12.0	69.3	0	30.7
Other urban					
Teens	36.8	6.1	44.5	8.9	27.6
Young adults	2.5	5.0	67.2	0	30.4
Prime-age adults	0	15.7	89.2	0	10.8
Rural					
Teens	34.3	18.6	76.2	16.9	6.5
Young adults	1.2	21.3	92.4	0.7	7.1
Prime-age adults	0	47.4	95.1	0	4.9

Source: Integrated Labour Force Survey 2000/01.

survey. The data include people who have a job but are temporarily absent from it. While about 20 percent of male teenagers are working in Dar es Salaam, the corresponding proportion is 43 percent in other urban areas and 76 percent in rural areas. Similar patterns can be identified for male young adults, with an employment-to-population ratio that increases from 47 percent in Dar es Salaam to 76 percent in other urban areas. By contrast, the majority of male young adults living in rural areas are employed, with an employment-to-population ratio of 92 percent. Teenager and young adult participation rates are always below those of prime-age adult men, which are about 95–97 percent with little variation across areas.

Table 10.1 clearly indicates that combining work and school is essentially a phenomenon affecting teenagers in rural areas. In other urban areas, a small proportion of male individuals do both activities, but this proportion rises to 22 percent in rural areas, probably because rural teenagers are able to provide their work services on the household farm, without the need for a lengthy job search or formal contractual arrangements. In addition, lower household income in these areas makes these individuals potentially more likely to work while still in school, while the lack of substantial alternative work opportunities other than on the household farm makes the return to search quite low.

Analysis of the proportion of individuals who are neither at work nor at school (sometimes defined as joblessness; see Ryan 2001) provides a first illustration of the problems young people face in Tanzania's labor market. Around 25 percent of male teenagers and 41 percent of male young adults are neither at school nor at work in Dar es Salaam. The corresponding proportions in other urban areas are 18 percent for both teenagers and young adults. In rural areas, joblessness is lower, about 7 percent for both groups.

There are some notable differences between the labor force status of men and that of women (table 10.1). Women are less likely to be in school than men of the same age. This is particularly evident in urban areas: in Dar es Salaam the proportions of female teenagers and young adults in school are 44 percent and 5 percent respectively (that is, 14 percentage points and 9 percentage points less than males of the same age). In other urban areas, the proportions of female teenagers and young adults in school are 37 percent and 2 percent respectively (14 percentage points and 5 percentage points less than males of the same age). In rural areas, where boys' school attendance is lower, differences between girls and boys are less evident, with a proportion of female teenagers in school of 34 percent and a proportion of female young adults in school of 1 percent (that is, 5 percentage points and 1 percentage point less than males of similar age).

The proportion of female teenagers and young adults who never attended school is about 4 percent in Dar es Salaam and 5–6 percent in other urban areas, exhibiting little difference from males. This suggests that conditional on enrollment, girls are on average less likely to remain in school than boys are. The proportion of female teenagers and young adults who never attended school is much higher in rural areas: 19 percent and 21 percent respectively, or 4–6 percentage points more than males. Although girls appear to do worse than boys with regard to school attendance, a comparison with older individuals shows that recent cohorts of women have experienced remarkable progress relative to men in both rural and urban areas. The proportion of prime-age adult women who never attended school is 12 percent in urban areas (10 percentage points more than men), 16 percent in other urban areas (12 percentage points more than men), and 47 percent in rural areas (28 percentage points more than men).

As with men, employment ratios for women increase with age in all areas, and they are at their lowest in Dar es Salaam and at their highest in rural areas. The proportion of female teenagers at work is 27 percent in Dar es Salaam, 45 percent in other urban areas, and 76 percent in rural areas. The corresponding proportions among female young adults are 37 percent, 67 percent, and 92 percent. In general, teenage girls are more likely to be working than teenage boys; the differences range from 6 percentage points in Dar es Salaam to 1 percentage point in other urban areas. Differences are statistically significant. No differences emerge in rural areas. The pattern is reversed among young adults, as young women are less likely to be at work than young men. Here, differences range from 10 percentage points lower in Dar es Salaam to 9 percentage points lower in other urban areas. No differences emerge between girls and boys in rural areas. One potential explanation for this pattern is that girls in urban areas drop out of school earlier than boys and enter the labor market earlier. However, as they age, some of them tend to withdraw from the labor market, as they become gradually absorbed by childrearing and other domestic activities, while potentially a smaller proportion of female school leavers enter the labor market. This is confirmed by an analysis of employment-to-population ratios among prime-age adult women, showing a negative female-male gap. The employment-to-population ratio of prime-age adult women is 28 percentage points lower than that of men in Dar es Salaam, and 5 percentage points lower than that of men in other urban areas. Differences in rural areas are only about 1 percentage point.

Girls are also less likely than boys to combine work and education. This is largely a reflection of the fact that fewer women are in school full time. If one standardizes the proportion of those combining work and school (see table 10.1) to the proportion in school, results are very similar for men and women. Conditional on being in school, then, the probability of work is similar for boys and girls. Finally, the proportion of women neither at school nor at work shows that in urban areas, females are more likely to be jobless than males. This likely reflects a lower labor supply of women together with a potentially lower demand for their work services. As with men, it appears that young women ages 20–24 are at greater risk of being neither in school nor at work. For example, the proportion of jobless women rises from 32 percent for teenagers in Dar es Salaam to 58 percent for young women and falls to 31 percent for prime-age adult women. The corresponding proportions in other urban areas are 28 percent, 30 percent, and 11 percent. There are no discernible differences in the prevalence of joblessness between males and females in rural areas.

In sum, there is evidence that a nonnegligible proportion of the population drops out of school and starts to work at an early age, especially in rural areas. In general, girls drop out and enter the labor market earlier than boys do. As an increasing proportion of students drop out of school, the chance of finding a job falls in urban areas. Whereas most men appear to eventually become absorbed into the labor market, a large proportion of women remain out of the labor market, especially in Dar es Salaam. Some of these women may be devoting their time to home production.

The data suggest a smoother transition in rural areas, where a large proportion of males and females transition into work at an early age. This smoother transition may result from the need for young people in rural areas to start work earlier to guarantee their own survival and that of their households, as well as from the lower returns to education and job search in rural areas. Rural jobs are likely to provide only a subsistence living for many individuals. More rapid transitions may therefore be associated with worse lifetime outcomes in rural areas than in urban areas.

Nature of Employment

Workers are divided into five categories: those in paid employment (employees), the self-employed with employees, the self-employed without employees, those performing unpaid work in the family non-agricultural business (typically shops), and those working on their own farms (table 10.2). Work for pay includes payment both in cash and in kind. The data refer to the individual's main occupation in the week before the survey. Male youth are in general more likely to perform work for the household farm or business and less likely to be in paid employment or to run their own businesses than prime-age adult men. For example, among teenagers the proportions of employees are 41 percent, 15 percent, and 4 percent in Dar es Salaam, other urban areas, and rural areas, respectively. For prime-age adult men these proportions are 55 percent, 37 percent, and 9 percent. Similarly, the proportions who are working in the family business (table 10.2, columns 4 and 5 together) in

Table 10.2. Nature of Employment in Tanzania, 2000/01

(percent, except where indicated otherwise)

Item	(1) Employee	(2) Self-employed with employees	(3) Self-employed, no employees	(4) Unpaid family worker	(5) Own farm	(6) Average weekly hours	(7) Multiple jobs	(8) Underemployed
Males								
Dar es Salaam								
Teens	40.76	0	27.20	22.75	9.29	53.061	0.3	6.6
Young adults	47.38	1.72	38.36	6.65	5.88	58.077	2.1	4.2
Prime-age adults	54.46	10.32	30.00	0	5.22	57.808	7.8	1.0
Other urban								
Teens	15.05	0.21	16.74	5.24	62.76	44.137	16.0	2.8
Young adults	21.77	3.06	22.49	3.82	48.87	58.180	10.4	3.7
Prime-age adults	36.94	5.54	28.48	0.38	28.66	62.288	21.1	2.1
Rural								
Teens	3.63	0.04	2.32	3.47	90.54	43.116	12.5	4.8
Young adults	5.62	0.34	4.63	0.83	88.57	52.876	18.3	5.7
Prime-age adults	8.95	0.99	4.44	0.25	85.37	54.701	24.0	3.3
Females								
Dar es Salaam								
Teens	52.06	0.42	26.12	15.24	6.16	56.324	3.6	7.1
Young adults	36.38	2.77	53.82	4.37	2.66	54.724	2.5	13.6
Prime-age adults	27.22	3.27	55.79	0.39	13.34	50.425	7.0	10.4

(continued)

Table 10.2. Nature of Employment in Tanzania, 2000/01 *(continued)*

(percent, except where indicated otherwise)

Item	(1) Employee	(2) Self-employed with employees	(3) Self-employed, no employees	(4) Unpaid family worker	(5) Own farm	(6) Average weekly hours	(7) Multiple jobs	(8) Underemployed
Other urban								
Teens	16.77	1.27	11.72	20.86	49.39	43.443	18.7	12.2
Young adults	19.08	1.08	35.18	6.51	38.14	48.976	15.0	7.8
Prime-age adults	14.12	5.85	28.40	2.88	48.77	52.829	26.3	9.5
Rural								
Teens	1.86	0.00	1.91	5.16	91.06	41.728	13.6	8.0
Young adults	1.32	0.28	1.94	1.38	95.08	46.943	14.9	10.9
Prime-age adults	2.29	0.19	3.03	0.78	93.70	48.642	19.9	8.2

Source: Integrated Labour Force Survey 2000/01.

the three areas are 32 percent, 68 percent, and 94 percent for teenagers and 5 percent, 29 percent, and 86 percent for prime-age adult men. Self-employment (columns 2 and 3 together) describes respectively 27 percent, 17 percent, and 2 percent of teenagers and 40 percent, 34 percent, and 5 percent of prime-age adult men. One possible interpretation of these figures is that paid employment might require a lengthy job search, and self-employment might require either capital or access to credit, with both these conditions probably harder to fulfill for younger individuals.[1]

In general, workers in urban areas tend to work more hours. Prime-age adult men work on average 58 hours a week in Dar es Salaam and 62 hours in other urban areas. In rural areas, average hours of work are lower, about 55 hours. Both teens and young adults tend to work less than prime-age adult men, but patterns across areas largely reflect those of prime-age adult men. The average number of hours of work among male teenagers is about 53 in Dar es Salaam, 44 in other urban areas, and 43 in rural areas. For young men, these numbers are 58, 58, and 53.

A nonnegligible proportion of individuals in Tanzania hold at least two jobs. Multiple job holding is particularly widespread in other urban areas and rural areas and is more common among prime-age adult men than among teenagers and young adults. For example, only 2 percent of young adults in employment have a second job in Dar es Salaam, compared with about 8 percent of prime-age adult men. In rural areas these figures are 18 percent and 24 percent. Overall, it appears that youth work fewer hours than prime-age adult men and are less likely to hold more than one job.

Do these differences in hours worked across different age groups reflect differences in either the supply of or the demand for labor? In an admittedly imperfect measure of the imbalance between demand and supply of hours of work across age groups, an indicator of underemployment is reported in table 10.2, column 8. This measures the proportion of individuals who work fewer than 40 hours a week and declare a desire to work more hours. It is interesting to observe that this proportion is always the highest among youth. For instance, in Dar es Salaam 7 percent of teenagers and 4 percent of young adults declare being underemployed. For prime-age adult men in Dar es Salaam, this proportion is only 1 percent. In rural areas the corresponding proportions are, respectively, 5 percent, 6 percent, and 3 percent.

Teenage girls appear to be more likely to work as employees than teenage boys in urban areas (52 percent and 17 percent in Dar es Salaam and other urban areas, respectively, versus 41 percent and 15 percent) and less likely to work in the family enterprise. Changes in the distribution of women's employment over the life cycle also appear rather different from men's. As with men, the proportion in nonagricultural self-employment rises with age in each area (from 27 percent to 56 percent in Dar es Salaam, from 13 percent to 36 percent in other urban areas, and about 2 percent in rural areas), and the proportion in unpaid nonagricultural family work falls (from 15 percent to less than 1 percent in Dar es Salaam, from 21 percent to 3 percent in other urban areas, and from 5 percent to 1 percent in rural areas). However, in contrast to men, the proportion in salaried employment falls with age or stays constant, while engagement in the household farm rises in Dar es Salaam. In urban areas, prime-age adult working women are less likely to be in paid employment or to be self-employed with employees than men, and they are more likely to be self-employed with no employees or to work in the family enterprise than prime-age adult men. In rural areas, most working women tend to engage in work on the household farm. These women account for 94 percent of working women in rural areas (compared with 85 percent of working men). These patterns might reflect different opportunities in access to salaried employment for women compared with men, possibly because of their poor labor market characteristics (for example, education) or as a result of gender discrimination. The need to take care of children and families might also make salaried dependent employment a less attractive option for women in Tanzania.

Information on hours shows that on average women tend to work fewer hours than men. Differences in average hours of work between prime-age adult women and men vary from nine fewer in urban areas to six fewer in rural areas. The same does not apply to teenage girls: the average differences in hours of work among teenage girls and boys range from three more hours in Dar es Salaam to one less hour elsewhere. This is consistent with the notion that women tend to engage increasingly in household chores, although an alternative explanation may be that women who start to work at very early ages are those with the higher marginal utility of consumption relative to leisure, that is, those from poorer backgrounds or whose leisure their parents value less, hence those who provide more hours in the market. Underemployment is higher for females than for males. For example, 14 percent of female young adults in Dar es Salaam declare being underemployed, compared with only 4 percent of male young adults.

In sum, the career profiles of men and women appear to be rather different. As they become older, urban men tend to move away from work in the household enterprise or farm toward salaried employment and self-employment. At the same time, they tend to work more hours. This change may reflect a combination of true job changes and the fact that those who leave school later are more likely to engage in salaried work or self-employment. A large majority of working men in rural areas work on the household farm, although they too tend to move toward salaried employment and self-employment as they age.

As they grow older, women in urban areas increasingly work for themselves (with no employees) or on the family farm. In part, this may reflect a move away from salaried employment due to the need for more flexible working arrangements to attend to domestic duties. In rural areas, women's participation is higher at every age, and there is little indication that rural women withdraw from the labor market. Almost all these women work on the household farm. Women tend to work fewer hours than men, but they are also more likely to report being under-employed. In this sense, the lower labor market attachment of women does not seem to be attributable entirely to their lower labor supply. There is evidence that women in Tanzania find it particularly difficult to access the labor market in urban areas, probably because of a combination of discrimination and lower market skills.

Inactivity and Unemployment

Not surprising, activity rates increase with age and are lowest in Dar es Salaam and highest in rural areas among teenagers and young adults, paralleling patterns of employment. Activity rates among teenagers increase from 39 percent for boys and 47 percent for girls in Dar es Salaam to 77 percent in rural areas (table 10.3). Activity rates for young adults vary between 79 percent for men and 68 percent for women in Dar es Salaam and 94 percent in rural areas. For prime-age adult men, participation is almost universal, with the proportion of inactive individuals varying between 1 percent in Dar es Salaam and 3 percent in rural and other urban areas. Unemployment rates—defined as the ratio of the number of (strictly) unemployed individuals to the number of active individuals (ILO 2000)—are remarkably high among teenagers and young adults in urban areas. There is virtually no unemployment in rural areas. For teenage males, these rates range from 47 percent in Dar es Salaam to 13 percent in other urban areas. Similar patterns emerge among young adult males: unemployment rates are about 40 percent in Dar es Salaam and 11 percent in other urban areas. Of interest, unemployment rates are virtually zero among prime-age adult men. Male unemployment in Tanzania is hence primarily an urban phenomenon disproportionately affecting young workers.

Table 10.3. Activity and Unemployment Status in Tanzania, 2000/01

(percent, except where otherwise indicated)

Item	Active	Unemployment rate	Unemployment-to-population ratio	Available and not searching for work	Not available	Long-term unemployment	Very long-term unemployment	Unemployment duration (years)
Males								
Dar es Salaam								
Teens	38.6	46.5	18.0	2.7	5.4	48.7	26.5	3.60
Young adults	79.0	40.3	32.0	2.0	7.3	79.8	48.8	9.13
Prime-age adults	98.9	1.5	2.0	0.4	0.7	59.9	49.9	3.39
Other urban								
Teens	49.8	12.6	6.0	3.5	8.2	70.1	52.5	5.03
Young adults	85.0	10.6	9.0	1.6	7.7	73.7	64.6	5.66
Prime-age adults	96.5	1.7	2.0	0.5	3.0	49.3	36.7	1.97
Rural								
Teens	77.3	1.6	1.0	2.5	3.7	24.5	20.8	1.78
Young adults	93.6	1.5	1.0	1.9	3.2	26.5	15.6	1.73
Prime-age adults	97.4	0.7	1.0	0.7	1.8	33.4	23.7	1.68

Females

Dar es Salaam								
Teens	46.6	43.1	20.0	6.1	7.0	59.9	37.3	4.72
Young adults	67.9	44.9	31.0	9.1	18.5	61.9	43.2	5.89
Prime-age adults	77.8	10.9	9.0	5.6	16.6	49.8	44.5	2.81
Other urban								
Teens	47.2	5.7	3.0	11.8	13.8	66.3	56.3	3.51
Young adults	75.0	10.4	8.0	8.3	14.3	78.4	63.4	5.43
Prime-age adults	90.6	1.5	1.0	4.1	5.3	83.8	61.6	9.27
Rural								
Teens	76.7	0.7	1.0	3.1	3.8	26.6	22.2	1.63
Young adults	93.5	1.2	1.0	2.1	3.9	31.0	19.0	1.58
Prime-age adults	95.4	0.4	0	0.7	3.9	22.4	18.9	1.43

Source: Integrated Labour Force Survey 2000/01.
Note: "Active" and "unemployment rate" are as defined by ILO.

Activity rates are higher among teenage girls than teenage boys in Dar es Salaam. In other urban areas, females are slightly less likely to be active than males. In rural areas there is no significant difference between the activity rates of teenage boys and girls. Although female activity rates increase with age, the rise is less pronounced than for males. As a result, men overtake women by the time they reach prime age. However, at least as high a proportion of active women are unemployed. Unemployment rates in Dar es Salaam are 43 percent among female teenagers (3 percentage points less than males), 45 percent among female young adults (5 percentage points more than men), and 11 percent among prime-age women (9 percentage points more than men). In other urban areas, females are less likely to be unemployed than males in their teens (6 percent compared with 13 percent) but equally likely to be unemployed at ages 20–24. As with males, there is virtually no unemployment in rural areas.

In urban areas, long-term unemployment accounts for at least half of total unemployment. The average unemployment duration is remarkably high in urban areas, especially for young adults.[2] In Dar es Salaam it ranges from 3.6 years for male teenagers to 9.1 years for young adults. In other urban areas the average duration is 5.0 years for male teenagers and 5.7 years for young adults. Among adult men, the duration of unemployment is higher in Dar es Salaam (3.4 years) than in other urban areas (2.0 years).

The rate of long-term unemployment is particularly high among young adults, among whom it accounts for more than 70 percent of unemployment. Among prime-age men it accounts for 36–60 percent of unemployment.

Females are generally unemployed for shorter periods than males, except for teenagers in Dar es Salaam. The average duration of unemployment among young adults in Dar es Salaam is 5.9 years for women and 9.1 years for men; in other urban areas average duration is 5.4 years for women and 5.7 years for men. The fact that a nonnegligible proportion of women enter into inactivity, an option largely unavailable to men, may explain why observed durations are shorter for women.

In rural areas, where unemployment is almost nonexistent, the few who declare being unemployed return to employment more rapidly. Long-term unemployment represents 25–33 percent of rural unemployment and decreases with age.

Do these data provide a good indication of the extent of the joblessness of different age groups? If individuals who are out of school have a lower probability of finding jobs, these figures overestimate the extent of unemployment for a random individual in an age group. By contrast, if those who have no job opportunities stay in school or declare themselves inactive, these figures underestimate the extent of unemployment for a random individual in an age group.

An alternative measure of joblessness relates the number of unemployed to the entire population, regardless of whether these individuals are in school (or even active). Even if unemployment is standardized to a much larger population at risk (that is, the entire population in an age group), unemployment is still higher among young adults and teenagers than among prime-age adults.

Not all of those out of work (or school) are unemployed: some are available to take a job if offered and some are unavailable for work. These are groups with lower labor market attachment. The proportion of individuals who are available to work but declare not having searched for work the previous week is small at all ages and in all areas. It is most prevalent among teenagers, about 3 percent of whom fall into this category.

A significant percentage of youth are not available: 5 percent of teenagers and 7 percent of young adults in Dar es Salaam, 8 percent for both age groups in other urban areas, and 4 percent of teenagers and 3 percent of male young adults in rural areas. These figures make the extent of joblessness even more worrisome and suggest that unemployment ratios may understate the magnitude of the problem.

Reasons for Inactivity

A large proportion of respondents indicate that they are not looking for a job because of their low expectations of finding one (table 10.4). This proportion is particularly high for teenagers and young adults in urban areas. In Dar es Salaam, 65 percent of teenage boys, 60 percent of teenage girls, and 67 percent of female young adults report this as the main reason for not looking for a job.

A significant share of those not looking report that they are waiting for a reply to a job application or waiting for a job to start. No systematic patterns are observed across areas or age groups, with figures ranging from 5 percent to 100 percent depending on age, gender, and location.

In both rural and urban areas, a large proportion of young people report not looking for work because of household responsibilities (except for male youth in Dar es Salaam). In rural areas, 31 percent of male and 29 percent of female teenagers and 38 percent of male and 47 percent of female young adults report that household duties prevent them from looking for work. In urban areas other than Dar es Salaam, 18 percent of

Table 10.4. Reasons Why Tanzanians Are Not Looking for or Are Not Available for Work
(percent)

| | Reason not looking | | | | | | Reason not available | | |
	(1) Thought would not find	(2) Waiting for job or reply	(3) Off-season	(4) Household duties	(5) Temporarily ill	(6) Other	(7) Household duties	(8) Ill	(9) Other
Item									
Males									
Dar es Salaam									
Teens	64.5	13.6	0	3.2	3.6	15.2	28.0	11.3	60.7
Young adults	25.6	32.5	0	2.7	0	39.3	18.7	24.7	56.6
Prime-age adults	0	100.0	0	0	0	0	0	100.0	0
Other urban									
Teens	28.3	48.8	0	7.5	1.5	13.9	25.8	31.7	42.5
Young adults	51.8	21.8	0	18.0	0	8.3	16.9	15.7	67.4
Prime-age adults	16.2	7.0	38.3	0	0	38.5	12.6	83.4	4.0
Rural									
Teens	17.4	22.1	8.3	30.7	1.3	20.2	22.7	45.9	31.4
Young adults	19.9	27.9	8.7	37.6	0	5.9	10.5	58.6	30.9
Prime-age adults	33.8	39.4	17.7	9.1	0	0	3.2	92.1	4.7

Females

Dar es Salaam									
Teens	60.0	8.5	0	12.5	1.0	18.1	43.0	17.6	39.4
Young adults	67.5	2.7	0	24.6	0	5.2	73.1	15.1	11.7
Prime-age adults	42.9	19.9	16.7	17.0	0	3.6	77.8	20.1	2.1
Other urban									
Teens	16.7	28.9	1.7	48.0	0	4.8	40.5	18.1	41.4
Young adults	15.4	17.9	3.5	47.1	1.8	14.4	45.8	27.6	26.6
Prime-age adults	36.5	20.5	10.3	29.1	0	3.7	46.4	46.9	6.8
Rural									
Teens	17.2	18.3	20.8	28.6	0	15.11	21.4	54.9	23.7
Young adults	22.4	5.2	18.5	46.6	0	7.4	24.3	57.1	18.6
Prime-age adults	47.2	25.3	14.3	0	8.1	5.0	12.8	85.8	1.4

Source: Integrated Labour Force Survey 2000/01.

male young adults, 48 percent of female teens, and 47 percent of female young adults cite this reason. "Inactivity" thus appears to hide some productive employment in the household, leading to an overestimate of the true extent of joblessness among young people.

Many inactive young people report being unavailable for work because of illness or disability. The figures are particularly high among urban teenage boys (32 percent), rural male young adults (59 percent), and rural female teens (55 percent) and young adults (57 percent). These very high figures probably reflect the impact of the HIV/AIDS epidemic.[3]

The proportion of people available for work but not looking is much higher among females than among males (table 10.3). In Dar es Salaam 9 percent of female young adults (compared with 2 percent of males) are available but not searching; 18 percent of young women (compared with 7 percent of young men) are idle (not available). Idleness is low and stable over age groups in rural areas.

More than half of female teenagers and young adults in Dar es Salaam not looking for a job report that they are not looking because they do not believe they will find a job. Women are more likely than men to report not looking for family reasons. Not surprisingly, a higher proportion of idle women report household duties as the main reason for not being available for work. This proportion tends to increase with age in urban areas, consistent with the notion that inactive women are engaged in productive work at home.

Job Search Methods

Tanzanians use a variety of methods to search for jobs (table 10.5). Formal inquiries of potential employers is the most widespread method. As individuals age, they are less likely to use informal search channels (asking friends or relatives) than to ask employers or to attempt to start their own businesses. Young people are more likely than prime-age adults to use informal channels, perhaps because they have a smaller chance of finding jobs through formal job applications. No substantial differences emerge in the patterns of job search between males and females.

Summary

Urban unemployment is primarily a youth phenomenon in Tanzania (and a problem for prime-age adult women in Dar es Salaam). Unemployment figures probably underestimate the extent of joblessness, because a small proportion of individuals declare that they are available but are not looking for work because of their low expectations of finding a job. Inactivity rates are also remarkably high (although some inactive people are engaged in

Table 10.5. Job Search Methods in Tanzania
(percent)

Item	Inquired with employer	Found job through family or friends	Attempted to start own business
Males			
Dar es Salaam			
Teens	75.3	19.0	5.7
Young adults	58.4	30.8	10.9
Prime-age adults	64.3	8.9	26.8
Other urban			
Teens	67.8	28.6	2.2
Young adults	79.3	12.9	7.8
Prime-age adults	89.5	0	10.5
Rural			
Teens	39.7	25.9	28.1
Young adults	51.1	20.2	24.8
Prime-age adults	64.6	5.9	29.6
Females			
Dar es Salaam			
Teens	55.2	38.4	5.2
Young adults	53.6	29.2	17.2
Prime-age adults	36.5	19.4	41.2
Other urban			
Teens	63.1	21.9	15.0
Young adults	59.1	17.4	20.3
Prime-age adults	56.9	12.0	31.2
Rural			
Teens	44.3	0	55.7
Young adults	67.7	0	27.6
Prime-age adults	69.1	0	30.9

Source: Integrated Labour Force Survey 2000/01.

household chores). A small but nonnegligible proportion of Tanzanians are inactive because of health reasons (4 percent of men and 2 percent of women between the ages of 20 and 25 in Dar es Salaam). It is plausible that the inactivity rates reflect the widespread prevalence of HIV/AIDS.

Women seem to fare worse than men. Although dropping out of the labor force is an option for a nonnegligible proportion of women in urban areas, possibly itself the result of lower labor demand, joblessness remains higher for women even conditional on participation.

Long-term unemployment is particularly widespread, especially among young adults. Rather than cycling in and out of the labor market in an attempt to gain employment for life, young adults in urban Tanzania remain out of the labor force for very long periods. Females tend to be unemployed for shorter periods than males, probably because some of them transition to inactivity, an option rarely pursued by males.

Prime-age women have very high rates of unemployment and underemployment in Dar es Salaam. Participation is also lower for females in other urban areas. Although this may signal that their productivity at home is higher than the wage they are offered in the market (or that they have stronger preferences for home production relative to market activities), it may also reflect poor labor market prospects.

Unemployment and underemployment are not major problems in rural areas, where both participation and employment are high. These statistics, of course, reveal nothing about the quality of jobs these individuals hold or their standards of living.

Determinants of Labor Force Status among Youth

This section investigates the labor force status and schooling choices of teenagers and young adults using simple regression tools. It examines the role of aggregate indicators of the state of the local labor market and the individual characteristics that predict employment, unemployment, and school attendance.

For different labor market outcomes Y, we run the regression

$$Y_{iR} = \beta_0 + X'_R \beta_1 + X'_i \beta_2 + u_{iR'} \tag{1}$$

where i denotes a generic individual living in region R, the X'_Rs denote regional characteristics, the X'_is denote individual characteristics, and u is an error term.

One might expect lack of job opportunities to be a major factor explaining the poor labor market outcomes of teenagers and young adults in Tanzania; if wages are far from perfectly flexible, low labor demand will increase joblessness. To measure the level of local labor demand, the ratio of the employment of prime-age adults to the population in the region of residence is used. Employment of prime-age individuals is used because they are presumably the group with the highest labor market attachment and the group in which employment is most likely to be exogenous to that of youth.[4]

A rise in the supply of young workers is likely to have an effect on their employment prospects. The model includes the share of teenagers and young adults in the working-age population (ages 15–60) in each region.

Because rural-to-urban migration is high in Tanzania (about 28 percent all teenagers and young adults in urban areas are rural migrants), only those who report being born in the area are included. This allows us to control for the potential bias that would stem from endogenous migration. If migration toward cities in which labor demand is stronger is greater (see Card 2001), including the share of all young residents (rather than only natives) would overestimate the (presumably negative) correlation between youth labor supply and the youth employment rate.[5]

Average travel time to the closest secondary school (in hours) is included as an additional measure of local opportunities. These data come from the 2000/01 Household Budget Survey (NBS 2002). The data were aggregated by region and rural-urban status and this variable was included on the right-hand side of the regressions.

A number of individual controls are also included. The first is a dummy variable denoting whether the individual received any type of training in his or her life. This includes both on-the-job training, such as apprenticeship, and off-the-job training, such as formal vocational education. The second is a dummy variable indicating whether the individual is a migrant, which measures returns to migration. Because the aim is to investigate the role of individuals' family backgrounds in determining their labor market outcomes, we also include the average years of education of the head of household.

All of the regressions control for the following covariates: Four education dummy variables are included—never attended school (zero years of education), incomplete primary (one to six years of completed education), completed primary (seven years of completed education), and at least one year of secondary education (eight or more years of education). To control for the circumstance that labor force participation rises and school attendance falls as individuals get older, unrestricted dummy variables are included for potential experience. To control for different household structures, dummy variables are included for the individual's relationship to the household head (head, spouse, child, other relative, domestic employee, or unrelated family member). Quarter-of-year dummy variables are also included to allow for potential seasonal patterns in employment. To control for potentially unobserved differences between Dar es Salaam and other urban areas, we include a dummy variable for residence in Dar es Salaam.[6] Standard errors are clustered by region of residence.

The regression coefficients (table 10.6) should be interpreted with caution. Ideally, only exogenous variables should appear on the right-hand side to keep the ordinary least squares estimates consistent; this is

Table 10.6. Determinants of Labor Force Status and Schooling Choices of Youth in Tanzania

Item	(1) Work[a]	(2) School[b]	(3) School and work[c]	(4) Work only[d]	(5) School[e]	(6) No work and no school[f]
Males						
Urban						
Adult employment rate	1.075**	0.092	0.581**	0.494**	-0.489*	-0.586**
	(0.378)	(0.186)	(0.228)	(0.218)	(0.268)	(0.277)
Youth share	-0.480**	0.004	-0.322***	-0.159	0.326**	0.154
	(0.213)	(0.118)	(0.110)	(0.138)	(0.135)	(0.176)
Time to school	0.055	0.111	0.050	0.005	0.061	-0.116
	(0.112)	(0.081)	(0.067)	(0.079)	(0.087)	(0.091)
Training	0.137***	-0.185***	-0.004	0.141***	-0.181***	0.044
	(0.024)	(0.023)	(0.013)	(0.025)	(0.022)	(0.028)
Migrant	-0.034	-0.052*	-0.009	-0.024	-0.043*	0.077
	(0.038)	(0.026)	(0.015)	(0.034)	(0.022)	(0.046)
Head of household education	0.001	0.020***	-0.004	0.006	0.024***	-0.025***
	(0.007)	(0.004)	(0.005)	(0.004)	(0.007)	(0.003)
Number of observations	2,004	2,004	2,004	2,004	2,004	2,004
R-squared	0.331	0.517	0.241	0.381	0.427	0.163
Rural						
Adult employment rate	0.762	0.141	0.544	0.218	-0.402	-0.360*
	(0.465)	(0.182)	(0.390)	(0.221)	(0.440)	(0.181)
Youth share	0.275	0.066	0.199	0.076	-0.133	-0.142
	(0.334)	(0.140)	(0.337)	(0.164)	(0.300)	(0.114)
Time to school	-0.044	-0.004	-0.025**	-0.019	0.021	0.024
	(0.026)	(0.007)	(0.012)	(0.018)	(0.014)	(0.019)

	(1)	(2)	(3)	(4)	(5)	(6)
Training	0.032	-0.094***	-0.040**	0.072***	-0.054***	0.022
	(0.023)	(0.024)	(0.015)	(0.024)	(0.014)	(0.027)
Migrant	-0.007	-0.009	0.016	-0.023	-0.025	0.031
	(0.037)	(0.013)	(0.020)	(0.028)	(0.017)	(0.031)
Head of household education	-0.016***	0.010**	0.002	-0.017***	0.009**	0.007*
	(0.002)	(0.004)	(0.004)	(0.004)	(0.003)	(0.004)
Number of observations	3,971	3,971	3,971	3,971	3,971	3,971
R-squared	0.150	0.464	0.247	0.380	0.197	0.059
Females						
Urban						
Adult employment rate	0.410*	0.068	0.067	0.344*	0.002	-0.412**
	(0.197)	(0.097)	(0.065)	(0.181)	(0.120)	(0.152)
Youth share	-0.552*	0.165	-0.164	-0.488	0.329**	0.323
	(0.326)	(0.179)	(0.136)	(0.288)	(0.147)	(0.278)
Time to school	-0.202	0.075	0.023	-0.026	0.052	-0.050
	(0.189)	(0.098)	(0.082)	(0.163)	(0.062)	(0.193)
Training	0.148**	-0.177***	-0.027**	0.174***	-0.150***	0.003
	(0.059)	(0.024)	(0.010)	(0.053)	(0.027)	(0.052)
Migrant	0.031	-0.036	-0.007	0.038	-0.029	-0.001
	(0.038)	(0.021)	(0.018)	(0.046)	(0.022)	(0.034)
Head of household education	-0.015	0.013	-0.010	-0.005	0.023***	-0.008
	(0.012)	(0.009)	(0.007)	(0.007)	(0.008)	(0.011)
Number of observations	2,383	2,383	2,383	2,383	2,383	2,383
R-squared	0.272	0.446	0.161	0.311	0.384	0.196

(continued)

Table 10.6. Determinants of Labor Force Status and Schooling Choices of Youth in Tanzania (continued)

Item	(1) Work^a	(2) School^b	(3) School and work^c	(4) Work only^d	(5) School^e	(6) No work and no school^f
Rural						
Adult employment rate	0.079	0.368***	0.168	−0.089	0.200	−0.279
	(0.540)	(0.123)	(0.323)	(0.301)	(0.338)	(0.283)
Youth share	−0.017	−0.025	−0.041	0.025	0.016	0.001
	(0.285)	(0.093)	(0.165)	(0.191)	(0.212)	(0.152)
Time to school	−0.017	−0.028***	−0.023**	0.006	−0.005	0.022
	(0.019)	(0.004)	(0.010)	(0.014)	(0.011)	(0.013)
Training	0.046*	−0.085**	−0.030	0.076***	−0.055***	0.009
	(0.024)	(0.030)	(0.022)	(0.021)	(0.019)	(0.031)
Migrant	−0.010	−0.009	−0.006	−0.004	−0.003	0.013
	(0.028)	(0.012)	(0.011)	(0.032)	(0.006)	(0.028)
Number of observations	2,383	2,383	2,383	2,383	2,383	2,383
R–squared	0.272	0.446	0.161	0.311	0.384	0.196

Source: Integrated Labour Force Survey 2000/01.
Note: Standard errors in parentheses.
* Significant at the 10 percent level.
** Significant at the 5 percent level.
*** Significant at the 1 percent level.
a. Probability of working, regardless of whether in school.
b. Probability of being in school, regardless of whether working.
c. Probability of combining work and school.
d. Probability of only working.
e. Probability of only going to school.
f. Probability of neither working nor going to school.

probably not the case here. If individuals with otherwise better labor market prospects are more likely to acquire education and receive training, the erroneous conclusion might be drawn that education and training boost employment. Similar concerns arise with the variables capturing the age and education structure of the household or the child's relationship to the household head, because living arrangements may be endogenous to latent labor market outcomes. Along the same lines, one has to be extremely cautious in interpreting the coefficient on the migrant dummy variable as the causal effect of migration. Those who migrate are most likely those with larger potential gains from or lower costs of migration (Borjas 1999). Their performance can thus not be extrapolated to the population of potential migrants at large.

Among urban males, a 10 percentage point rise in adult employment leads to an increase in youth employment of about 10 percentage points (column 1). The increase does not affect school attendance. However, a rise in local labor demand leads to a significant increase in both the probability of combining work and school (0.58) and the probability of working full time (0.49) (columns 3 and 4). The rise in employment following a rise in local labor demand hence comes in about equal proportions from a rise in part-time work among students and a decline in inactivity (column 6).

Local labor supply also affects urban males' labor force status. A 10 percentage point rise in the share of youth in the working-age population leads to a drop in employment of 4.8 percentage points and a rise in full-time school attendance of 3.3 percentage points. An improvement in the state of the local labor market appears to have no effect on overall school attendance, but it tends to reduce the share of urban males who combine work and school.

Distance from school (proxied by time to school) does not appear to be a binding constraint for urban males. Training is associated with higher employment and lower schooling. This could mean that training boosts employment. Alternatively, it could mean that people who are working or have a higher probability of working are more likely to receive training. Migrant males are less likely to be in school, but there is no apparent correlation with employment or inactivity. The negative effect of migration on school attendance probably reflects the fact that most individuals migrate after they have left school. Higher household education increases males' probability of school attendance and reduces joblessness. One additional year of education by all other household members is associated with a rise in school attendance of 2 percentage points and a drop in joblessness of 2.5 percentage points. This suggests that family background is an important predictor of labor market outcomes in Tanzania: urban individuals from more educated households are more likely to be in school and less likely to be inactive.

Results in rural areas are qualitatively similar. Neither local labor demand nor the youth share of the labor force has a statistically significant effect on males' labor force status, probably because most males work on the household farm. An alternative explanation is that emigration from rural areas occurs when labor market opportunities weaken, so that youth employment falls as labor supply increases, leading to a regression coefficient that is biased toward zero.

Unlike in urban areas, distance to school appears to be an important determinant of youth labor force status in rural areas. This is consistent with the notion that distance to school acts as a fixed cost of school attendance, reducing the incentives for individuals to combine work and school.

The coefficients on the other variables appear in line with those in urban areas. As in urban areas, higher household education increases school attendance, but in rural areas it is associated with a decline in employment and a slight rise in inactivity. Males from more privileged backgrounds give up work in exchange for either school or leisure in rural areas, while in urban areas they stay in school rather than remaining unemployed or inactive.

Results for females are qualitatively similar. One difference is that changes in local labor demand appear to affect inactivity and full-time work for urban females. A 10 percentage point increase in employment of adult women is associated with about a 4 percentage point rise in female youth employment. Unlike for males, school in combination with work does not appear to be important for urban females in response to changes in the state of the local labor market. Aggregate labor supply (as represented by the adult employment rate) also appears to be an important determinant of labor force status among females in urban areas. No appreciable differences can be detected between males and females with regard to the other coefficients.

Local labor market conditions do not appear to matter for females. Surprisingly, stronger labor demand is associated with higher school attendance. Distance to school is an important determinant of labor force status, with longer distance to school associated with a decline in part-time school attendance and hence an overall fall in school attendance in rural areas.

A number of robustness checks were performed on the data (not reported). First, the ratio of employed prime-age adults to the population was computed. The fact that some prime-age adults live in the same households with youth might bias the estimates of the effect of local labor demand. This potential bias stems from the correlation between different household members' labor supply arising from reasons other than local labor demand and supply (for example, patterns of substitution or complementarity in individuals' labor force status within the household or added worker effects). In fact, the results are essentially unchanged.

Second, adult employment was computed using different age brackets for adults. In general, the results are qualitatively similar, although less precise.

Third, the effect of local labor demand and supply was estimated, ignoring most of the other (potentially endogenous) covariates included in the models in table 10.6. We ran these estimates to address the concern that the inclusion of endogenous variables might affect the consistency of the estimates of the arguably exogenous indicators for the state of the local labor market. Results were qualitatively unchanged, although point estimates were less precise.

In sum, there is evidence that the labor force status of teenagers and young adults in Tanzania is strongly affected by local labor demand, as proxied by adult employment, especially in urban areas. While an increase in local labor demand translates into an increase in employment for both males and females, the effect is larger for males, because a nonnegligible proportion of males (but not females) tend to combine work with school as demand increases. For both males and females, stronger local labor demand tends to reduce joblessness—that is, to increase employment rates among those who would otherwise have been out of school. There is no evidence that local labor demand affects school stay-on rates. This may suggest that widespread early dropout in Tanzania is not due to the need for children to engage in work but rather to the potentially high costs of or low returns to schooling (for evidence on low returns to education, see Söderbom and others 2004). This conclusion is consistent with the observation that school in combination with work is not uncommon and that labor market prospects are poor in urban areas. At a given level of local demand, a rise in the aggregate supply of youth to the labor market also appears to depress young people's labor market prospects.

Local labor demand and supply indicators appear to explain little of the variation in employment across rural areas. This may be because rural youth are disproportionately employed on the household farm and hence isolated from the local labor market. Endogenous out-migration may also partly explain the lack of correlation.

Distance to school appears to be a constraint only in rural areas. Greater distance to school tends to reduce the incentive to combine work with school, reducing school attendance, with no significant effect on work.

Socioeconomic background, as proxied by the average education of other household members, is a strong predictor of labor force status. It is associated with a decline in work (in rural areas) and joblessness (in urban areas) and a rise in schooling.

Conclusions and Policy Implications

Joblessness in Tanzania is largely due to the lack of sufficient aggregate demand for labor relative to aggregate supply. The problem is particularly acute among urban teenagers and young adults, who are four to five times more likely than prime-age adults to be jobless. This ratio is much higher than in most developed countries, where youth unemployment is about twice that of prime-age adults (ILO 2000).

The evidence from Tanzania is not consistent with the widespread view that joblessness in developing countries is a luxury for the better off. Youth unemployment does not appear to reflect queuing by young people for rationed well-paying jobs: in urban areas young people from more advantaged families are more likely to attend school and less likely to be jobless, suggesting that joblessness is a more severe problem for the poor.

Girls in urban areas start working earlier than boys, sometimes in menial jobs characterized by long working hours, but their transition to the labor market during the life cycle is slower because a substantial proportion of females are absorbed in home production (particularly childbearing and childrearing). A large number of women classify themselves as being involuntarily unemployed or underemployed; improvements in labor market conditions lead to declines in women's inactivity rates. These findings indicate that a substantial proportion of women, particularly young women, are inactive because of poor labor market prospects, suggesting that labor market outcomes for women do not simply represent culture or preferences.

Despite increasing joblessness in urban areas, migration from rural to urban areas continues to grow. This suggests that the employment prospects of rural youth may not be rosier than those of their urban counterparts.

Analysis of the Tanzanian labor market's inability to absorb all available workers goes beyond the scope of this chapter. One can speculate, though, that the economic reforms of the mid-1990s, which put the country on a path of fiscal discipline and macroeconomic stabilization and led to extensive privatization, disproportionately affected those attempting to enter the labor market for the first time. The sustained GDP growth registered since the mid-1990s does not appear to have compensated for this effect. The increase in the proportion of youth in the labor market and increasing urbanization have further weakened the labor market prospects of recent cohorts of urban workers. Some of the reasons invoked for youth unemployment in developed countries (minimum wages, union power, employment protection legislation, the perverse incentives associated with welfare) are unlikely to apply to Tanzania (or to most developing countries), where the labor market is largely unregulated, welfare is essentially nonexistent, and unions operate only in the formal public sector (Freeman 1993; LO/FTF 2003).

How do young people cope without jobs? One possibility is that they engage in informal work that is not recorded in the Integrated Labour Force Survey. To the extent that this is the case, the measures of unemployment and joblessness in this chapter overestimate the nature of the problem. This point merits further research.

A second possibility is that young people engage in illegal activities. Evidence from the United States indicates that criminal behavior is responsive to labor market opportunities, especially among youth with poor labor market prospects. This behavior does not show up in the Integrated Labour Force Survey, although data from the United Nations Development Programme (UNDP 2005) based on victimization rates indicate very high property crime and robbery rates in Dar es Salaam. Prostitution may be another way for young people to make ends meet. If young people in Tanzania respond to poor labor market prospects by engaging in criminal or hazardous activities, this might provide an additional rationale for policy intervention aimed at the youth unemployment problem.

A third possibility is that households provide support. Young people may live with family members or pool resources with relatives living in different households. Migration of some household members from rural to urban areas may be a way for rural households to spread the risk of economic downturns affecting cities and rural areas differently (Rosenzweig 1988). More rural-biased development (after decades of urban bias), in particular land redistribution, might relieve some of the pressure on the urban labor market (Mjema 1997), although it is not obvious that such development can guarantee sustained growth.

Youth can react to labor market shocks in various ways. One strategy is to stay in school. If the alternative to school is inactivity or unemployment, why do so many youth in Tanzania appear to drop out early in the absence of work opportunities? We find no evidence that school enrollment is affected by the state of the local labor market, although urban males are more likely to combine work with school in good times. In rural areas, distance to school remains an impediment to attendance. Policies aimed at improving stay-on rates, possibly by improving school quality and building new schools, could potentially alleviate some of the problems in the youth labor market.

Another mechanism for coping with joblessness is migration. Potential gains might come from increasing mobility across urban areas by providing more effective information systems about job vacancies.

A third strategy is self-employment. Young people are substantially less likely than prime-age adults to be self-employed. Difficulty accessing credit, a lack of entrepreneurial culture and skills, and a legal framework that has long discouraged small (informal) enterprises (Mjema 1997) are all likely to explain why this avenue is rarely pursued by Tanzanian youth. This seems to suggest room for policy intervention.

The government of Tanzania is not indifferent to the problem of youth unemployment. Since the mid-1980s it has implemented policies, and the government, nongovernmental organizations, and international organizations have launched activities. Analysis of the policies proposed and partly implemented during the 1990s suggests that these efforts were generally ineffective (Shitundu 2005).[7] Underinvestment, the very limited number of beneficiaries, mismanagement, lack of coordination, and political patronage among the different agents involved all hampered these efforts.

In recent years the government has intervened more actively to reduce youth joblessness, creating the National Youth Development Fund, the Women's Development Fund, the National Entrepreneurship Fund, and the Local Government Youth and Women Development Funds. It adopted the National Employment Policy of 1997, the National Poverty Eradication Strategy of 1998, the National Youth Development Policy, the Poverty Reduction Strategy of 2000, the National Strategy for Growth and Reduction of Poverty of 2004, the New Empowerment Policy of 2004, and the Income Tax Act of 2004.

Several supply-side interventions have been launched. The Primary Education Development Programme of 2002 abolished school fees and is apparently responsible for the unprecedented rise in primary school enrollment after more than a decade of stagnation. Access to and quality of secondary education have also improved, as a result of halving school fees, constructing schools, and introducing scholarships (under the Secondary Education Development Programme). Complementary Basic Education in Tanzania, a program in force since the 1990s to provide remedial education to school dropouts, has proved effective. The ILO project, Promoting Gender Equality and Decent Work Throughout All Stages of Life, provides apprenticeship and skills training. Efforts to reform the vocational school system (Vocational Training and Education Authority and Folk Development Colleges) are on the agenda but still to be implemented.

Major interventions on the demand side have sought to improve the business climate, provide credit to microentrepreneurs (through, for example, the Small Entrepreneurs Loan Facility program, cofinanced by the Inter-African Development Bank and the government), and provide public jobs with potential training content (through public-private partnerships, such as the Dar es Salaam Solid Waste Management Programme, the ILO Integrated Urban Employment Promotion, which is part of the Jobs for Africa Programme, and Community-Based Programmes under the Tanzania Social Action Fund scheme). Other efforts, such as the Labor Exchange Centre in Dar es Salaam, are being made to increase the match between the supply of and demand for labor and to strengthen technical capability in government offices dealing with employment issues.

Policy makers appear to be placing much greater emphasis on youth unemployment in Tanzania. Financial resources have increased substantially to match the scale of the problem, and a much greater level of coordination has been achieved.

Notes

1. A compositional effect is also likely to be at work, because as the labor force ages, an increasing proportion of it is made up of individuals with higher education. These trends potentially reflect the circumstance that more educated individuals are more likely than less educated individuals to enter into paid employment or to start their own businesses (especially businesses that hire employees). Regression results (not reported) show that conditional on education, the probability of being an employee does not increase with age. However, for self-employment with employees there is a pronounced age event, even conditioned on education. This suggests that compositional effects are important in explaining the growth in dependent employment over the life cycle but not the growth in self-employment with employees.

2. Cross-sectional data typically report information on unemployment duration only for the unemployed. The simple average of these durations underestimates actual unemployment duration, potentially by a large amount. To derive duration here, we use the following identity, which holds in steady state: $u = i/(i + h)$, where u is the unemployment rate, i is the inflow rate, and h is the outflow rate (Machin and Manning 1999). In steady state, average duration equals the reciprocal of the outflow rate (that is, $1/h$). To obtain these figures, we compute unemployment rates as the number of individuals available (that is, strict and nonstrict unemployed) divided by the number of people working, in school, or available. We compute inflow rates as the number of people with at most three months of unemployment, standardized to the sum of those working and those in school.

3. Tanzania has one of highest prevalence rates of HIV/AIDS in Sub-Saharan Africa. Recent estimates indicate a prevalence of 8.8 percent among the population ages 14–49—considerably higher than the 7.3 percent average for Sub-Saharan Africa (UNDP 2005).

4. After experimenting with the data, we chose individuals ages 35–44, segregated by sex.

5. In principle, one would want to reimpute those who migrated to urban areas back to their rural area of origin to measure local labor supply net of outmigration (exactly as we do in urban areas, where migrants are excluded). Unfortunately, the Integrated Labour Force Survey does not identify where urban migrants come from (except, generically, whether they are from an urban or rural part of the country).

6. This implies that we do not exploit differences between Dar es Salaam and other urban areas to identify the effect of aggregate indicators. These coefficients are completely identified based on differences across other urban areas. Observations from Dar es Salaam, however, contribute to the identification of the effect of all other variables in the model.

7. An exception is the microfinance programs implemented during the 1990s, which benefited some young entrepreneurs.

References

Beegle, Kathleen, and K. Burke. 2004. "Why Children Aren't Attending School: The Case of Rural Tanzania." *Journal of African Economies* 13 (2): 333–55.

Beegle, Kathleen, Rajeev Dehejia, and Roberta Gatti. 2006. "Child Labor and Agricultural Shocks." *Journal of Development Economics* 81 (1): 80–96.

Blanchflower, David G., and Richard B. Freeman. 2000a. "The Declining Economic Status of Young Workers in OECD Countries." In *Youth Employment and Joblessness in Advanced Countries*, ed D. G. Blanchflower and R. B. Freeman. Chicago: University of Chicago Press.

———. 2000b. "Introduction." In *Youth Employment and Joblessness in Advanced Countries*, ed D. G. Blanchflower and R. B. Freeman. Chicago: University of Chicago Press.

Borjas, George. 1999. "The Economic Analysis of Immigration." In *Handbook of Labour Economics*, vol. 3, ed. O. Ashenfelter and D. Card. Amsterdam: Elsevier.

Card, David. 2001. "Immigrant Inflows, Native Outflows, and the Local Labour Market Impacts of Higher Immigration." *Journal of Labour Economics* 19 (1): 22–63.

Card, David, and Thomas Lemieux. 2000. "Adapting to Circumstances: The Evolution of Work, School, and Living Arrangements Among North American Youth." In *Youth Employment and Joblessness in Advanced Countries*, ed D. G. Blanchflower and R. B. Freeman. Chicago: University of Chicago Press.

———. 2001. "Can Falling Supply Explain the Rising Return to College for Younger Men? A Cohort-Based Analysis." *Quarterly Journal of Economics* 116 (2): 705–46.

Freeman, Richard B. 1991. "Crime and the Employment of Disadvantaged Youths." NBER Working Paper No. 3875, National Bureau of Economic Research, Cambridge, MA.

———. 1993. "Labor Markets and Institutions in Economic Development." *American Economic Review* 83 (2): 403–8.

———. 1996. "Why Do So Many Young American Men Commit Crimes and What Might We Do About It?" *Journal of Economic Perspectives* 10 (1): 25–42.

———. 1999. "The Economics of Crime." In *Handbook of Labour Economics*, vol. 3, ed. O Ashenfelter and D. Card. Amsterdam: North-Holland.

Freeman, Richard B., and William M. Rodgers III. 1999. "Area Economic Conditions and the Labor Market Outcomes of Young Men in the 1990s Expansion." Working Paper No. 7073, National Bureau of Economic Research, Cambridge, MA.

Freeman, Richard B., and David A. Wise. 1982. "The Youth Labor Market Problem: Its Nature, Causes, and Consequences." In *The Youth Labor Market Problem: Its Nature, Causes, and Consequences*, ed. R. B. Freeman and D. A. Wise. NBER Conference Volume. Chicago: University of Chicago Press.

Government of Tanzania. 2003. "Unemployment Issues: Perspectives from the Ministry of Labour, Youth Development and Sports." Poverty Policy Week 2003: Speeches, Presentations and Papers.

Guarcello, Lorenzo, Marco Manacorda, Furio Rosati, Jean Fares, Scott Lyon, and Cristina Valdivia. 2005. "School-to-Work Transitions in Sub-Saharan Africa: An Overview." Working Paper No. 15, Understanding Children's Work Project, Rome.

ILO (International Labour Organization). 2000. *Employing Youth: Promoting Employment-Intensive Growth*. Geneva: ILO.

Koreman, Sanders, and David Neumark. 2000. "Cohort Crowding and Youth Labor Markets: A Cross-National Analysis." In *Youth Employment and Joblessness in Advanced Countries*, ed D. G. Blanchflower and R. B. Freeman. Chicago: University of Chicago Press.

LO/FTF (Danish Trade Union Council for International Development). 2003. "Profile of the Labour Market and Trade Unions in Tanzania." Project No. 036/002/01, Copenhagen.

Machin, Steve, and Alan Manning. 1999. "The Causes and Consequences of Long-Term Unemployment in Europe." In *Handbook of Labour Economics*, vol. 3, ed. O. Ashenfelter and D. Card. Amsterdam: North-Holland.

Mjema, Godwin D. 1997. "Youth Unemployment in Tanzania: New Strategies for Combating an Old Problem." *Journal of Population Studies and Development* 4 (1).

NBS (National Bureau of Statistics of Tanzania). 2002. "Household Budget Survey 2000/01." Dar es Salaam.

———. 2003. "2000/01 Integrated Labour Force Survey." Dar es Salaam.

O'Higgins, Niall. 2003. "Trends in the Youth Labour Market in Developing and Transition Countries." Social Protection Discussion Paper No. 321, World Bank, Washington, DC.

OECD (Organisation for Economic Co-operation and Development). 1996. *1996 Employment Outlook*. Paris: OECD.

———. 1998. *1998 Employment Outlook*. Paris: OECD.

———. 1999. *Preparing Youth for the 21st Century: The Transition from Education to the Labour Market*. Paris: OECD.

———. 2000. *From Initial Education to Working Life—Making Transitions Work*. Paris: OECD.

Rama, Martin. 2003. "The Sri Lankan Unemployment Problem Revisited." *Review of Development Economics* 7 (3): 510–25.

Rees, Albert. 1986. "An Essay on Youth Joblessness." *Journal of Economic Literature* 24 (2): 613–28.

Rosenzweig, Mark R. 1988. "Labor Markets in Low-Income Countries." In *Handbook of Development Economics*, vol. 1, ed. H. Chenery and T. Srinivasan. Amsterdam: North-Holland.

Ryan, Paul. 2001. "The School-to-Work Transition: A Cross-National Perspective." *Journal of Economic Literature* 39 (1): 34–92.

Shitundu, Joseph M. 2005. "Youth Employment Inventory of Existing Policies and Programmes in Tanzania." Background Paper, Social Protection Unit, World Bank, Washington, DC.

Söderbom, Måns, Francis Teal, Anthony Wambugu, and Godius Kahyarara. 2004. "The Dynamics of Returns to Education in Kenyan and Tanzanian Manufacturing." Working Paper WPS/2003-17, Oxford University, Centre for the Study of African Economies, Oxford, United Kingdom.

UNDP (United Nations Development Programme). 2005. *Human Development Report 2005*. New York: UNDP.

U.S. Census Bureau. 1995. *Population Trends Tanzania*. PPT/92-10. U.S. Department of Commerce, Economics and Statistics Administration, Bureau of the Census, Washington, DC.

Welch, Finis. 1979. "Effects of Cohort Size on Earnings: The Baby Boom Babies' Financial Bust." *Journal of Political Economy* 87 (5): S65–S97.

World Bank. 2007. "Tanzania: Sustaining and Sharing Economic Growth—Country Economic Memorandum and Poverty Assessment." Report No. 39021-TZ, World Bank, Washington, DC.

CHAPTER 11

How Did Universal Primary Education Affect Returns to Education and Labor Market Participation in Uganda?

Lisa Dragoset and Lars Vilhuber

Uganda implemented its universal primary education program in 1997. As a result, primary school enrollment rose from 3 million in 1997 to 7.6 million in 2002 (World Bank 2005; Deininger 2003). This chapter examines how primary school enrollment rates, returns to education, and employment patterns changed in Uganda after universal primary education was implemented. The focus is not on estimating the returns to education or the labor participation rate but rather on estimating a credible, time-consistent model for two time periods and analyzing the changes in the estimates.

The chapter first describes how participation in the educational system changed over time. It then examines changes in the returns to education and in the relative shares of formal and informal (or entrepreneurial) employment. It compares sets of repeated cross-sections of Ugandan society from various household surveys and investigates how different (synthetic) cohorts have fared at similar points in their careers.

Several phenomena may keep children from enrolling in school, even if it is free. First, households bear the opportunity cost of forgone earnings of children in school, a potentially significant barrier to expanding education. A large literature discusses the trade-off faced by families in developing countries in choosing whether to send children to school or to work, whether at home or on the family farm (Psacharopoulos 1997; Ersado 2005; Drèze and Kingdon 2001; Hazarika and Bedi 2003; Ravallion and Woodon 2000; Burke and Beegle 2004; Ranjan 2000, 2001, 2002; Singh 1992; Gisser 1968). "Engaging in income-generating activities" is the primary reason why boys and one of the top five reasons why girls do not attend school in Uganda, despite universal primary education (World Bank 2003). As the investment climate improves, the earnings potential of these out-of-school children also increases—and with it the likelihood that at least some children continue to stay away from school.

Second, job opportunities for the educated may be lacking. If jobs are not available once students finish school, schooling merely delays entry into poverty and there is no incentive to enroll. Acknowledging this problem (World Bank 2003), policy makers have implemented policies to alleviate credit constraints, improve infrastructure, and create a better business environment—with the goal of facilitating wealth creation by existing businesses and removing barriers to the creation of new enterprises, particularly small businesses and opportunities for self-employment. A better investment climate goes hand in hand with a better educational system: the educational system creates the skills to feed the investment climate; a successful economy creates incentives to participate in the educational system in the first place.

Third, if access to secondary and higher education is not also widely available, participation in primary education falls—again, it only delays entry into poverty. Demand for primary education may be high as an entry ticket to secondary education. According to Appleton, Hoddinott, and Knight (1996), the rate of return to primary education in Uganda may be even higher than usually estimated if the economy has high demand for postprimary educated workers and secondary education is easily accessible. Court (1999) studies the impact of changes in the fee structure of Uganda's Makerere University, finding that enrollment rates doubled as a result of financing reform.

Fourth, schooling quality may decline as enrollment rates increase. Indeed, Deininger (2003) found that student-teacher ratios rose to near the highest in the world, regardless of efforts to increase quality, and that in 1999, only three-quarters of participating students passed final examinations in primary school. Moll (1996) finds that decreases in school quality in South Africa between 1960 and 1990 reduced the returns to primary education. Many empirical studies demonstrate the importance of schooling quality for economic growth and increasing returns to education (Lee and Barro 2001; Rangazas 2002; Behrman and Birdsall 1983; Schultz 1999; Harmon and Walker 2000; Moll 1992). Fuller, Edwards, and Gorman (1986) find that increases in educational quality had significant effects on economic growth in Mexico from 1888 to 1940 but that increases in quantity (school expansion) had inconsistent effects. Card and Krueger (1992) show that higher school quality created higher returns to education for men born in the United States between 1920 and 1949. These findings suggest that investments in schooling quality must accompany those in universal primary education for the increase in primary school enrollment rates to translate into higher human capital and social welfare.

Education and Earnings in Uganda

The education-earnings profile in Uganda is steep—more schooling translates rapidly into more income—suggesting that families have positive incentives to send their children to school (figure 11.1). However, only a small fraction of the work force actually derives its income from the formal sector (table 11.1).

Figure 11.1. Income Rises with Level of Education in Uganda

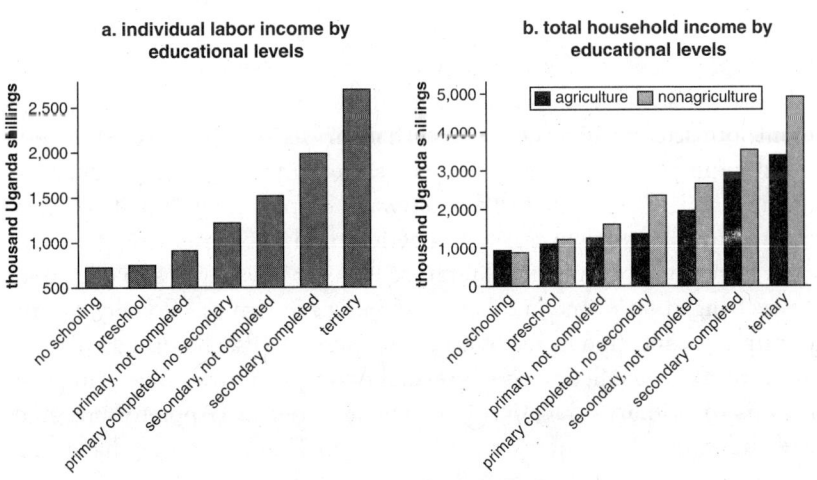

Source: 1999 Uganda National Household Survey data.

Table 11.1. A Large Proportion of Uganda's Labor Force Works Outside the Formal Sector

Industry	Percentage of work force not earning labor income
Agriculture	83
Mining and quarrying	83
Commerce	81
Manufacturing	68
Other	37
Transport	27
Construction	20
Banking/financial services	12
Utilities	11
Professional	10
Public administration	4
Total	72

Source: Authors' calculations based on Uganda National Household Survey, 1999.

The Literature on Educational Participation in Developing Countries

The most direct evidence on educational participation comes from Deininger (2003), who finds a dramatic increase in primary school enrollment in Uganda from 1992 to 1999. Inequalities in enrollment rates by gender, income, and region also declined significantly over this period.

Appleton (2001) examines returns to education and employment patterns in Uganda during the 1990s. He finds that returns to education increased for all three major income sources: farming, nonagricultural self-employment, and wage employment. Both secondary and tertiary education had large and significant effects on access to wage employment, but this positive effect for secondary education was offset by a negative impact on nonwage earnings. In contrast, primary education did not have a significant effect on wage employment, but it did raise income by increasing access to nonagricultural self-employment.

A large body of empirical literature looks at how returns to education have changed over time in other developing economies. Globally, returns to primary education have continued to increase (Psacharopoulos 1994), but returns have failed to rise in several African countries. The Mincerian returns to primary education have fallen in Kenya (Appleton, Bigsten, and Kulundu 1999) and South Africa (Moll 1996), and they have stagnated in Ethiopia (Krishnan, Selaissie, and Dercon 1998).

Other studies examine the effect of education on occupational attainment and employment patterns. They find that education has a significant effect on the probability of nonfarm labor market participation and increases wages earned in nonfarm work in both Ghana (Abdulai and Delgado 1999) and Pakistan (Fafchamps and Quisumbing 1999). Schiefelbein and Farrell (1984) find that schooling quality was a strong predictor of occupational attainment in Chile during the 1970s.

Several studies estimate the impact of large-scale education policies in developing countries. Duflo (2001) finds that Indonesia's 1973 school construction program increased both years of education (by 0.12–0.19 years) and wages (by 1.5–2.7 percent). Mingat (1998) studies the impact of education policies in high-performing Asian economies. He finds that countries with higher proportional investments in primary education were significantly more likely to have greater development afterward. In addition, both the quantity (average duration of schooling) and the quality (retention rates and levels of student learning) of education had increased in the high-investment countries relative to other Asian economies. Other studies confirm the increase in educational attainment and wages resulting from educational reform (Paxson and Schady 2002; Clark and Hsieh 2000; Patrinos and Sakellariou 2005; Pomponio and Lancy 1986; Dronkers 1993; Post 1994).

The Model

Consider the choice faced by families with children in school (Becker 1975). The child's earnings are a function of the child's identity i, the fraction of total hours h spent earning such income, the level of schooling s achieved, and the policy environment p in effect at the time of work. If the child does not go to school, earnings are $I(i,1,s,p)$; if the child goes to school for one additional year, earnings are $I(i,0,s)$ during the school year and $I(i,1,s+1,p)$ a year later.

To send a child to school, parents must be able to cover direct schooling costs, $k(p)$, which include books, school fees, food, and possibly lodging. Some of these components, such as school fees, are directly related to policy. Uganda's universal primary education reduced some costs, but others persist. Parents will send their children to school if

$$I(i,0,s)+\delta I(i,1,s+1,p)-k(p) > (1+\delta) I(i,1,s,p) \tag{1}$$

where δ is the discount factor. This expression can be rewritten as

$$\delta[I(i,1,s+1,p)-I(i,1,s,p)] > I(i,1,s,p)-I(i,0,s)+k(p) \qquad (2)$$

where the left-hand term is the discounted benefit from investing in an additional year of schooling and the right-hand term includes the direct and indirect costs of that additional year of schooling.

Two points about this simple specification are important. First, the condition is satisfied at all levels of education, including after the end of free primary education. As long as the condition holds, the child will go to school; when the condition no longer holds, the child will leave. Second, policy decisions affect both sides of the expression—costs and incentives. While universal primary education reduces direct costs, the improved economic climate can lead to a presumably short-term reduction in school enrollment at certain levels of schooling if the decrease in schooling costs does not offset the increase in alternate employment opportunities. This is unlikely in the early years, given the substantial reduction in schooling costs from free universal primary education, but k remains positive. Other economic changes, such as an increase in the price of essential food, can be integrated through changes in the discount factor or through explicit modeling of credit and budget constraints.

Results

Cross-sections of the Uganda National Household Survey for 1992 and 1999, using data for 2002 where available, were examined.[1] For part of the analysis, synthetic 5- and 10-year cohorts of young people are constructed based on their age in 1992. Because the data are not in true panel form, these individuals cannot be followed over time. We can, however, identify survey respondents in later surveys who would have been in the same age group in 1992. Their outcomes serve as proxies for the unobserved outcomes of the actual 1992 survey respondents. The assumption is that these two largely distinct groups have the same characteristics and thus experience similar outcomes on average. Some of the measured outcomes suggest that this condition is not always satisfied.

Two indicators of education are focused upon: some primary education and some secondary education. The information available on the highest achieved education level varies across years and has been standardized.

Primary education has seven levels (grades), denoted by P1 through P7. We aggregate any completed level of primary into one category and any level of completed postprimary education (J1 through J3, S1 through S6) into a second category. Formally,

$$EDUC_{it}(1) = I(EDUC_{it} \in \{P1-P7\}) \tag{3}$$

and

$$EDUC_{it}(2) = I(EDUC_{it} > P7) \tag{4}$$

where i is individual "i" in time period "t." For the regression analysis, we use years of education, linearized from the educational achievement categories.

Changes in Enrollment

Enrollment (and consequently education levels) increased between 1992 and 2002, as other studies have pointed out (Deininger 2003; World Bank 2005). The number of girls and boys ages 5–10 and ages 10–15 who completed some level of primary school rose significantly (table 11.2). Among 15- to 20-year-olds, the number of Ugandans with no more than a primary education fell, reflecting the increase in postprimary education in older groups.

By 1997, when universal primary education was implemented, the first cohort was ages 10–15, possibly still young enough to benefit from the program (table 11.3). The schooling rate for males of the first cohort rose to 83 percent in 1999. As they aged another three years, the rate dropped again with their acquisition of additional education.

By the time universal primary education was implemented, the third cohort was in its early 20s. In 1992, 70 percent had obtained some primary education and another 20 percent had completed some secondary education. By 2002, another 14 percent had gone on to some secondary education.

The second cohort (children ages 10–15 in 1992) falls between these two groups. Some members may have benefited from universal primary education to prolong their stay in the educational system. Between 1999 (when the youngest members of this cohort were 17) and 2002, the number of males with some primary education rose 2 percentage points. The number of people in this cohort who obtained some secondary education also increased almost 2 percentage points.

Compared with the cohort that was ages 15–20 in 1992, the cohort of the same age in 2002 has a significantly higher educational level. More than 95 percent of the males in the younger cohort had at least a primary education, compared with only 90 percent in the older cohort. Only 20 percent of males in the 15–20 cohort in 1992 had any secondary

Table 11.2. The Percentage of Ugandans with Some Secondary Education Rose between 1992 and 2002

	1992	1996	1999	2002
(a) With no more than primary education				
Male				
5–10	39.87	—	54.58	53.40
11–15	85.25	—	89.27	90.59
16–20	70.05	—	59.95	58.09
21–25	59.57	—	52.37	52.15
Female				
5–10	39.25	—	54.56	54.95
11–15	77.67	—	87.66	90.09
16–20	63.55	—	55.69	57.13
21–25	55.91	—	53.73	55.20
(b) With some secondary education				
Male				
5–10	0.00	—	0.15	0.00
11–15	1.75	—	2.95	4.86
16–20	20.44	—	31.27	37.45
21–25	28.41	—	38.43	41.52
26–30	28.45	—	28.26	35.01
31–35	26.55	—	30.28	33.11
36–40	23.74	—	29.96	29.48
41–45	21.54	—	27.33	30.31
Female				
5–10	0.00	—	0.03	0.02
11–15	2.20	—	4.27	5.09
16–20	15.76	—	28.38	33.65
21–25	16.23	—	23.56	30.38
26–30	13.45	—	16.84	21.79
31–35	10.82	—	14.90	18.58
36–40	8.01	—	10.23	14.75
41–45	8.09	—	9.77	13.25

Source: Authors' calculations based on data from the Uganda National Household Surveys.
Note: — = Not available.

education, compared with 41 percent in the 10–15 cohort. For women the primary education differential increased with age.

The older cohorts (ages 15–20 and ages 20–25) were not directly affected by universal primary education. However, their secondary educational achievement increased between 1992 and 2002. Free universal primary education may have freed household resources, allowing households to keep children in school longer (a demand-side explanation).

Table 11.3. The Free Primary Education Policy Has Freed Household Resources, Allowing Families to Keep Children in School Longer

	Observed in			
Age in 1992	1992	1996	1999	2002
(a) With no more than primary education				
Male				
5–10	39.87	—	82.73	58.09
11–15	85.25	—	50.85	52.15
16–20	70.05	—	56.18	56.36
21–25	59.57	—	57.78	58.42
Female				
5–10	39.25	—	77.84	57.13
11–15	77.67	—	52.09	55.20
16–20	63.55	—	54.35	57.77
21–25	55.91	—	52.57	51.19
(b) With some secondary education				
Male				
5–10	0.00	—	10.25	37.45
11–15	1.75	—	39.63	41.52
16–20	20.44	—	32.95	35.01
21–25	28.41	—	27.73	33.11
26–30	28.45	—	32.25	29.48
31–35	26.55	—	27.22	30.31
36–40	23.74	—	29.32	27.14
41–45	21.54	—	28.77	37.25
Female				
5–10	0.00	—	13.34	33.65
11–15	2.20	—	27.25	30.38
16–20	15.76	—	21.98	21.79
21–25	16.23	—	16.67	18.58
26–30	13.45	—	12.75	14.75
31–35	10.82	—	8.77	13.25
36–40	8.01	—	10.18	9.79
41–45	8.09	—	8.65	12.33

Source: Authors' calculations based on data from the Uganda National Household Surveys.

Alternately, decreases in the cost of secondary education may have increased participation.

The fraction of young (ages 20–30) male heads of households with at least a primary education increased from 86 percent in 1992 to 93 percent in 2002 (table 11.4). Of interest, heads of household were neither more nor less likely to have more education than other household members.

Educational attainment of household heads increased in all regions. Male household heads in the Central Region still have a higher educational level than those in other regions. However, in the Western Region, where only half as many household heads had some secondary education as in the Central Region, educational levels caught up with those of the rest of the country. By 1999, all regions attained the 1992 level of the Central Region. Education levels increased over 1992 in both rural and urban areas, with particularly strong gains for rural women (table 11.5).

Changes in the Returns to Education

Returns to education are reported for both wages and a measure of household income. A large portion of earnings are nonlabor earnings, which cannot be consistently attributed to individuals.[2] Those earnings therefore are attributed to the head of the household. For consistency in the sample selection, some of the wage earning regressions are restricted to household heads as well.

Table 11.4. The Average Educational Level of Household Heads in Uganda Rose between 1992 and 2002

	Some primary	Some secondary	At least primary
(a) All ages			
Male			
1992	56.80	20.11	76.91
1999	56.74	25.15	81.89
2002	57.96	29.32	87.28
Female			
1992	33.44	10.67	44.11
1999	36.87	13.08	49.95
2002	45.87	19.56	65.44
(b) Young (20–30) heads			
Male			
1992	63.20	22.99	86.19
1999	64.73	25.01	89.74
2002	60.92	31.86	92.78
Female			
1992	46.27	23.21	69.47
1999	47.99	26.21	74.20
2002	54.14	31.64	85.77

Source: Authors' calculations based on data from the Uganda National Household Surveys.

Table 11.5. Educational Levels Increased in Both Rural and Urban Areas

	1992	1996	1999	2002
(a) With some primary education				
Male				
Rural	59.99	—	63.41	63.24
Urban	51.85	—	50.97	50.69
Female				
Rural	48.32	—	56.00	60.32
Urban	56.71	—	54.92	52.24
(b) With primary or secondary education				
Male				
Rural	70.75	—	76.81	80.49
Urban	86.77	—	89.16	90.52
Female				
Rural	53.19	—	63.43	70.81
Urban	81.29	—	85.36	87.64

Source: Authors' calculations based on data from the Uganda National Household Surveys.
Note: — = Not available.

The basic reduced form regression we estimate is

$$\log Eht = \beta0 + \beta1 \; f1(\text{demographics}) + \beta2 \; f2(\text{age})$$
$$+ \beta3 \; f3(\text{education}) \tag{5}$$

with linear effects for demographic characteristics (gender, marital status, region) and quadratic effects for age and years of education. *Eht* can be either the labor income of the household head or the total earnings of the entire household. Depending on the left-hand side variable, equation (5) can be interpreted as a Mincerian wage equation or a reduced-form household production function.

Because education is generally considered endogenous in this type of equation, we instrument it. Candidate instruments are the distance to school, other household members' education, and parental education. For none of these measures are data consistently available for all years. The results presented generally use as an instrument a quadratic in distance to school and a quadratic in the difference of an individual's education from the average household education.

Ten different specifications were estimated. Across most of them, the increase in the returns to education between 1992 and 1999 was strong, robust, and statistically significant. Some of the ordinary least squares results are weakened or do not hold up when returns to education are instrumented. The result no longer holds for women, for men in some regions, and for the oldest age group. It does hold for men in general and for younger age groups (ages 21–30 and ages 31–40)—precisely the age groups one might expect to benefit directly from greater access to the education system.

The instrumented variable results for the younger cohorts are very similar to the ordinary least squares results, suggesting that positive selection is not driving the ordinary least squares results: all workers with higher education enjoyed higher returns to education in 1999, not just the high-ability workers. Some of the specifications and samples show signs of weak instruments.

Including only wage income for the household head is restrictive, particularly for women, who are not usually household heads but often contribute outside wages to household earnings. Although the returns to education of female heads of household do not increase significantly when other wage income is included, the returns to education for other female household members do.

The returns to education can also be measured by considering total household income. While the ordinary least squares results show the same increase in returns to education across genders, regions, and age groups, the instrumented variables results confirm the results only in some regions and only for the youngest male cohorts. For the oldest male cohort, the instrumented variables results show a decrease in the returns to education when using household income. Instruments are generally weak, indicating that the model that successfully explains wage income works less well for household income and that the results should be interpreted with caution.

Changes in Employment Patterns

Employment increased across all age groups between 1992 and 1999 (table 11.6). Except among men ages 15–20, the generally small increase in employment reflected primarily increases in the "employer" category.[3] For men ages 15–30, overall employment rose about 1 percentage point. The increase in employment was much higher among young women, particularly women ages 15–25.

In the cohort of men ages 20–25 in 1992, employment rose from 94.2 percent to 95.5 percent. This compares with a 1992 employment rate of 94.5 percent among men ages 25–30. Among all male cohorts, the rate of unemployment was higher for the younger cohort. This pattern does not hold for all female cohorts. The employment rate of most

Table 11.6. Employment Rose between 1992 and 1999, Particularly among Young Women

	1992			1999		
Age in 1992	Salaried	Employer	Overall	Salaried	Employer	Overall
Employment status by age, weighted results						
Male						
15–20	22.51	68.19	90.70	25.03	67.78	92.81
21–25	21.05	73.15	94.20	20.90	75.40	96.29
26–30	24.20	70.27	94.46	24.34	71.60	95.94
31–35	24.11	71.64	95.75	25.32	70.90	96.22
36–40	23.85	72.06	95.91	22.93	73.52	96.45
41–45	25.71	67.62	93.33	16.20	79.30	95.51
Female						
15–20	22.69	47.94	70.62	13.11	69.92	83.03
21–25	17.77	57.78	75.56	18.38	60.78	79.16
26–30	16.97	65.82	82.79	14.22	71.50	85.72
31–35	9.80	73.25	83.05	11.63	71.09	82.72
36–40	13.13	70.77	83.90	7.75	78.12	85.86
41–45	7.06	76.16	83.22	10.56	74.83	85.39
Employment status by cohort, weighted results						
Male						
15–20	22.51	68.19	90.70	24.78	71.65	96.43
21–25	21.05	73.15	94.20	23.45	72.10	95.54
26–30	24.20	70.27	94.46	25.83	71.21	97.05
31–35	24.11	71.64	95.75	20.14	76.03	96.17
36–40	23.85	72.06	95.91	15.85	79.72	95.57
41–45	25.71	67.62	93.33	19.58	74.83	94.42
Female						
15–20	22.69	47.94	70.62	18.25	56.21	74.46
21–25	17.77	57.78	75.56	14.67	74.20	88.87
26–30	16.97	65.82	82.79	9.07	72.88	81.95
31–35	9.80	73.25	83.05	8.81	80.09	88.90
36–40	13.13	70.77	83.90	7.99	71.94	79.93
41–45	7.06	76.16	83.22	3.22	85.39	88.60

Source: Authors' calculations based on data from the Uganda National Household Surveys.
Note: All means are weighted.

cohorts rose, appearing to reflect the economywide upswing in employment opportunities.

Cross-sectional analysis does not indicate a pattern in how this increase was achieved. For some age groups of men, a strong increase in salaried employment accounted for most or all of the increase in employment. For other age groups, salaried employment was stagnant or declined, and employment gains stemmed from increases in self-employer status.

Cohort rather than cross-sectional age group analysis sheds some light on this phenomenon. The younger male cohorts saw strong increases in salaried employment, while older cohorts saw a decline. Salaried employment generally declined for female cohorts, coupled with strong increases in employer status. All increases in female employment rates were driven by increased self-employer status. Most of the increase in female employment was driven by increases in employment from a low base.

Concluding Remarks

Educational participation and achievement in Uganda rose significantly between 1992 and 2002. The fraction of the population with no formal education declined by about a third (13 percentage points), and the fraction of the population with at least some secondary education increased by more than 6 percentage points.

At the same time, the returns to education increased substantially for many demographic groups, particularly for some of the younger male cohorts, and in some geographic areas. Much of this increase reflected increases in returns to secondary education, which may be related to pull factors in the labor market. The strong result for younger men is robust to some specification of the endogeneity of education, and instrumented variables results are very similar to ordinary least squares results. This suggests that the result is valid across a broad ability spectrum of the young male population, with little polarization. Results for household income, rather than formal wage earnings, are broadly similar, albeit weaker.

Self-employment (or entrepreneurial employment) rose among both men and women. While the returns to education are similar for the two earnings measures, it is difficult to determine whether the increase in employment was due to push factors (reduction in public sector employment) or pull factors (higher returns). Government programs aimed to facilitate entrepreneurial activity. Whether they succeeded is difficult to determine because the data do not allow distinguishing formal employment from informal employment in a time-consistent manner. Further study is warranted to investigate this point.

Notes

1. Weighted data are not available for 1996. Data for 2002 are available on education, but the earnings data are not comparable. We therefore exclude 2002 data from the regression analysis.

2. Each individual reported labor and nonlabor income for up to three activities in 1992. Nonlabor income is reported only at the household level in 1999.

3. In this case, employer actually means self-employed.

References

Abdulai, A., and C. Delgado. 1999. "Determinants of Nonfarm Earnings of Farm-Based Husbands and Wives in Northern Ghana." *American Journal of Agricultural Economics* 81 (1): 117–30.

Appleton, S. 2001. "Education, Incomes and Poverty in Uganda in the 1990s." Working Paper 01/22, University of Nottingham, Centre for Research in Economic Development and International Trade, Nottingham, United Kingdom.

Appleton, S., A. Bigsten, and M. Kulundu. 1999. "Have Returns to Education Changed over Time? Evidence from Kenya, 1978–1995." Centre for the Study of African Economies Working Paper 1999/6, University of Oxford, Oxford, United Kingdom.

Appleton, S., J. Hoddinott, and J. Knight. 1996. "Primary Education as an Input into Post-Primary Education: A Neglected Benefit." *Oxford Bulletin of Economics and Statistics* 58 (1): 211–9.

Becker, G. S. 1975. *Human Capital: A Theoretical and Empirical Analysis, with Special Reference to Education.* Cambridge, MA: National Bureau of Economic Research.

Behrman, J., and N. Birdsall. 1983. "The Quality of Schooling: Quantity Alone Is Misleading." *American Economic Review* 73 (5): 928–46.

Burke, K., and K. Beegle. 2004. "Why Children Aren't Attending School: The Case of Northwestern Tanzania." *Journal of African Economies* 13 (2): 333–55.

Card, D., and A. Krueger. 1992. "Does School Quality Matter? Returns to Education and the Characteristics of Public Schools in the United States." *Journal of Political Economy* 100 (1): 1–40.

Clark, D., and C.-T. Hsieh. 2000. "Schooling and Labor Market Impact of the 1968 Nine-Year Education Program in Taiwan." Working Paper 1009, Hong Kong Institute of Economics and Business Strategy, Hong Kong, China.

Court, D. 1999. "Financing Higher Education in Africa: Makerere, the Quiet Revolution." Tertiary Education Thematic Group Series 22883, World Bank, Washington, DC.

Deininger, K. 2003. "Does Cost of Schooling Affect Enrollment by the Poor? Universal Primary Education in Uganda." *Economics of Education Review* 22 (3): 291–305.

Dréze, K., and G. Kingdon. 2001. "School Participation in Rural India." *Review of Development Economics* 5 (1): 1–24.

Dronkers, J. 1993. "Educational Reform in the Netherlands: Did It Change the Impact of Parental Occupation and Education?" *Sociology of Education* 66 (4): 262–77.

Duflo, E. 2001. "Schooling and Labor Market Consequences of School Construction in Indonesia: Evidence from an Unusual Policy Experiment." *American Economic Review* 91 (4): 795–813.

Ersado, L. 2005. "Child Labor and Schooling Decisions in Urban and Rural Areas: Comparative Evidence from Nepal, Peru, and Zimbabwe." *World Development* 33 (3): 455–80.

Fafchamps, M., and A. Quisumbing. 1999. "Human Capital, Productivity, and Labor Allocation in Rural Pakistan." *Journal of Human Resources* 34 (2): 369–406.

Fuller, B., J. Edwards, and K. Gorman. 1986. "When Does Education Boost Economic Growth? School Expansion and School Quality in Mexico." *Sociology of Education* 59 (3): 167–81.

Gisser, M. 1968. "On Benefit-Cost Analysis of Investment in Schooling in Rural Farm Areas." *American Journal of Agricultural Economics* 50 (3): 621–9.

Harmon, C., and I. Walker. 2000. "The Returns to the Quantity and Quality of Education: Evidence for Men in England and Wales." *Economica* 67 (265): 19–35.

Hazarika, G., and A. Bedi. 2003. "Schooling Costs and Child Work in Rural Pakistan." *Journal of Development Studies* 39 (5): 29–64.

Krishnan, P., T. Selassie, and S. Dercon. 1998. "The Urban Labour Market During Structural Adjustment: Ethiopia 1990–1997." Centre for the Study of African Economies Working Paper 98-9, University of Oxford, Oxford, United Kingdom.

Lee, J., and R. Barro. 2001. "Schooling Quality in a Cross-Section of Countries." *Economica* 68 (272): 465–88.

Mingat, A. 1998. "The Strategy Used by High-Performing Asian Economies in Education: Some Lessons for Developing Countries." *World Development* 26 (4): 695–715.

Moll, P. 1992. "Quality of Education and the Rise in Returns to Schooling in South Africa." *Economics of Education Review* 11 (1): 1–10.

———. 1996. "The Collapse of Primary Schooling Returns in South Africa 1960–90." *Oxford Bulletin of Economics and Statistics* 58 (1): 185–209.

Patrinos, H., and C. Sakellariou. 2005. "Schooling and Labor Market Impacts of a Natural Policy Experiment." *LABOUR* 19 (4): 705–19.

Paxson, C., and N. Schady. 2002. "The Allocation and Impact of Social Funds: Spending on School Infrastructure in Peru." *World Bank Economic Review* 16 (2): 297–319.

Pomponio, A., and D. Lancy. 1986. "A Pen or a Bushknife? School, Work, and 'Personal Investment' in Papua New Guinea." *Anthropology and Education Quarterly* 17 (1): 40–61.

Post, D. 1994. "Educational Stratification: School Expansion, and Public Policy in Hong Kong." *Sociology of Education* 67 (2): 121–38.

Psacharopoulos, G. 1994. "Returns to Investment in Education: A Global Update." *World Development* 22 (9): 1325–44.

———. 1997. "Child Labor versus Educational Attainment: Some Evidence from Latin America." *Journal of Population Economics* 10 (4): 377–86.

Rangazas, P. 2002. "The Quantity and Quality of Schooling and U.S. Labor Productivity Growth (1870–2000)." *Review of Economic Dynamics* 5 (4): 932–64.

Ranjan, P. 2000. "Child Labor, Child Schooling, and Their Interaction with Adult Labor: Empirical Evidence for Peru and Pakistan." *World Bank Economic Review* 14 (2): 647–67.

———. 2001. "Credit Constraints and the Phenomenon of Child Labor." *Journal of Development Economics* 64 (1): 81–102.

———. 2002. "The Determinants of Child Labour and Child Schooling in Ghana." *Journal of African Economies* 11 (4): 561–90.

Ravallion, M., and Q. Woodon. 2000. "Does Child Labour Displace Schooling? Evidence on Behavioural Responses to an Enrollment Subsidy." *Economic Journal* 110 (462): 158–75.

Schiefelbein, E., and J. Farrell. 1984. "Education and Occupational Attainment in Chile: The Effects of Educational Quality, Attainment, and Achievement." *American Journal of Education* 92 (2): 125–62.

Schultz, T. 1999. "Health and Schooling Investments in Africa." *Journal of Economic Perspectives* 13 (3): 67–88.

Singh, R. 1992. "Underinvestment, Low Economic Returns to Education, and the Schooling of Rural Children: Some Evidence from Brazil." *Economic Development and Cultural Change* 40 (3): 645–64.

Uganda, Republic of. 1992. "Integrated Household Survey 1992: Main Questionnaire." Technical Report. Ministry of Finance, Planning and Economic Development, Statistics Department, Kampala.

———. 1996. "Uganda National Household Survey 1996/1997: Labour Force Pilot and Socio-Economic Survey Questionnaire." Technical Report. Ministry of Finance, Planning and Economic Development, Statistics Department, Kampala.

———. 1999a. "Multipliers for Uganda National Household Survey 1999/2000." Technical Report. Uganda Bureau of Statistics, Kampala.

————. 1999b. "Uganda National Household Survey 1999/2000—Socio-Economic Survey Questionnaire." Technical Report. Uganda Bureau of Statistics, Kampala.

————. 2002a. "Uganda National Household Survey 2002/2003: Manual of Instructions." Technical Report. Uganda Bureau of Statistics, Kampala.

————. 2002b. "Uganda National Household Survey 2002/2003: Socio-Economic Survey Questionnaire." Technical Report. Uganda Bureau of Statistics, Kampala.

World Bank. 2003. "Poverty Reduction Strategy Paper Annual Progress Report." Report 26567-UG, Washington, DC.

———— 2005. "Uganda: From Periphery to Center, A Strategic Country Gender Assessment." Report 30136-UG, Office of the Sector Director, Poverty Reduction and Economic Management, Africa Region, Washington, DC.

Index

Boxes, figures, notes, and tables are indicated by b, f, n, and t, respectively.